Designing for Play

BARBARA E. HENDRICKS
Play Environment Designer

170201

Ashgate

Aldershot • Burlington USA • Singapore • Sydney

Published by
Ashgate Publishing Ltd
Gower House
Croft Road
Aldershot
Hants GU11 3HR
England

Ashgate Publishing Company
131 Main Street
Burlington, VT 05401-5600 USA

Ashgate website: http://www.ashgate.com

British Library Cataloguing in Publication Data
Hendricks, Barbara E.
    Designing for play. - (Design and the built environment)
    1.Playgrounds- Design and construction
    I. Title
    711.5'58

Library of Congress Control Number: 00-111538

ISBN 0 7546 1320 8

Printed and bound by Athenaeum Press, Ltd.,
Gateshead, Tyne & Wear.

Contents

Foreword

This book is aimed at the designer who would like to design well for the children. It is intended as a reference to introduce current issues and ideas relating to children in public spaces. The large body of literature and expertise relating to child development and child psychology may seem inaccessible to a designer; in this book I hope to whet their appetite to come to know more about this important population.

This is a book, but I hope it is not a typical book. A book about play should also signal that it is to be played with, it is for people who play, who play seriously. It is not necessary to start at the beginning and read toward the back. You can also start in the middle and read toward the front. Boxes of information and highlighted ideas that catch your attention can be the starting point. Some statements that are important to me are repeated – this is not a mistake in the editing – it is deliberate. Repetition is part of he way we play and the way we learn and remember; the repetition is part of the rhythm of this book. The whole aim is to increase the quality of designing for play – and we can only do that when we feel freer as adult designers to use play as a tool for our own further development as well as enjoy it for the fun of it. Enjoy!

Acknowledgements

The author and publishes would like to thank the following publishers and organisations for permission to reproduce material or illustrations. While we have made every effort to contact and acknowledge copyright holders and sources, the many changes of publishers and merger of publishing companies have sometimes made it difficult to find the actual copyright holder. If there are any errors or emissions, please contact the author and we will gladly correct this in further printings.

Illustrations:
The Osborne Collection of Early Children's Books, Toronto Public Library for two illustrations from *Healthful Sports for Young Ladies*, pages 19 and 23.
The Victoria and Albert Museum, V&A Picture Library for Reitveld's Beach Buggy of 1916, page 37.
Notts Sport for photographs of school yards, pages 86, 115 and 195.

1 Designing for Play

Designing for play has been the rightful field of work for anyone who wishes to set themselves up as a playground designer. There is no clearly identified body of knowledge required nor any particular design skills. Architects, landscape architects, sculptors, engineers, technicians, builders, gardeners, sportsmen, educators and former children all have tried their hand at playground design. The multitude of angles from which we approach playground design could be seen to bring in a wonderful diversity to this field. Unfortunately that is not so. Public playgrounds have been part of western cities for a little over one hundred years now and yet as we enter into the twenty first century there is no other aspect of public provision that has changed so little over the past century and is so boringly the same around the world as public playgrounds.

Why is this so?

- Is this because there is so little professional competence in the design of play areas?
- Is it because designing for children has little or no prestige in society?
- Is it because societies do not prioritise good quality space design for children as a public service?
- Is it because children have no political power?
- Is it because the adults are too busy taking care of their own needs?

The list of questions could continue – there is no simple answer to the problems in public playgrounds design. The solution lies in the will of society to want to offer children a quality childhood, where children are recognised as citizens and not extensions of their parents. To date there are few role models to follow when trying to establish new levels of service for children. We need to look to the basic characters of play and of childhood. Yet if there is no agreed upon body of knowledge – where do we start?

How do we know something?

We recognise as right or accurate pieces of information that seem to make sense to us. When we are new to a subject and learning about it for the first time we tend to accept without question the first pieces of information we are told about that subject. After that all further incoming information is filtered through the first set of knowledge we have.

When we are learning about children's play out of doors, a subject where there are a multitude of meanings and theories, we need to consider carefully those first pieces of information we have accepted and identify our biases, otherwise we are in danger of discarding salient knowledge about children and children's play in favour of that information we first received.

Some excellent articles and books have been written on designing for children's play – and there have been many nostalgic and romanticising publications as well. The design profession have been busy contributors – mostly landscape architects or architects, however the majority of reference books have been written by pedagogues and early childhood experts.

Many of the playground design books now published are a type of do-it-yourself playground design guide. Playground design has been seen to be a distant cousin of garden design at the amateur, home-gardener level. Anyone can do it, if they just follow a few technical tips and guidelines. This book takes playground design seriously – like play itself. It is a book aimed at bringing the issue of designing for play up to a professional level – a subject for designers about design.

Looking through the literature on designing play areas I have renewed my acquaintance with Arvid Bengsston's *Environmental Planning for Children's Play*. I have enjoyed the text and photographs every time I read the book and I have found that at different stages in my professional development I would find more material for thought and inspiration. This last time with the book I was struck with the sections dealing with the problems facing children living in cities – it sounded so immediate, as if he was writing about the situation in 1999. Actually it was 1970 when he wrote it.

What has happened in these 29 years? Little has changed to alter conditions in public spaces in cities in favour of use by children. In fact, Bengsston starts the book by referring to a 1958 European seminar on the problem of playgrounds. Forty years later the list of problems is almost the same and just as long. Is there a real intent on the part of society to provide well for children's use of public spaces? There seems to still be a great gap between people like Arvid Bengsston and other advocates of children's welfare and right to play and those professionals who are responsible for the form and content of the everyday public spaces used by children. Often the technical literature intended to inform these professionals only seems to widen the distance because each new text increases the height of the mountain of opinion and ideas we are trying to get an overview of.

I hope this book will help give perspective over the mountain – and give designers an overview over the current ideas and knowledge about children's interaction with their environment and about play as a cultural activity.

The century of the child - children as VIC's

The twentieth century was early on called the century of the child and the United Nations has celebrated the International Year of the Child and made a declaration of the Rights of the Child. Yet have conditions for children improved over this century?

In the western world children today have better access to medical care, protection by law from physical punishment and many children have bedrooms filled with mountains of toys – paradise on earth for children, you might think. Children are celebrated in the market economies as Very Important Consumers – they have a great influence on how the family income is used. But do children really have it better? Why then are there so many children with symptoms of stress and related problems?

Children today in most western societies have rights as individuals established and protected by law, although they are not permitted to vote for their governments. In this book I will address one aspect of western society that seems to be going in the opposite direction relating to children's rights, the children's right and freedom to use outdoor public spaces and the opportunities children have to come to explore in their own terms about living on Planet Earth.

The Right to Explore Planet Earth
This planet has rhythms of day and night, the sun moving across the sky, the moon's phases, the stars, and the rise and fall of the tides, the seasons as well as local geography and living things. All these items are part of our human heritage. Yet modern urban children are kept apart from the planet and its forces - we need to make a Charter with our children and give them the freedom of this earth.

In many traditional societies and developing countries children have better conditions relative to access to outdoors and exploring the world around them than do children in many modern western cities. Not that children in developing countries have access to designed playground – they do not; but they have the freedom to explore the outdoor environment around them and come to know about it in their own terms and make it their own. Children in modern western cities are not so free- they are very restricted by traffic and fear of violence to children. Their movement is often so restricted throughout their childhood that they become adults with little or no understanding of how their city is organised. They are taken to public playgrounds and supervised while at play and then escorted back into the adult private sphere of the home. They have no sense of the lay of the land around them and may even have a fear of animals, birds and nature. Many city children do not ever see the stars in the sky and have no idea of how to determine north from south – they are cut off from the planet and its rhythms.

Children really are not so dangerous. It is the perceived dangers in the outside world this gate is to protect them from.

One mother of a five year old boy tells the story how one night in the winter when she put him to bed the full moon was shining into his bedroom window. After kissing him good night and turning off the light she left the room. A short time later a little voice called to her "Mommy you forgot to shut off the moonlight".

I am not suggesting that all is negative in western cities for children – cities are grand places to live. They are the epitome of our culture and civilisation. They are treasure houses of ideas, architecture, art, music and spiritual developments. The problem is that children are not permitted to use much of the city as children or to get the most out of city living. Children are not content to just be driven past and look at the city, they want to touch, to feel, to interact with things; and the way in which we now organise city living and childhood access to public spaces severely limits the child's possibility for exploring city on their own terms. They should not need to be bussed out to the forest to be able to play freely in the outdoor environment. In the twenty first century, if we adults act wisely on behalf of all our citizens, children in cities can enjoy the best of city living and those cities that take good care of the children will be seen to be the best cities for all to live in.

Play environment design requires reasonable competence in both the natural sciences of the environment and the social science of childhood as well as design. Theories of play area design all too often are based in adult mythology and clichés – not in knowledge. It seems the more we know about natural sciences and about childhood the more unnecessary it is to have a theory – what is important then is to design well.

> *I Ching:*
> "Those with little experience have little wisdom."

Playing means it is possible to take risks that would otherwise be too dangerous. Designing play areas requires a playful approach to designing, to taking risks, to testing the boundaries of trends in design, it means to risk being seen as not serious. Play area design should be executed with humility, recognising that we adults are but tourists in the land of children; we are not experts in their culture and their ways. Childhood experts are experts in an adult definition of childhood – not in life as experienced by children. While we have played as children we lack the experience of contemporary childhood.

> Cities are grand places to grow up in – they are the treasure houses of our civilisation.

Reference

Walker, Brian Browne. (1992), *The I Ching or Book of Changes*, New York: St Martin's Griffin.

2 People Play

About the role of play in our lives

"Play is a constant happening, a constant act of creation in the mind or in practise" Arvid Bengsston, 1970.

The twentieth century has been the first century in this civilisation where children and childhood has been under the microscope. In the nineteenth century the state started to differentiate between children and adults with laws against child labour and requirements for school attendance. Children's and mother's medical care became specialities of experts. During the twentieth century we have seen an ever greater expansion of expert professions who specialise in children and childhood, in parenting and child care - psychologists, educators, educators of early childhood educators, childhood historians, sociologists and anthropologists. Children and childhood are now acceptable as an adult profession but not yet as prestigious as being in the business of automobiles, computers or aeronautics. It is an area of expertise that is often connected to "women's issues" and one where the value to society is not recognised in the pay packets those experts receive. And those professions that are experts on children are also seen to be experts on play and play spaces. This is an expertise arrived at by association – not by a competence in the subject itself. Play area design is often carried out by persons who know something about educating children but nothing about physical space design, or by physical space designers who know very little about children or play.

Children and childhood are now acceptable as an adult profession but not yet as prestigious as being in the business of automobiles, computers or aeronautics.

Play is a phenomenon that is exceptionally complex and not so well understood – as witnessed by all the unsuccessful attempts to scientifically define play. Play is such an intrinsic part of being human that it is difficult for us to get the scientific distance to study it. Play has often in the past

7

been associated with childhood and free time – something people do when they aren't working or producing something useful. Play wasn't seen to produce anything useful.

The environment of play

Not so long ago we discovered that play could be made useful as a tool for learning and as a means for forming children into useful adults. As a result some kinds of play became more acceptable – and it was even acceptable to spent tax money on such things as playgrounds. The kind of play opportunities provided by public funds needed to be defended in terms of child development and building up physical skills and good health. Children's play is still, however, somewhat of a black sheep in the herd of useful sheep.

When early childhood psychologists or educators focus on play it is always with the explanation that play is so important to the development of the children- and what they, as specialists, are interested in is the process of acquiring knowledge and skills – i.e. moving the child from the realm of childhood into the realm of adulthood, not in the act of play. Research on child's play has often been carried out so the adult expert could discover more about the development of human intelligence and the process of education.

Views of childhood

The Science of Childhood	The Poetry of Childhood
Hierarchical development, children develop into people through education /a series of progressive developmental stages. (adapted from Chawla, L. (1994).)	Romance of children as closer to nature, ideas of Rousseau, children as pure, as inherently competent.

Playgrounds are promoted as places for outdoor learning, such as the "Landscapes for Learning" on school grounds. Play area design is seen to emphasise and promote those kind of play activities that are most understood by experts to be developmental – or in the jargon of the commercial play equipment manufacturers- they have "play value".

Today we are beginning to realise the importance of play and a playful attitude toward life, both as an intrinsic healthy human drive and as a means of developing and growing in a complex and stressful environment. Developing, not just in terms of developing muscles and physical skills but also in terms of spiritual, intellectual, creative, social and emotional growth. The twenty first century should be the century when it becomes acceptable to be a lifelong player – and when it is recognised that players often enjoy a long life.

Playing is living!

Children's play occupies all aspects of young children's lives and many modern homes are fitted with play rooms and play yards to accommodate the activities of the children. Many adults however have difficulty when the child doesn't stop playing when they are in other environments – at the table, in the car, shopping and so forth. While children are very quick at picking up the understanding that in different places and with different people one behaves differently - the urge to play still comes to the surface.

Children are well known to play everywhere and play with everything. The recognition that children play everywhere has lead one or two local politicians to ask out loud why it is necessary to spend money on playgrounds – after all the children are all over the streets and corners and not in the playgrounds. In 1982, I was asked by a city councillor in a Canadian city, "Those little buggers are everywhere but on the playground, so why are you recommending that we spend money on these playgrounds?" My best answer then – and still is today – that city governments have a duty to create special, outdoor play places for children. Today, I will add that they also have a duty to make them places where children like to be and where they find challenging play possibilities.

Playing at life

Asking "why people play?" is like asking why we breathe. Both are essential activities that satisfy needs. "Play is life for young children" writes Cosby Rodgers in *Play in the Life of Young Child*. There are some big questions that must be lived out – not answered. These are questions like "what is the meaning of life?" and similarly "what is the meaning of playing?". Our verbal language may not have words for this yet – but we are still developing as human beings - at all ages.

How people play reflects the multiplicity of human nature and is a forever fascinating study. People never stop playing – not really. Adults tend to have absorbed the play into their daily life and give it important and serious sounding labels – but if seen as play many of the activities of adults can be better understood.

Playing is an expression of the joy of life

•Playing alone or together?

•Playing alone, permits one to explore the environment and find out about being alive on this planet, it can be fantastically satisfactory when the playing takes place in a richly varied outdoor environment.

•Playing alone, when the play is about social interaction and finding out about what it is like to be human, can be most unsatisfactory.

•Children must be permitted time to play alone in a varied environment and also time to play with others – with children of all ages and with adults.

•Play is about the pleasure of functioning – the joy of being alive and able to do things.

•Creativity is born in children's exploration of and relationship to the natural world and it is to this place that creative people return again and again for inspiration. (Cobb, Edith 1977.)

Playing at "office"

I have found great insight into the adult working environment –particularly the office environment -when one views it as another form of group role playing. I have come to understand my feelings of frustration and anger with a dictatorial and non -communicative supervisor when I realised that as a play leader he was not able to keep the play going, as he was not able to integrate the ideas and demands of all the players into the play. Children who are accepted as play leaders are very good at this (Andersen and Kampman, 1996). Perhaps these children will also better managers when playing "office".

Also when I play/work at "office" I want to be able to negotiate what role I am to play in the game and I want to know what role others are playing. I don't want to spend a lot of time guessing what role I have been assigned for that day. Good working environments can be developed using the model of how groups of children keep a role play going. Adults who are good leaders are using similar behaviour models. We have studied play as a tool in child development and there is a future potential to using play as a way of understanding adult behaviour. Play too is a tool for further development of our culture.

Playing brings insight

One of the benefits from children's play is that it gives the person insights into the nature of people and the world around them that last a lifetime. Not only do most people have fond memories of those places and things that were part of their childhood play, these memories can help them through difficult periods later in life. Some countries, like the Scandinavian ones, have put an emphasis on the importance of play in young children's lives – and have very little organised, formal educational content in the early childhood centres – much to the surprise of early childhood specialist from the USA and Japan.

In countries like Denmark and Sweden it is recognised that children need to play with the world around them. They need to find out about the physical environment and the people they live with through using their whole bodies and minds before they are ready to sit still in an indoor classroom situation and learn in a more conceptual way. In these countries children start kindergarten class at 6 years and first class at 7 – and if the parent chooses the child can stay out of the formal education system until 7 years of age – kindergarten class is not mandatory, although almost all children do attend. Recent studies show however that there is no advantage or edge gained by children who enter kindergarten class earlier at age 4 or 5 or 6. Seven year olds entering the school system for the first time very quickly are on the same learning level as their peers who have been in school for a year already.

People play – but so do other living creatures

While play is an important drive in people - and one that shows our most human abilities in terms of body and verbal language and our use of symbols - we are not unique in playing. Animals too, play - we have been aware of this watching young lambs in the spring or a group of puppies or kittens - and have passed it off as just part of being young - and practising using their bodies. Today we are becoming more aware that there is much more to animals play than just

---

The shape of play

Each child's play is unique, as is each play activity. There are a variety of factors which influence the form play takes.

There are the influences from within the child – the child's personality, gender and experiences.

There are the external influences – the physical environment, time available for play, other children and adults, the play environment personality and the cultural attitude toward playing. It appears that the influence of other children is greater than previously understood – this is perhaps a greater influence than the others

When examining or discussing children's play behaviour or pedagogical aspects of play items it is necessary to recognise the interconnectedness of these influences – and that play cannot be separated from the internal and external influences.

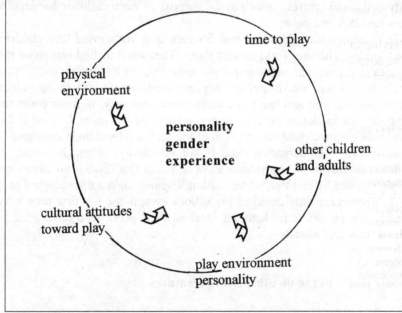

---

instinctive reactions and learning to hunt for food. Animals that have become domesticated also seek to get people to join in play with them. How do we know when an animal plays? Its body language clearly spells it out – if we know how to listen to the animals. During the twenty first century I expect we will also discover a lot more about our fellow human beings by being more alert to non-verbal communication, much of which is learned and reinforced while playing.

The advantage of playing is that you can test out actions and emotions that would be too dangerous to act out in real life. This is why play fighting is so important to young children - often boys but NOT confined to boys. Role playing also serves as a way of testing out rejection of a friend or playmate and feelings such as anger, revenge and a curiosity to see what it feels like to hit or hurt. To keep the play going all this must happen while all the players clearly know that it is "just playing". And children are for the most very good at keeping the play going and avoiding getting serious – unfortunately adults misread what is happening and put a stop to the play. Adults even forbid this kind of play. Perhaps as a result some children never really find out how to send out positive signals, to avoid getting into difficult situations with other people, how or why to avoid violence, and how to make and keep friends. Play is important in our socialising – and I will go into this more in the following chapters.

Playing at designing # 1
The advantage of playing is that you can test out actions and emotions that would be too dangerous to act out in·real life.

References

Andersen, O. Peter. and Kampmann, Jan. (1996), *Borns Legekultur*, Copenhagen Munksgaard Rosinante.

Bengsston, Arvid. (1970), *Environmental Planning for Children's Play*, Praeger Publishers New York.

Cobb, Edith. (1977), *The Ecology of Imagination in Childhood*, New York: Columbia University Press.

Chawla, Louise. (1994), *In the First Country of Places: Nature, Poetry and Childhood Memory*, Albany, New York: State University of New York Press.

Rodgers, Cosby. (1988), *Play in the Lives of Young Children*, Washington DC: National Association for the Education of Young Children.

3 History of the Play Yard – not a design story

The notion of setting aside outdoor spaces for children to use for play and to furnish it with devices to support the play is a relatively new idea in the development of our civilisation. While people have been making swings, seesaws and may poles for centuries – it was only in the 19th century that western society undertook to set up   public play yards for children. Provision of public play facilities was part of The Reform Movement– an attempt to improve the living conditions of workers in the rapidly growing and very polluted industrial cities of the 1800s. General health and living conditions were so poor that the average body size of the 19th century urban dweller was less than that of persons living in the Middle ages. Play provision for children was one of a set of new measures supported by public funds and charities following the passage of legislation against children's labour and the requirement for mandatory basic education for all children.

Play comes after daily bread and schooling

While we tend to think of this time of change in the lives of children as something belonging to the 19th century- - it is yet to become a reality for poor children living in the developing parts of the world. There too, play provision in terms of well furnished play yards will not happen (except for children of the elite) before these nations can find their way to legislate against child labour and to eliminate it in practise, as well as to ensure that all children have access to a basic education.

It is a fact that many of the world's children are very poor and for these children the issue of well furnished playgrounds seems far removed from the needs of daily life.

The public play yard

The public play area originated as a response to urban problems – poor health, lack of sanitation and was originally argued for by agencies and persons who undertook this reform as part of their charitable good works towards the poor and unfortunate. The idea of public funds being used to provide for play spaces was argued for by various playground movements and women's movements at the turn of the century but only took hold when it was discovered that boy children growing up in 19th century industrial cities did not meet basic physical tests for entering military service. The wars at the beginning of this century, culminating in World War 1, did more for the development of public playgrounds than we would like to think. The great need for young men as soldiers resulted in a very clear pattern of successful recruitment of country lads while boys growing up in poor sections of western industrial cities were not deemed physically fit to fight for their country. The need for a supply of ordinary soldiers led to an acceptance that city living for poor children must be improved by public action rather than left solely to charitable good works and reform idealists.

The development of the profession of urban planning is also tied into the history of public play provision. Playgrounds were seen to be a utility; a matter of functional equipment, not an issue of spatial design or architecture. While public buildings and public gardens were being developed with an aesthetic component; places for children were purely functional. It was and still is possible and acceptable for politicians to argue for a good architecture and high quality public parks as an element of civic pride and well being, playgrounds have always been relegated to the category of a functional necessity.

Children and charity

Play provision has maintained some aspects of its first beginnings as charitable good works and public funding is deliberately kept at an inadequate level because it is relatively easy to use adult feeling for children to get them to "give" something to the children. Thus we still see playgrounds in wealthy western cities developed only through fund raising or through charitable contribution from a charity such as the Elks Lodge or Rotary Group. In many western lands playgrounds for children are installed by parents on a weekend. It is a "feel good" act to provide a playground for children.

Adults like to give children toys – this explains why so many poor quality toys are sold at Christmas time. The same sentiments drive the construction of playgrounds developed by local parent groups through fund raising and charity. They give to the children so they can feel better and be part of an adult group working toward a common goal. The driving force is not to provide well for the children but to give the children something so the adults can feel good, preferably without it costing very much. If the driving force was to provide well for children these places would look much different.

> Adults like to give children toys – this explains why so many poor quality toys are sold. The same is true of playgrounds developed though fund raising or charity.

The emphasis on cost has always determined the quality of children's environments supplied by public funding and has influenced the quality of these places both in terms of their physical environment and their social environment. Even governments in the wealthiest western countries with a sound economy and well established public service, fast public transport, great opera houses and theatres and a high standard of living argue that they cannot afford to provide adequate space and well designed settings for children. Adult's work with children is also greatly undervalued and underpaid by society. Salaries of professions who work with children's play are at the lowest level and funding to research at a university level in children's play or designing for play is often very much limited. It is of course an issue of political priorities and children are not a high priority; they have no political power. Those adults who lobby governments on behalf of children still approach children, for the most, as charity cases, and present themselves as doing good works for the community.

Playground design - using a rubber stamp

The public provision of play has also become very much a stereotype in most western cities. Already in 1976 Thomas Burton wrote:

> There is a certain uniformity and repetition about leisure opportunities available both within and outside our urban centres. With a few notable exceptions, every neighbourhood park in Canadian cities is a facsimile of every other one. The facilities on urban playgrounds across the nation are repeated ad nauseam – swings, slides, sandpits, merry-go-rounds and baseball diamonds.
>   The cause of this lies, to a considerable extent, in the traditional approach to planning. Since planning is an activity which takes place in a political context and since it is usually undertaken without direct reference to those who will be most immediately affected, it tends to emphasise majority goals. The

planners – and their masters, the politicians- have sought to derive goals which, they believe, will be endorsed by a majority of citizens.

Burton's observations are just as true today as they were 25 years ago. New playgrounds are established using the same old formula that was developed early in the twentieth century – and despite all the criticism of this quality of provision from play organisations and academics, cities continue to provide for play as if they have only a small number of rubber stamps to use when making the plans for these spaces. Swings, sandpits, merry go rounds and combination structures with a number of slides continue to dominate public play facilities; although the social element is the most important to the children when they play in public playgrounds. However the majority of voting citizens know about swings and slides – this is their idea of what should be in a playground.

A typical playground – could be found in any city.

Play things of the wealthy and idle

The ideas of what should be in a public playground were found in equipment and facilities that were used for amusement in the private gardens of the wealthy as well as adaptations of elements taken from the developing kindergarten movement.

For centuries, people in Europe and the Orient knew about swings and seesaws. We can see paintings hanging in art galleries showing the amusements of the wealthy class including swinging and playing games. Archaeologists in Rome and Greece have uncovered urns and other pottery painted with adults engaging in many sorts of activities that today we would call children's play. It of course was a time when wealth meant that one did not need to work and therefore showing people at play was a way of showing their wealth.

In ancient times until not so long ago there seemed to be less distinction between adult play and children's play. St Sernin writes in 1822 "Persons of a more advanced age, and distinguished by grave occupations, did not look upon it as any disgrace to take the exercise of swinging..." (St Sernin, (1974) pp 3 and 4.). Of course this writer describes the activity as exercise – making it much more acceptable as an adult activity. Indeed throughout the book, written in 1822, the activities of the girls was referred to as exercise, sport, pastimes and amusement. In China swings became popular in the period of the Tang Dynasty (618 – 907 AD), particularly for women (Lu Pu (1990), p.137).

> **"Nothing is useless to people of sense"** (attributed to La Fontaine in St Sernin (1974), p.6)

Illustration reproduced with permission, The Osborne Collection of Early Children's Books, Toronto Public Library. St Sernin Mme. (1974), *Healthful Sports for Young Ladies*, original drawing by Jean-Démosthène Dugourc.

The playful water gardens and pleasure grounds built by the wealthy in the 16th and 17th century – such as the gardens at Versailles in France, the Ville d'Este, and Villa Garzoni at Collodi in Italy were adult playgrounds built for the wealthy to show to the world that they had power and wealth. Another reason for their existence was to amuse and to be the stage for entertaining and impressing friends and business connections. The 16th and 17 centuries were still times when the rich enjoyed their pleasures at home with large gatherings of family and courtiers. The enjoyments of these people included elaborately engineered water tricks seen at Fountain of Venus at the Villa d'Este. Games of hide and seek, of grass bowling and nine pins were everyday events. Swinging was a popular women's amusement (Berrall, (1978), p 204). Special effects were created for special events like weddings and festivals – where elaborate mechanical devices were created as well as enormous flower displays (Berrall, (1978)). It was a time when it was known, in the western belief system, that man was lord over the whole of the earth and wealthy men loved to show their power over nature and to enjoy playing with it.

Children are ahistorical – they live in the here and now.

At this time playing was still an acceptable behaviour for adults – even for serious adult men. One example of this is seen in the fashion for playing with the yo-yo during the period around the French revolution. It was the sport of kings, princes and even generals. It is written that even Napoleon and his troops used the yo-yo to calm their nerves the evening before the Battle of Waterloo in 1815 (Rydahl, (1999)). Today's generals will likely feel the need much more sophisticated diversion to calm their nerves – and if they play with a yo-yo they are unlikely to go public about it.

Kite flying began also as a activity for adults – and Chinese history records the use of kites as early as the Han Dynasty (206 – 24 BC). This activity still seems to have retained some legitimacy for adults with kite flying festivals and competitions still attracting many participants.

Fireworks and firecrackers also have a long history of association with play used already two thousand years ago in China – both as a element in extravagant festivals of the wealthy, and as a feature for the ordinary people on set festivals, such as Halloween, New Year or Mardi Gras. Fireworks in Europe was a feature of the elaborate parties of kings and the wealthy, and the design of their large pleasure gardens often took into consideration good view positions for firework displays.

"Long live our childish games…these at least do not occasion any remorse" (St Sernin p. 11).

Many landscape architects take pilgrimages to visit the historic gardens in Spain, in Italy and France and today these places are considered worthy of restoring and preserving – often using public funds. when we visit these places today we conduct our selves in a appropriate manner of this day – we are serious students of garden design. Ordinary man has had rules of appropriate comportment for ways to use parks and gardens – already in place when the first royal gardens were opened to the public and very predominant in the 19th century. By this time public parks and gardens were not for pleasure but for promenade – to dress up in finest clothing and be seen by other fashionables. Playing was prohibited in these first large public parks and gardens. Crystal Gardens in London, designed for the World Exposition of 1851- at the height of Victorian era- is a fine example of how appropriate dress and style were used to impose behaviour patterns of propriety, while serving to inhibit the human urge to be playful (Zuylen, (1995)).

The playful garden landscapes at Villa Garzoni were designed to amuse impress and to serve as a setting for grand parties; today they are a destination for serious garden enthusiasts, many failing to understand or appreciate the fun or playful aspect in the garden.

Playing was something done at home, in private if at all. The Puritans saw pleasure as sin – and those modern societies, which developed under the influence of the Puritans, like the USA, still today retain a tendency to suspect public support for play and recreation and are characterised by a minimum of public spending on children's play. During the Victorian era however few wealthy people were constructing adult playgrounds – the public garden became a more serious place, a place for an airing, dress up in fancy dress, and at the same time gardening became a popular pleasure in itself for the wealthy who had the land and the staff (Brown, J.(1999)).

Today it would not be acceptable for a man of enormous wealth to build a play garden like those at Versailles, Villa Garzoni or Ville d'Este – as is underlined by the suspicion and criticism of Michael Jackson's Neverland. In fact it would be seen to be inappropriate to play in the gardens at Versailles today. When we play, we look to Disneylands and Legolands as well as the many other amusement parks with elaborately contrived amusements; and this kind of amusement has become a major industry. It is one of the puzzles of human nature that for centuries people were driven to amass wealth and then to show themselves above the ordinary person by developing elaborate outdoor gardens for their amusement, while today people who want to amass great wealth develop elaborate outdoor gardens to amuse the ordinary people. Is this an advancement in our understanding of the human urge to play? I think not.

When we want to find grand landscaped park settings for play we look to Disneyland or similar amusements parks. The high cost of admission is offset by secure and high quality playful environments where it is fully legal to play – even as an adult.

Today's wealthy elite play with things like jet planes, yachts, cars, gambling, race horses, drugs, sex, heli-skiing, the entertainment industry and other adventures that are seen to be fashionable. These kinds of play often involve defying death. The pleasures are not home and family based but take place in exotic locations. Playing, really playing, like fooling around in water, jumping, skipping, swinging are no longer fashionable adult activities. Nor is building gardens where adults can enjoy playful activities that so thrilled the European nobility of several hundred years ago. Adults who like to play, do so on the sly – they take their grandchildren out to the park or amusement centre as an excuse so they can play. We all benefit from playing this type of play –we shouldn't need to have a child beside us as an excuse to hop on a swing in the park and take a good high swing. It is okay to call it exercise, if you wish!

> **There can be no *Recreation* without delight** (Locke, J. *Some Thoughts Concerning Education*, Lasdun S. (1983), *Making Victorians*).

Playthings we inherited from the pleasure grounds of the wealthy

The seesaw. Illustration reproduced with permission The Osborne Collection of Early Children's Books, Toronto Public Library. St Sernin Mme, *Healthful Sports for Young Ladies*. Original drawings by Jean Dèmosthène Dugourc.

Play things adopted from the play of the wealthy were the swing, the seesaw and the wading pool/ water play. These were reduced to functional structures set out in the play yard under the guise of providing exercise and clean water.

Playthings we inherited from the educational movement

Already existing on the school yards for the elite were playing fields and some climbing/gym equipment and something called a giant stride or maypole. In 1846, Charlotte Brontë described a schoolyard in her novel *The Professor*, in this way: "A bare gravelled court, with an enormous 'pas de géant' in the middle, and the monotonous walls and windows of a boys schoolhouse round" (Bronte, (1989) p. 96). The pas de géant is explained in

Giant stride – 1970 version. Still to be found in playgrounds – and still enjoyed when well designed and well located. While clothing, architecture, transport, furniture and nearly everything else that is "designed" has changed greatly in form since 1850 – items for children's play often appear much as they did 150 years ago. Time truly stands still when we play!

the notes to the Penquin edition as "Giants step, a playground structure of a pole with ropes attached to a revolving head" (p. 297). These traditional facilities have continued to appear on playgrounds throughout the twentieth century. With the development of public schools in the nineteenth century there was often a school teachers residence attached, with space for gardens for the teachers. These gardens were often also tended by students. Outdoor areas for handwork, wood crafts and other practical lessons also were present in the early school yards in countries like Denmark. Today these items are often appearing on playgrounds both school playgrounds and kindergarten yards, and presented as a new trend in playgrounds.

Taken from the developing pedagogy around child care were the sandbox and climbing equipment brought outdoors from the gym. The function was to develop better physical health in city children – and there was no need for the space to be attractive – it should be neat, tidy and not cost very much. Later came outdoor building blocks and construction material, also adapted from the educational movement.

Playing at learning

Among the early advocates of special educational setting for young children were people like Johann Heinrich Pestalozzi (1766-1827), Friedrich Froebel (1782 -1852) and Dr Maria Montessori (1874 –1952). Pestalozzi established a school in Yverdun where he searched for new ways to educate children using the natural curiosity and desire to learn of the children. Froebel visited the school and took the search for a better education system further and began working with very young children. He was the originator of the idea of the "Kindergarten" – a garden for children. His school was closed in 1851 because the government disapproved of his work.

Maria Montessori was an Italian medical doctor and pedagogue who started her work based on observations of mentally ill children. Dr Montessori argued that children should be permitted greater freedom to explore the world around them and to be children, not forced to conform to adult norms. She was among the first to recognise the importance of childhood as a life phase and the need to respect children as persons. Today children's rights as persons is entrenched in the laws of most western countries and also based in a UN declaration of November 1989. While national governments today give official support to the idea of children as persons with rights, in daily practise local governing bodies still allocate children's need a relative low priority.

While many politicians and university wise men are heard making statements like "*our country's most precious resource is our children*" - there is however still a very general idea that society need not put too much emphasis on providing well for childhood as it is only a passing phase of life. It is built into our modern society that adulthood, particularly young adulthood, is the ultimate stage of life the time when one is a "real person".

The rest of life is either to be spent waiting to become a person or regretting having become too old to be a person. What a waste of the gift of life.

> Childhood is something we grow out of

The Seven Ages of Man
William Shakespeare In *As You Like It*, Act 11 Scene V11

All the world's a stage,
And all the men and women merely players:
They have their exits and their entrances;
And one man in his time plays many parts,
His acts beings seven ages. At first the infant,
Mewling and puking in the nurse's arms.
And then the wining school-boy, with his satchel
And shining morning face, creeping like snail
Unwillingly to school. And then the lover,
Sighing like furnace, with a woeful ballad
Made to his mistress' eyebrow. Then a soldier,
Full of strange oaths and bearded like a pard,
Jealous in honor, sudden and quick in quarrel,
Seeking the bubble reputation
Even in the cannon's mouth. And then the justice,
In fair round belly with good capon lined,
With eyes severe and beard of formal cut,
Full of wise saws and modern instances;
And so he plays his part. The sixth age shifts
Into the lean and slipper'd pantaloon,
With spectacles on nose and pouch on side,
His youthful hose, well saved, a world too wide
For his shrunk shank; and his big manly voice,
Turning again toward childish treble, pipes
And whistles in his sound. Last scene of all,
That ends this strange eventful history,
Is second childishness and mere oblivion,
Sans teeth, sans eyes, sans taste, sans everything.

Just a child

There is a generally accepted notion that childhood and playing are things we grow out of – so there is no need to design well for it. Childhood lasts for the first 16 to 18 years of ones life and then for the next 20 to 25 years one is "a person" – before old age begins to set in – and again there is no need to concern society to do anything lasting or well for this older age group. Playgrounds for children today, unlike gardens for the wealthy, are seen to have no requirement for design or aesthetic considerations in most communities – rather it is an issue of providing a minimal facility with the least inconvenience to "adult" i.e. serious interests. After all it is just for children. Design is serious adult business.

> Show me a city's playgrounds and I can tell you what is in the heart of the people who run the city .

References

Berrall, Julia S. (1978), *The Garden, An Illustrated History*, Penguin Books: Harmondsworth.

Brown, Jane. (1999), *The Pursuit of Paradise*, Harper Collins: London.

Burton, Thomas L. (1976), *Making Man's Environment: Leisure*, Van Nostrand Reinhold Ltd.: Toronto.

Lasdun, Susan. (1983), *Making Victorians, The Drummond Children's World, 1827-1832*. Victor Gollancz Ltd: London.

Lu Pu. (1990), *China's Folk Toys*, New World Press: Beijing

Rydahl, Klaus. (1999), "Yoyo jorden rundt" *Samvirke*, page 67, Februar.

St Sernin, Mademoiselle. (1974), *Healthful Sports for Young Ladies*, originally published by Rudolph Ackerman in 1822, reproduced in facsimile by the Osborne Collection of Early Children's Books, Toronto Public Library: Toronto.

Zuylen, Gabrielle van. (1995), *The Garden, Visions of Paradise*, Thames and Hudson Ltd.: London.

4 Design and Aesthetics – in relationship to play

Aesthetics in the playground

> "aesthetic – adj & n (US esthetic) - adj. 1.concerned with beauty or the appreciation of beauty. 2 having such appreciation, sensitive to beauty. 3 in accordance with the principles of good taste. – n. 1(in pl.) the philosophy of the beautiful, esp. In art. 2 a set of principles of good taste and the appreciation of beauty." *The Concise Oxford Dictionary*, (1990).

Children's outdoor play and playgrounds have not been seen to be a design issue and the need for beauty in the play yard has rarely been mentioned – in western societies. Therefore, it was a great surprise to me to find that in the statement of purpose for Kindergartens in China is found the statement "The gardens should be made green and beautiful".

Later, after learning just a little bit about the important of aesthetics in the Chinese culture I realised I shouldn't be so surprised. That there is a specific statement of beauty as a requirement in a public institution for children is not surprising considering the importance aesthetics plays in the Chinese culture. That there is NO similar statement in western societies statutes on the establishment of kindergarten is a shocking omission; considering how important aesthetics is to western civilisation. As shown the last chapter however, play spaces for children in the west have been seen to be functional spaces – used only by children who were not yet considered to have developed into real human beings.

Statute of Kindergartens in the People's Republic of China
Article 30

Kindergartens should have playgrounds for outdoor activities commensurate with their scale, facilities necessary for games and physical education should be available. Conditions should be created to provide sandpounds, animal-raising corners as well as the plantation gardens. The gardens should be made green and beautiful through plantation in accordance with the characteristics of kindergartens.

Aesthetics and play

To play is one most basic aesthetic experiences. Play has its roots in the human sense of aesthetic and our civilisation is based on the human urge to play. This is a big claim for something as overlooked as play but we have overlooked it partly because we took it for granted and partly because aesthetics is such a serious philosophical issue. Aesthetics is the relevant study of well educated adults while play is something childish and unimportant. However there are some adults who take play seriously for example the well known child psychologist, Bruno Bettelheim. He states:

> (Play) is the most important activity of human beings. I believe one can be successful and serious, deep down serious, only in an activity that also, to some degree, has the satisfaction that the child derives from play (Play – Ideas programme/CBC June 18 1987).

When we take play seriously then the connections between play and aesthetic are also more obvious.

Aesthetic impressions arise when one is conscious of one's surroundings and are most acute when one is aware that one is experiencing something for the first time. The first glimpse of the Alps, of the Parthenon, of the gardens of the Ville Lante or of Picasso's Guernica are the most moving. Of course we want to see more, experience more, to come to know more about the place or the object that aroused our aesthetic appreciation. We all have memories of similar impressions, of being moved to a higher state of aesthetic appreciation. We may mistakenly assume that such experiences are only for adults. This is not so.

Children – and particularly young children are very receptive to aesthetic experiences. Young children – as travellers in this world for the first time – see and are aware of the beauty of many things – things we adults have come to overlook. That is the advantage of experiencing things for the first time in a state of heightened awareness. Persons in the adult stage of life today have, for the most, lost this freshness; this condition of the child may be part of the explanation for the adult perception that children are closer to nature than are adults.

Aesthetic experiences are not limited to visual appreciation of beauty. We can appreciate beauty with all of our senses – all at the same time or, most often one or two at a time. We can enjoy the perfume of the rose, lavender and lilac, the sound of an orchestra and the song of the lark, the feel of velvet or modelling clay, the taste of chocolate and good wine. And what about that sensation experienced during takeoff of an aeroplane or on a swing – these are other pleasurable sensations that are also part of our aesthetic experiences.

> **Anaesthetic** is the opposite of **aesthetic** and means insensible or the absence of sensation.

Play happens in the search for aesthetic experiences.

The playful activities of young children are rooted in the children's innate urge to seek out sensory stimulation – and to repeat the pleasant ones again and again. Young children use all their senses to explore this world – they don't just stand and look at it. The sensations that comes into the brain from seeing, smelling, hearing, moving, touching, tasting, are the basis for the child's accumulation of knowledge of the world around them. Over time we come to know unpleasant and painful sensations are to be avoided and pleasant ones sought out.

Young children want to find out what they can do; they are seeking a response to their existence from the world around them. Children are masters of "hands on aesthetics" –they want to experience with the whole of their senses. It is not an issue of what something looks like but more an issue of what the child can do with it. With repetition they develop further skills and explore further what they can do. To have an aesthetic experience is to be attracted to the source of the pleasure or beauty. Creativity arises with the urge to recreate the aesthetic experience, perhaps in another way, to make an even greater sensation happen. Creativity arises in play as a means to make things happen, to see what happens when things are used in another way. Play happens in an effort to seek out an aesthetic experience.

Playing leads to culture

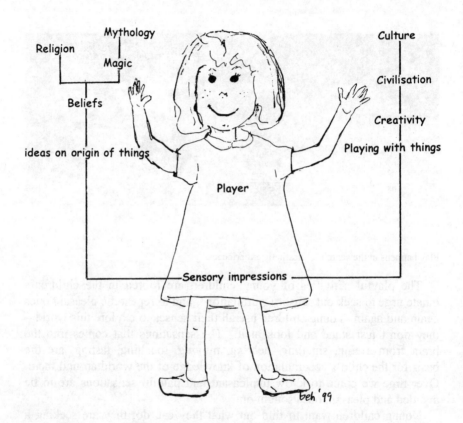

Playing leads to Culture

The human urge to play with things and to experience sensory stimulation is the source of civilisation, culture and religion – it should be held in great respect.

An aesthetic experience can be sensed – it cannot be scientifically analysed.

But is it good taste?

The aesthetic pleasures of young children often include appreciation of simple elements in the world around them —a shadow, playing in water, swinging and rocking, dancing, the beauty of sunlight on a dragonfly wing. They find beauty in the ordinary.

Young children, like early civilisations, value impressions of the world around them and do not concern themselves with the idea or concept of good taste – but with what tastes good, feels good and so forth. They have an innate appreciation of the beautiful, not a learned appreciation. Our culture teaches us another set of rules of beauty – a lecture in good taste.

The ultimate practitioner of good taste is the expert designer who leads the modern society in establishing what is the current trend in good taste and what is no longer good taste. This is a culturally learned appreciation and is not the same as the children's aesthetic. However designers and those who create children's play yards, if they think of beauty and aesthetics at all, use the learned adult designers criteria as the basis for determining what is beautiful in a play yard, not the children's.

"Cute" and play design

Another stream in designing for children has been the "make it cute" movement – where forms and images from illustrations used in children's stories are reproduced at large scale for outdoor spaces. This approach comes from the "feel good sensation" adults get when they give children toys and the basis for selection is the same – the adult pleasure and pleasant memories associated with childhood. This urge in adults has resulted in so many "sweet" little playhouses, play tree houses, and many decorative images painted onto the sides of play structures suggesting flowers, trees, animals and so forth. The most outstanding examples of "cute" are the plethora of designs of spring rides and rocking devices, depicting animals, vehicles and mythical figures which are intended for children to be rocked in. Many are coin-operated and are set out in shopping malls and stores. The design is intended to send a signal that this is for children but all to often mistreats children's sense of beauty and good design.

It is possible to make beautiful things for children that children appreciate and that also integrate adult good design values. "Cute" design talks down to children, treats their sensory experiences as second rate design. Look at children's own art – its originality, its vitality. It is not lame and "cute". Children should have access to good adult design and children's spaces should be designed well in accordance with the children's aesthetic as well as the adult. Children are very good at reading the environment around them and poor quality design for children is understood by them to state that children are not considered as important as adults. They may not be able to put words on their feelings and they may not be able to read street signs but they have already understood where they are placed in the hierarchy of society when the see the quality of the places they are given to play in.

I play therefore I am.

Play is a creative act and human play with objects, with symbols and ideas is the basis for the development of civilisation and culture. Play yards then, are breeding places of culture and creativity. The design of such places should recognise this much more than it has in the past.

Ludic elelments of design

Design is a serious business and designers are serious people. Yet designers and artists are among those adults whose approach to the world around them is closest to that of the children. Artists use their intuition and their senses to arrive at some new interpretation of the world around them and express this message in their creations. This is true for both the visual arts as well as dance, music and literature. Artists *play* with ideas, with words, with materials to create new impressions and interpretations. There is a relationship between play and the arts – not only demonstrated by the words we use for these activities but also demonstrated by the way in which both activities are practised. Artists play that is manipulate with words, with shapes, forms, colours, music notes, with material and ideas until such time as the parts all make the whole that the artist is seeking.

In the past several centuries art has become more available to the middle class and is no longer just for the very rich and nobility. Artists - as members of new art movements - set out their way of thinking in manifestos and essays in an attempt to have a wider understanding amongst their public and to disseminate their ideas to other realms of life. Art movements attracted all kinds of creative people – painters, musicians, architects and writers. They did not restrict their creative efforts to the "high arts" but applied their ideas to everyday life. This has resulted in aspects of art and design being applied to everyday things such as household objects, kitchen utensils and sometimes items for play. Architects and sculptors frequently have undertake to design furniture and decorative elements for homes. They have also tried to apply the principles of the art movement to urban design. Only on rare occasions have they applied their thinking to play furniture for the outdoor room.

The act of designing for play

Designing for play should be seen to be an art form – like composing music, writing a new stage play or creating a new painting. It is an act of creativity that in some way informs on the culture that it was developed within and contributes to the further development of that art form. It falls as a category of design most logically in the realm of garden design and like garden design has the elements of time and weather as factors that influence the design. Play area design is however more than just a spatial design issue. Designing for play should also contribute to the collective understanding of the role of play to humans and, at its best, interpret human playfulness or contribute to the possibility for playfulness in a new way.

Good art gives insight to the individual on life, beauty and the individuals place in this world. Good art must communicate to the beholder of the work in such a way that the artist's experiences and inspiration can touch and inform the perceiver – and for this reason good art is art which is more than just a personal private expression by an artist but is an artistic communication reaching out to touch other people. Good art for children must touch and communicate to the children and good design in children's play spaces would be designs that communicate some insight into life on this planet and some elements of playfulness in a way that children perceive and appreciate the messages in the design. The design must add to the quality of the playfulness to the space and something more – which is the artist or designers unique way of telling something to the players about life here on earth.

> If the designer is a good artist he will not, however, content himself with existing materials and conventions. He will try to change things or at least explore the possibilities for change (de Lucio Meyer 1973 p. 205).

Who designs for play? There are a number of streams of design for play. First we have the designer of toys – and there has been a good foundation for quality toy design in the past century. Designers like Antonio Vitali, Kurt Naef, Patrick Rylands and Kay Bojesen have created toys that just demand you take them into your hands and do something with them. Corporate toy designs like Lego and Mattel also excel at making things that appeal to the player both in children and adults. These are individual things that evoke an aesthetic response – an urge to reach out and see what can be done with it.

Art theories applied to a play item are rare in the history of modern art – one such example is the Rietveld Beach Buggy of 1918, by the architect Gerritt Thomas Rietveld. Several versions of the buggy were made from 1918 to 1923 for the private pleasure of the Rietveld family and friends. Rietveld was a member of the NeoPlasticism movement. Other members of this movement included the painters Mondrian and Theo Van Doesburg. They believed that their ideas of abstraction could be applied to the urban scene. In a statement to explain their ideas they wrote " The word *art* no longer means anything to us. In its place we demand the building up of our environment according to creative laws, deriving from a set principle. These laws, linked to those of economics, mathematics, engineering, hygiene, etc. lead to a new plastic unity." (Benevolo, L.(1977) p 407).

In the case of the Beach Buggy, colours and forms are applied as if onto a three dimensional painters canvas. In no way does the artist attempt to create a new way to play but applies his artistic views of colour and form to a typical homecrafted item for children. The individual forms and colours of the parts that make up the body of the buggy express this new idea of building up an environment in accordance with a set principle. It is a way of decorating or disguising a more mundane object, not a rethinking of a Beach Buggy.

The application of art principles as decoration on functional objects for everyday use happens because much of modern art has been about abstraction and testing aesthetic responses. After the invention of the camera and other industrial means of reproduction art needed to find a new niche as it no longer was needed as a visual record. Artists moved into the word of the intellect, and focused on new ways to interpret and capture impressions of the senses, light, colour, form, movement were all removed from their association with objects but were elements of intellectual and artistic curiosity. The play was in the act of creation, and the viewer could appreciate the playfulness.

This approach to forms and colours, once accepted by the public, were then taken into industrial design where it is still very necessary to work with actual objects where only the form, colour and material can reflect designers taste and attitudes – there is still an inherent functional aspect that must be retained.

Reitveld Beach Buggy of 1918 – an application of artistic principles to an everyday child's play thing. Illustration courtesy of Victoria and Albert Museum.

Educational toys were developed, not by designers, but by educators and technician. Froebel (1752 – 1852) worked out a system of building blocks according to scientific principles. Further refinements led to the invention of interlocking building blocks such as that made of rubber by Minibrix (a precurssor to the Lego block) in 1935.

An engineering enthusiast, Frank Hornsby, invented the Meccano in 1901 to teach children the principles of engineering. Mass production and international distribution of educational toys began in Europe around 1930 and by the late 1930s there were manufacturer's catalogues showing "the best toys for every age" (Burton, A. (1996) p 92). These catalogues include the first versions of many of the bright colourful toys we know today in 2001.

This was one stream of design for play where the play items are small and intended for private purchase for an individual child. The adults who designed the toys were professional educators or adults who had a passion or a particular activity. They were not artists. Toys and toy design originated as a craft rather than a serious act of design or high art.

Another stream of modern "design" for play is the corporate and individual design of large play items to be set up for collective play – for everybody's children- in outdoor playgrounds. Originally these items would be produced by small local firms who worked with metal – welding firms and smithies. After the second world war companies began to expand their business and some became national and international. Today there is a bewildering array of play equipment producers – some very small and local, others selling around the world.

Design for outdoor play

Playground equipment was intended to develop children's physical skills or to use up their excess energy so they would behave when they went back indoors, so the emphasis was and still is on physical activity such as swinging, climbing, seesawing and sliding. Most manufacturers of playground equipment offer a minimum of design and a maximum of function. Most products available today clearly show their roots in gymnastic equipment and rustic home-made structures. Design in terms of original artistic solutions is not often found in this commercial sector; it is much more a matter of modification, "redesign" and material substitution.

Designing structures to be mass produced for public play areas has been almost anonymous – with few individual designers or design styles to be recognised. One exception is the Dane, Tom Lindhardt Wils, one of the founders of the play equipment company KOMPAN A/S, who has achieved recognition for designs such as the "Spillophøne" - see photo next page (designed ca 1970). This item is a design that very successfully combines an aesthetics of playfulness with the possibility for the child to be playful with the item.

One of the ironies of the play world is that this beautiful design is scorned by many Danish early childhood experts based in a variety of unfounded arguments and a distrust of successful play equipment manufacturers. Beautiful design in play equipment is not an important issue to early childhood experts – which is one reason why there is so little design found in children's play yards attached to child care centres. Playground design is also not taken seriously by the design profession. In a book published in 1999, *Designmaskinen,* focusing on design as an outcome of processes with the culture, there is not one mention of playground equipment. Only briefly mentioned are toys for private consumption like Lego.

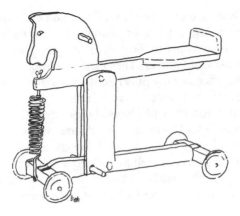

A rocking horse for indoor use – 1937. Design by Betty Bashall Toys, original at the Bethnall Museum of Childhood- Sketch by Barbara Hendricks.

A rocking horse outdoors on the playground. This design (from 1970s) for play combines good design and good fun. Even adults can enjoy this in terms of visual quality. The design talks directly to children who know immediately that this is something for them.

The artists playground

Individual architects and artists have set their hand at designing unique play structures and even whole plays for children, but for the most these places serve more as a monuments to the play of the designer than as places for the creativity of the child player. These sites are established as an element of civic pride and often occupy prestigious locations within the city. Artists like Isamu Noguchi, F. Hundertwasser, architects such as Richard Dattner and Louis Kahn (worked with Noguchi on the Riverside Drive Park Playground in New York) have all created one or several play equipment or sculptures for playing. Landscape architects also have designed play structures for public spaces as well as the play yard. Arvid Bengtsson in his work in Swedish public parks demonstrated an outstanding sensitivity toward children's life in cities and a fine intuitive understanding of the role of play.

In nearly every city one can find one or two play yards where an artist or an architect have set their hand at making play structures for children's play – and some are successful at creating items that make a contribution to the development of designing for children's play – but for the most these are just another artists rendering of a swing, a slide or a climbing structure. For example, in 1998, Stockholm was celebrated as the European cultural capital. As part of the cultural experiences in Stockholm an artist was

The Fruit Playground designed to celebrate Stockholm as the European Cultural Capital, 1998.

commissioned to create a new type of art playground – the result was "The Fruit Playground". In this playground there is great innovation and skill in the use of materials and paint but there is no innovation in providing for play here. There is nothing in this playground that contributes to the development of design for play. After the designer was finished the creative play was also over – playing here is limited to the usual swinging (if you can find out how or someone helps you), sliding and twirling around.

The play environment

The third stream of play design is the design of the whole play area – or "play environment" as it has come to be known. This area of work has not been seen as any kind of prestigious design work - and is often taken up by gardeners, engineers, teachers and early childhood experts. Landscape architects are getting more involved in this work but there is often not enough funding to permit payment of professional fees. If there is enough money for professional fees, all too often the architect takes on the work. It seems that playground design is the work of anybody – and therefore nobody. It shouldn't be a puzzle anymore that playgrounds are all so alike- as Thomas Burton (1976) criticised in Chapter 3. There is no profession of playground design – many other professions take on the task of playground design – using the "usual" as the template for their work. Playground design, not being a profession, has suffered from a lack of innovation and new thinking. Changes that have occurred have resulted from small innovations as new materials are used, redesign of traditional structures and forms and demands for improved safety.

Playground design, not being a profession, has suffered from a lack of innovation and new thinking.

This is a somewhat harsh judgement applied to playground design – there is some innovative work done – but far too little in comparison to the number of play areas established or renovated every year. One of the primary reasons that innovation in design is so limited is that there is so little funding available for this work. The other is that there is so little space set aside for children's outdoor play.

Space is an element of quality and lack of space for playing is also a lack of quality play opportunities. Squeezing a play structure into a too small space shows a lack of sympathy for children and their lives.

Money and space are two of the main determinants of quality – this is true for architecture as well as for landscape architecture – and for playground design. Modern and post modern architecture has failed to address good quality design for low cost housing as well as other aspects of modern city life where there is little money available. And playground design continues to be the poor relation which always needs to be on the look out for another source of a handout or donor.

Play area design is serious

There was a movie shown on TV once featuring an American social reformer trying to deal with the issue of the homeless. He asked some poor people how poverty could be eradicated. This is a question that has consumed many a thesis and report of university students who want a make a difference in their world. The answer from the poor was – "That is easy – just give us enough money". The same is, to some extent true of playgrounds – one way to deal with the proliferation of poor quality playgrounds is to put more money into the development and operation of play areas.

The other reason for the failure of so many play area designs is the failure of the design professions to take children's play seriously as a professional area of design. In my own experience I know well respected landscape architects who have developed specialities in Zoo design, in Golf Course design, but those who have branched off to specialise in play area design are destined to remain mostly unknown and underpaid. All general offices in landscape architecture feel fully competent to design playgrounds whereas they would not undertake a zoo or a golf course.

There are some exceptions of course – let us celebrate them. These include landscape architects like Jan Lindahl, a Swedish landscape architect, whose work on the grounds of the housing projects in Hällefors moves playing beyond the edges of the sandpit and blends art and playfulness into the residential landscape in a special Swedish way. There are also some enormously talented play area designers working in countries like Japan and Korea. At the same time many designers in Japan are introducing an element of playfulness into their architecture and art.

Colour and design for play

Toys seem to always have been colourful. Chinese traditional toys as early as the tenth century AD, were produced for sale in an array of traditional colours of red, green, yellow purple and black and white. Colour was applied to achieve a sharp, contrasting effect (Lu Pu, (1990), p 141).

From the early beginnings of the toy industry in Germany in the 16th century the toys manufactured for sale were brightly painted. This is perhaps a carry over from their peasant craft origins. Nevertheless, for centuries toys for children have been produced in the colours of the rainbow and these colours have come to be associated with childhood – much like a set of wax crayons. These colours of red, yellow, orange, blue, green, and purple, along with black and white, are often referred to as primary colours – however technically they are not all primaries. In association with childhood these colours have been applied in high saturation and they are not mixed with white or black to produce a tone or shade. Colour choice and application was a matter of local tradition as well as the availability of colour pigment at low cost.

With the introduction of synthetic dyes, colour became separated from those forms with which they traditionally appeared and industrial objects could be produced in just about any colour. Modern art movements experimented with the separation of colour from form. Since the middle of the 20th century, with the advent of colour photography and colour printing, colour images has come to be easily reproduced and manipulated at little cost. Today, humans are surrounded by a greater variety of images and forms in colour than every before and colour has become a matter of choice, with almost no relationship to the form, function or meaning of the object.

Modern art and industry have succeeded in removing colour from form only in the sense that adults no longer automatically associate a particular colour with a manufactured object, except where it is an element of brand recognition. In many cases this way of applying colour has led to visual chaos in instances where there is not an overall design approach, for example signage and storefronts in some commercial areas. Each sign and storefront is competing for the attention of the customer and the result is that the eye is totally overwhelmed. Bright colours in the outdoor adult world have come to symbolise commercialism and consumerism as well as poor design or absence of design. They also signal festivals, markets and circuses and a party atmosphere.

This chaotic use of colour in the adult commercial world, has resulted in a reaction to the use of colour and a mistaken idea that very strong colours and too many colours are confusing and disturbing to children. With regular intervals in the last half of the 20th century there has been the

Reappearing at intervals through the 20th century is the idea that playthings in the outdoors should not have any applied colour. An example of adult giving children what the adults want them to have, while ignoring what the children like.

theory set forward that children are best served by that which is pure – that is with no bright colour. Thus the regular resurgence of the purist movement in toys – non treated wood with no colour applied. (See also Chapter 12 – Green Children.) This is an adult idea based in belief with no consideration given to the visual aesthetics of children. These adults are trying to develop a particular adult aesthetic in the children.

Certain educational movements as well as life style movements, in their wish to disassociate themselves with commercialism and mass production have proclaimed that colour should be removed from the world of the child. The latest movement of this type is the Green/Environmental movement but elements can also be found in the Rudolf Steiner education movement and other pedagogical circles.

Another approach is that adults need to teach children what is good taste, so the adults will impose current adult fashion in colour harmonies on the children's rooms, their outdoor environments as well as in the clothing put on the children. This can be done because the purchasing power for these items still is with the adults, not with the user- the children. What the adults are missing is that the children have another perception of the world – a perception where colour is still important as a signal giver and where children get pleasure from bright colours. Children have learned from infanthood that bright colours are associated with toys, with play, with things that have to do with children, and these colours appeal to them; minimally as signals that children are welcome here. When used with consideration, the colours in an outdoor space can also help the children understand how the environment is put together. Here, it is not an issue of *what* colour but of strong colour *contrasts*.

Most manufactured children's toys for sale in western countries continue to be produced in bright colours. This is particularly true of toys for the infants and toddlers up to three years of age. For children of pre-school age and young-school age there is a tendency toward series of boys colours and other series of girls colours. The trend toward toys associated with movies and videos has brought with it also particular corporate branding of shapes and colours in toys.

Traditionally toy designs have always included bright colours, however playground equipment throughout most of the history of playgrounds was relatively colourless. Metal supports were left uncoloured or painted the traditional colours used for objects in public parks and gardens. The idea was that the play area should blend in with the park atmosphere. Wood was not used much in the manufacture of play equipment for public spaces until the late 1960s where it appeared as material used to construct multi-functional play structures. These first structures were also with little or no colour.

Colour was introduced with the increased use of plastic and plywood in the early 1970s. For the most, colour appeared with individual components and was a characteristic of the manufacturing process or source. The deliberate and careful application of colour, based in an artistic design, appeared in playground equipment in 1970. This was an influence from the modern art movements and the beginning of the interest of designers in playground equipment. Since that time the use of bright colours has spread throughout the play equipment manufacturing industry, mostly applying colour with no artistic theory, no relation to the shapes or forms or understanding of how children use colour to explore the environment. Some manufacturers are so uninterested in design that they offer their play equipment in a wide range of colours and the buyer makes the final selection. This has led to a reaction amongst educators of young children and outdoor designers, and there is a tendency today amongst certain education movements toward removing colour from the play equipment and going back to the conditions of the 19th century.

Art and the art of playing

Art, real "adult" art in public spaces often serves children as places to play –that kind of short term, explorative physical play which is what most play in public spaces is limited to. Sculptures that are set at ground level or on low pedestals almost always are attractive places for children to climb through and explore. Fountains are even more interesting as bases for playful activities. They have for the most been created with no consideration that children would play on them.

Playing is the art of finding out "what can I do with this?"

Adult designers sophisticated aesthetic versus children players hands on aesthetic

Design of children's play spaces requires some form of union or marriage between the adult designer's sophisticated good taste and the children's immediate sensory response to their environment. This combination is a powerful when it happens.

Playing is the art of finding out "what can I do with this?". It seems often that the best settings for play are ones that are chaotic and not designed. Playgrounds like the adventure playground or building playground offer some of the most satisfying play experiences for school age children. Here the children are the "designers" of the play but not of the play space. Not all public playgrounds can be building playgrounds however – and objects that form the stage for playing should be set up in places around the city – whether these places are called playgrounds or some other kind of public space.

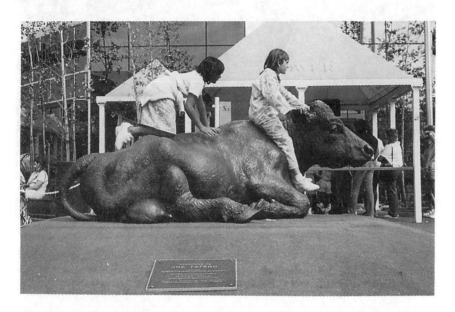

Rounded forms of sculptures– seem to be very attractive to children and where such sculptures are accessible children are found on them.

> "Paradoxical as it sounds, it is often only by going back to early or primitive sources that truly individual aesthetic expression can be found." (de Lucio-Meyer, JJ. (1973) p 101.)

References

Benevolo, L. (1977), *The History of Modern Architecture* vol. 2, The M.I.T. Press, Cambridge, Mass.

Bettleheim, B. (1987), "Play-Ideas Programme"/Canadian Broadcasting Corporation, June.

Burton, A. (1996), *Children's Pleasures*, V&A Publications: London.

Burton, T.L. (1976), *Making Man's Environment: Leisure*, Van Nostrand Reinhold Ltd. Toronto.

de Lucio-Meyer JJ. (1973), *Visual Aesthetics*, Harper & Row: New York.

Engholm I and Michelsen A. (1999), *Designmaskinen*, Gyldendal: Copenhagen.

Lu Pu. (1990), *China's Folk Toys*, New World Press: Beijing.

The birds were much more interesting to play with than the play items. Children look for possibilities to make movement, to change, to make something happen when at a playground. Their aesthetic response is spontaneous and expressed through activity.

5 Society's Criteria

Adults in control

Playgrounds for public use began as a means of reforming the industrial city, they took hold as a standard offering of modern city planning after world war one and became even more important when the automobile took over the streets. It became essential to get the play off the streets where it had always happened so that the cars could be free to move at greater speeds. Adult considerations and convenience have always been the motivating factor in the provision of public playgrounds. Controlling where the children were and ensuring that they were engaged in appropriate activities was and remains the underlying goal.

Today the provision of playgrounds has become integrated into the planning process for most western style residential developments and as part of the space attached to a child care centre or a school. A small space is set aside in the planning stage. How well it is furnished is an indication of the value that society places on childhood as a time of life. The

Child development theories in western society

Classical child development theory (Prevailing approach in government institutions.)	Romantic child development theory (related to alternative life styles, model cities, "new" thinking.)
Based in the scientific approach to childhood. Child is to be shaped and educated into human being. Control of children. A child is an empty vessel to be filled by society. Children are at varying levels of responsibility as they develop. Adults need to protect, guide and teach.	Based in the poetic approach to childhood. Children will develop naturally. children should be free. Children are close to nature. Childhood is related to the primitive, innocent, inherently competent. Children know what they need, will learn when they are ready.

prevailing approach to child development in western governments is the classical child development theory based in a hierarchy of ages and this theory of children has formed the programmes of most of the public institutions that deal with childhood in society.

While both the classical and romantic theories have existed side by side in western thinking since before the beginning of the industrial era, the classical theory has been found to be the most practical in terms of organising institutions around childhood and children. It is in the nature of the romantic movement that institutions would have difficulty administering such an approach. Nevertheless the romantic theories routinely are aired as an alternative or improvement over the existing institutional approach, and sometimes even today is presented as new thinking. The romantic theory has been a great influence on "new thinking" in playground provision such as the so-called "nature" and forest playgrounds (see chapter 12).

Play contributes to learning

Society in general is in agreement that children's play provision is linked to children's development and learning. This is the basis of arguing for play – even in the children's convention of the United Nations where the Children's Right to Play (1989) is a subsection of The Child's Right to Education.

> **"If children only learned what they were taught, the human race would have died out long ago – perhaps after the first generation"** source – unknown.

Who are the adult experts in children's play?

Earlier it was pointed out that there is no one profession of play experts but that many professions claim to have an expertise in children's play. This has meant that there is no common body of knowledge of expertise in children's play – and therefore no specific professional organisation to further the development of skills and knowledge. In general society has accepted that play is a subsidiary of education and educators are the society's play caretakers. For the most the educators do their best and have endeavoured to serve the children's needs by keeping some aspect of play provision on the agenda at the local political level.

Education is a goal that most adults today can accept and even value for children. As play is accepted as a necessary auxiliary to education and learning, teachers have taken on the hat of supervising and supporting children's playground activities. It is also accepted without question that educators are also the experts in our society about children's development and about children's play and educators of educators – that is university professors in Departments of Education - sit in many positions of highest authority and are seen as the ultimate spokesman and opinion leaders around society's attitudes toward children's play.

Experts on play and play spaces

	Experts in play	Outdoor space to play
1800s	☐	☐
1900s	☐	☐

Developmental theories – very briefly

The rationale for public play provision is based in the belief that playing contributes to learning. This has led to the idea of *the developmentally appropriate play area,* which means that the play possibilities provided are in step with the level of mental, physical and emotional development of the children as set out in prevailing child development theories. The theories of development are based in the notion that young children's play goes through various stages which reflect their level of development and that child development is hierarchical, that is that at each succeeding stage of childhood we are "more developed" than the stage before.

A classic example of play developmental theory is the idea that children's social play goes through various stages which reflect the mental and social development of the child. This notion is based in a study was carried out by M. Parten in 1932 and is still referred to today. This theory of social play or interpersonal play sees young children engaging in six stages of social play starting out with unoccupied behaviour, moving on to playing alone, called solitary play, the third stage was onlooker – watching other children at play, then engaging in playing side by side but not really interacting – this is called parallel play. The next stage is associative play where the child plays with others but holds to own interests rather than support the groups interest, and the final stage is co-operative activity where there the children negotiate different roles and organise themselves into complementary play actions, also called role playing. This theory was based on observations of children in a pre-school care setting.

Parten's categories of social play

Unoccupied behaviour ▶ solitary play ▶ onlooker ▶ parallel play ▶ associative play ▶ co-operative play.

Another view of play assigns even more clearly ages and developmental stages to ways of playing. This approach was taken by developmental researchers such as Piaget and Smilansky. Here play is categorised as: functional play, construction play, dramatic play and games with rules. Functional play begins in infanthood, while construction play was seen to start around two years as does dramatic or symbolic play. Games with rules come later in the child's development around the age of 7. This is a very broad generalisation of the approach which fills many academic books in its details (Frost and Klein, 1983).

Infant	**24 months**	**24 months**	**6-7 years**
Functional	Construction	Dramatic	Games with rules

Play area design to enhance development of the child

The general outcome of these theories was the broad acceptance that play and stages of development - physically, intellectually and socially were connected - and it was concluded that play spaces should be furnished and set out in such a way that it was appropriate to the level of development of the child. It should be pointed out that most of this work involves input from child educators and is limited for the most to child care institutions where children are segregated from each other by age grouping.

Recent work by researchers such a Jan Kampmann (Kampmann and Andersen, 1996) show that play is much more nuanced and is influenced by the norms of the children in the group and by the formation of play groups amongst the children. The activities of the group and the learning of social skills seems to be the most important aspect of play to the children. Nevertheless in a very broad brush approach one can see the logic in designing play spaces that support the children's play interests and stages of development.

What should a playground do?

The purpose and content of a playground will differ depending on whether it is a play facility attached to a pre-school child care centre, a school yard, an after-school programme or a public parks. The care centres and the schools are places where children are grouped according to ages and gender

> Society today will only provide for children when they are seen as future adults, and society expects them to go to pre-school and then to school to train to be capable members of adults society in the future; yet this same society does not act responsibly towards children and young people. How are children to learn to be responsible to society?

Adult cynicism forms outdoor play provision. Children should learn while they play – this is the clear message here. The producer has manipulated adult values to sell play items for children to adults who do not know how to evaluate good play experiences for children. That the subject for learning here is about nature is not surprising- adults today feel children aren't exposed enough to nature. Rather than providing a quality nature experience- learning about nature comes in the form of graphics on a very traditional climbing structure. This is a playground in mid-London.

in some parts of the world, and therefore it is easier to identify the appropriate level of development for such play areas.

Public parks, however, pose a greater problem in that they are to be used by all. This is one of the reasons why public playgrounds look so much alike – the same recipe was used. The idea is that the play opportunities that are placed there are for all ages and interests, with the result that the play items are really of little interest to any. Standard public park playground design today consists of structures and facilities that support primarily physical activities and are aimed at the average age of user of between 6 to 9 years of age, primarily boys. Sometimes this fits the user – more often it doesn't. Chapter 6 addresses the needs of the children in the playground. It is however a likelihood that eventually the play that occurs there fits the equipment, as only those who find the play equipment interesting will continue to play with it, (other than very young children who are taken there by their parents and who have no choice.) Sometimes though the only players at the place are very young children – all those who can exercise a choice go elsewhere. The non-use of public parks and playgrounds by children may not be because they prefer to be watching television or playing at computers but because public playgrounds just aren't interesting and challenging enough. Often it is because they are located in the wrong places.

Adult demands on a playground in a public park

As we have already seen there is no consensus about play and playgrounds and no common body of expertise. This means it is not possible to be precisely accurately about all the various ideas that adults have about what should a playground be like; here I have prepared a very general outline that reflects most adult demands.

Demands on a public playground from the adult society
1. Safety/ meets established regulations for safety
2. No maintenance/lasts "forever"
3. Easy to construct/install/amateur/unskilled labour
4. Can be used by all
5. Gets children off the streets and out of malls
6. A place where children wear off energy/get fresh air
7. Pleasant view for adults/harmonises with park atmosphere
8. Civic pride
9. Minimal expense

While some communities can quite rightly argue that they do not prescribe to all of these, these are the considerations that appear again and again in discussion with public park providers around the world.

Who uses public playgrounds?

While it is generally agreed that public parks are for all, not all use public parks. Who uses public parks and playgrounds in public parks varies from city to city and place to place. This also seems to vary over time –both in terms of time of day and season but also over decades. There was a time, now past, where it was known that children were the greatest uses of public open space. But in many cities the children have disappeared from public parks. Many parks seem to be relatively unused much of the time –however we must not forget the benefit of just being able to look out at a green open space. The reasons for the non-use of public parks are many and varied, from the institutionalisation of childhood, lack of time by young parents, time taken up watching television, videos and playing computers. But one of the most compelling factors resulting in the reduction of young children's use of public spaces is the issue of fear of violence and "stranger danger". In small communities where everybody knows everybody's children and in places where there still is a strong custom of public use of parks, children are still seen playing in the park.

In southern European countries there is a somewhat different pattern of use of public spaces than one finds in northern European countries. In countries like Italy and Spain the outdoor public spaces are used much more as gathering places for the neighbourhood –primarily because the weather permits this more often but also because the social life is still more based in the immediate neighbourhood. In countries like Italy it is also still a custom that fathers and grandfathers take the children to the park on Saturday or Sunday. In northern countries people use the outdoors in good weather but they tend to use private terraces and gardens. On Saturdays and Sundays families drive out of the neighbourhood to an amusement park, zoo or other place for family entertainment – often a commercial centre. Furnishing these private places is a big business these days, while the nearby park lays neglected with only a minimum of facilities. Life styles then of the adult population has a great influence on the use patterns of public parks.

Demands on a supervised pre-school play yard attached to a child care centre

In a typical kindergarten setting the demands on a play area are more specifically oriented toward child development and can be more targeted to the development level of the children who play there. This is easier to do because the user group is easily identifiable and shares a narrower spectrum of stages in their level of development. These play yards can be made more varied and interesting because there are adults who are working there with the children.

What society demands from a play yard attached to a care centre:

1. Encourages play
2. Stimulates senses
3. Nurtures curiosity
4. Encourages children's interaction with resources
5. Promotes interaction amongst children.
6. Promotes children's interactions with adults
7. Supports social and physical needs
8. Complements cognitive play
9. Complements social play
10. Promotes social and intellectual development

(Monroe, M. in Frost and Sunderlin, (1985), p 197.)

Play is the first consideration in this listing of the function of a playground – and was the reason why I choose this one. It is one where the author has tried to achieve a balance between the play possibilities and the developmental opportunities. This listing is very much a product of the U.S approach to providing for children's play but changes only marginally around the world.

School play yards

The demands on a school yard are tremendous, in terms of the concentration of numbers of children at play and also because these children have a great need to be able to move about and be free in between the times they are in the classroom. Today, there is a move to integrate a form of playfulness into the teaching methods in the formal curriculum and to look to the outdoor space around the school building as a resource to supplement the facilities of the indoors. This movement has come to be called "The Outdoor Classroom" or landscapes for learning.

In her work with a community group in Grand Rapids Michigan, Aase Eriksen identified the following demands or criteria from the community: (This site was a public park adjacent to a school.)

What society demands from a school yard
The site design should:
-serve the needs of student and faculty
-be an amenity to the surrounding community
-invite young and old to visit, linger and relax
-afford children with opportunities to explore and wonder
-provide children with experience of well designed, lively settings
-provide for the needs of all age groups, and for the interaction between
 age groups
-provide for a variety of sensory experiences through the use of varying
 textures and materials
-support learning and development
-provide for supervision, so children can be permitted to move freely.
 (Eriksen, A. (1985) p 47.)

Translation of criteria

The stated demands of society for a public playground tend to be idealistic and general. It is the designers role to translate these statements into specific physical facilities –and this process of translation is a very subjective one. For example while neither the statements from Monroe or Eriksen mention funding – the designer will have been given a budget and they will always be translating with available funding in mind.

Another un-stated and subjective factor is the type of interaction between adults and children that will take place on the playground. If the adults who work on the playground see their function as playground policemen, stopping any unacceptable play activity, then the form of the playground is determined by the need for one or two supervisors to be able to see all the children all the time. If the role of the supervisor is to enable play to happen and to support playful exploration, then there may be a demand for places for children where they can hide from the adult. Such criteria are not stated because it is assumed that all members of the adult society share the same understanding of the role of the adult on the playground.

Global versus local cultural criteria

While in many ways playgrounds look alike around the world, there are some local differences in both design, supervision and construction practises that the designer must be aware of. The designer who works across cultures will find that he or she needs to be careful with their assumptions and translation of the adult criteria and work within the assumed cultural reference of the local society. For example it is a standard demand in Denmark that good play areas have places where the children can get away from the adult supervisor. In this culture there is a concern that childhood has become too much supervised, that children are always being watched by adults and it is felt that this is not a healthy situation for children. In the USA however it is a rare play area designer who would dare to suggest that the play area design include corners that are deliberately designed so the children can hide away from the adults. Here it the responsibility of the adult caregivers to ensure that the children are safe at all times and it is the adult concern that must be served. These are two different views of adults and children on the play yard – and each is to be respected as part of the design criteria.

Scene 1. "Fire is a necessity on a playground. Young children are fascinated with it and they need to learn how to safely deal with fire through experience with it."

Some cultural differences in adult demands and prohibitions on the playground

Many of the cultural differences in demands on the playground come up in terms of prohibitions based in safety demands. Some of the most remarkable prohibitions are:

1. Firepole
A firepole is not permitted in some countries or prohibited for use by children under five or six. Yet some other countries children at the age of three are encouraged to learn how to use a firepole and by age of four most children in these countries are very good at using one – even when wearing slippery winter clothes and mitts.

2. Materials used in the playground - metal or wood
The material used to construct items on a playground can also be a matter of local and cultural preferences, with some consideration for climate. Some countries playground safety requirements prohibit metal on playground structures because there is a fear that in freezing weather children will get their tongue stuck on the metal. Just outside the playground lamp posts, signs and fence posts are metal. Children don't touch them in cold weather!

3. Hygiene
Countries such as France have almost eliminated sand on the playground due to a concern for hygiene and the fear that dogs and cats will soil the sand creating a health hazard to children. No real effort has been made to provide adequate space for dogs and cats as well as children's sand play.

4 Clean play
Water play and playing with sand and water tend to be messy activities-and in countries where adults take great pride in dressing their children up in expensive fashionable clothes when they go to the park, sand and water play are not acceptable on the playground This is true of countries like France where children's dress reflects the status of the parents. The children should not get very dirty while playing. In other countries, like in USA and Denmark, a child who is dirty after a tour on the playground is seen to be a child who has played well.

Towards developing a new set of society's criteria for play area design

During much of this century attitudes toward children and children's play have been based in our society's value for education and child development, focussing on the child as a human becoming. At the end of the century there have been some new voices. Play has begun to be seen in a much wider context and it is recognised that children have rights as persons and are members of society. Children and childhood are moving from being invisible in society –or at least having been kept in the shadow of the family, and are becoming more visible. Play too is moving from being a stepchild of education and learning to being a legitimate human activity that doesn't need excusing. The twenty first century society can be a time when human beings of all ages come to better understand the joy of living.

Children's playgrounds are filled with play equipment that adults want to give children, *not* with the things that children want to play with. This explains why there are so many unused playgrounds.

As play moves out from being a section of education, designers and artists will become more important as form givers for playful spaces – not only the types of public play spaces being built today – but including elements of human playfulness in all types of public spaces. Such work has started already. Forerunners like Hundertwasser have shown us how very attractive such spaces can be to all ages.

Protecting children from society

One of the major focuses of work and study on children's playgrounds over the last ten years has been the issue of safety of the playground. After thousands of hours of meetings and discussion there has been developed a whole range of standards and guidelines for playground safety –for the most focussing on the construction of manufactured playground equipment for public spaces. This has been carried out with major input from the playground manufacturing industry assisted by safety officers and safety inspectors. This work was carried out as a reaction to the concern over the number of injuries that were occurring to children on playgrounds and the problem that arose in an industry where there was a whole jungle of standards and local guidelines which could be used to protect local industry more than local children at the playground. The result has been the publication over the last several years of standards in the USA, in Canada and in most of Europe.

Who's Having All the Fun?
Expert professions who study play or influence play opportunities

Profession	View of Play
Biologist Psychologist Educator Pedagogue	Adaptive/contributes to growth, development and socialisation.
Sociologists	Imperial social system
Communication theorists	Play preceded language
Mathematicians	Strategy and probability
Anthropologists	Ritual vs. play
Folklorists	Traditional play and games
Mythology scholars	Play is the sphere of the gods
Psychiatry Medicine	Play as a diagnostic tool Play as therapy
Leisure science/recreation	Relaxation, fun
Architects Landscape architects Urban designers/planners Industrial designers	Play is a physical design problem
Engineers	Physical construction issue/safety
Politicians	Tax burden, funding, play policies, liability, the child's right to play

The work of the standard setting committees is by mostly voluntary workers, in that none of the committee are paid by the standard setting bodies but by other agencies who have a vested interest in playgrounds and child safety. One of the goals was to establish a standard of professional practise which eliminated foreseeable hazards from the construction and installation of playground equipment, while aiming at retaining some aspect of risk in the play. Another goal was to be able to reduce the chaos and hysteria that has arose as a result of courts of law awarding very large compensation to persons injured on a playground. A third goal was to establish some form of international standard to reduce the likelihood that national standards served as trade barriers. Design of playgrounds for the most was seen to be a functional issue – equivalent to the construction and assembly of the individual items.

The concern over the number of injuries to children on playgrounds is a curious society one. It is based in the idea that children should be able to play freely, without injury, more than that there have been a worrying number of injuries to children on playgrounds. In general, playground equipment is quite low down in the list of items as a source of injury to children.

Traffic in western cities, both children as passengers and as co-users of the street is the big sinner. It has become accepted in many parts of adult society that children should not be on the streets, ignoring the fact that this is where children and people have played for centuries before the invention of motorised vehicles. Traffic safety activities for the most are focussed toward separating children from the street, rather than making the street safer for children. Decreasing accident rate of children in traffic has been achieved at the cost of mobility of children around the city. Children's movements have become more restricted. Here, like in so many aspects of contemporary city life, the convenience of the adults in positions of power prevails over the needs of others.

Society acts like a fluid
Adult society can be likened to a stream of fluid – both will seek the easiest route to go – unfortunately also, like for fluids, that route always leads downhill unless activated in some way.

After traffic injuries, injuries to children occur mostly in the home with very ordinary elements like beds, stairs and floors being frequently the scene of the injury. Compared to the number of injuries indoors, injuries to children outdoors, on the playground, are quite low, which is also a reflection of the amount of time spent in each type of place. Nevertheless society seems more complacent about injuries to children in traffic and in the home than on the playground. This is perhaps related to the idea of the nature of play, where children should be carefree. It is also related to the fact that playgrounds are public places. This is two sided coin, on one side, public spaces are expected not to be the source of injury to citizens, yet on the other side, provision for good quality play demands that children be able to take risks.

Playgrounds where there are adult child caregivers or play leaders present are even more outset for the fear of injuries to children while at

Scene 2. "You must remove this fire! It is not safe for there to be fire where there are young children – they will play with it and maybe burn themselves."

play. First, because there is a greater possibility for more manipulative and construction activities on the playground. Secondly, because it is difficult for a parent to accept that a paid adult worker could be conducting themselves professionally yet their child was injured. This attitude is changing slightly, with a greater acceptance amongst professional injury prevention officers that small, superficial injuries at play are a sign that children are actually daring to try to do things they haven't done before. Some experts can now understand that there is no benefit to eliminating all possibility of injury from a play area, nor is it feasible.

"**Those with little experience have little wisdom** " *The I Ching.*

There seems to have been a positive secondary outcome from all these ten years of committee meetings on standards, which is that there is perhaps a better understanding of the play of children within this small circle of people who have participated in this long process of standard setting. Attitudes toward protecting children at play are become better informed, yet there is still along way to go. The indications are that when an adult sets themselves into the issue of children's play for about ten years or so then they begin to have some form of professional competence; unfortunately only few professionals do so and there are even fewer parents who can do so. Play provision will still continue to be hobbled by the amateur and layman understanding about children's play that prevails within society.

References

Eriksen, Aase. (1985), *Playground Design, Outdoor Environments for Learning and Development*, Van Nostrand Reinhold Co.: New York.

Frost, Joe L. and Klein, Barry. (1983), *Children's Play and Playgrounds*, Playscapes International: Austin Texas.

Kampmann, Jan and Andersen, Peter O. (1996), *Borns Legekultur*, Munksgaard Rosinante: Copenhagen.

Monroe, Marian L. (1985). "An Evaluation of Day Care Playgrounds in Texas", in Frost and Sunderlin eds., *When Children Play*, Association for Childhood Education International: Wheaton MD.

Walker, Brian Browne. (1992), *The I Ching or Book of Changes*, St Martin's Griffin: New York.

6 Children's Criteria

This is an impossible chapter to write as an adult cannot go into childhood to describe what it is like and adults do not have the communication skills to understand what children have to tell us about their lives. The result is that adults need to act as spokesmen for children, acting on their behalf. This places a great deal of responsibility on the adults who must screen their thinking very carefully to sort out what is wishful thinking, what is nostalgia about their own childhood, what is a rationalising of their own parenting style and what is professional interpretation on behalf of contemporary children. Although we cannot avoid all aspects of subjectivity it is necessary that we try to develop an understanding of what is the children's criteria.

There is a great deal of subjectivity in the way adults document their research on what the children want/need. The profession of the adult often forms many of the criteria – for example an educator will place great emphasis on learning opportunities. A landscape architect will more likely choose to emphasise nature and forms. An adult who prides himself on being a business professional will emphasise cost and efficiency. The gender of the adult also affects their approach to children and outdoor play yards. And that we are adults and see the world differently than children affects the way we value our surroundings. Adults see the physical environment very differently than children do, for example adults tend to see the bushes and trees in a park as attractive visual elements of no real function whereas, to children, this kind of landscape offers a world of play possibilities. These differences in values are aspects we can't avoid, so we should be aware of them. This subjectivity is also a part of this chapter and all professionals need to constantly be addressing the issue of assumptions and values they are imposing on the children.

"Sophisticates never understand children." (Bettelheim, Bruno.(1980) p. 172.)

Children are seen as human becomings

In our adult work we can perhaps better evaluate our assumptions if we look at children's position in society. Children occupy a number of roles – both as young persons who have a particular approach to the world around them, and secondly as future adults who are in training to take up adult roles. Our attitude to children's play has, for the most, been influenced by educators who are the dominant experts of early childhood and by prevailing marketing approaches. In general, in contemporary western society we take it for granted that public provision for children's play is part of the training of children to become adults, learning to be social humans, developing good physical skills as a prerequisite to being a good scholar. Brian Sutton Smith refers to this as the rhetoric of play as progress (Sutton Smith (1997), p. 9). This is the rationale for expenditure of public funds on children and has been discussed in Chapter 5 – The Adult's Criteria. But if not at play, when are children permitted to be children?

"**A civilised society is one which struggles to make the world better for its children.**"(Kline, Stephen (1993), p. vii.) .

Playing at being a child

In this chapter I will try to focus on the needs of players as children and not as future adults. Children live in the here and now – young children have no concepts of the future or history. Children have a need to be active participants in the world around them, to be engaged in events, to be part of society to the extent that their skills and abilities permit them. This means that children should be permitted to participate in routine daily activities and events that surround them such as household chores and food preparation, even through their playful approach to such activities may mean that such activities require much more time. From early on children should be participating otherwise they will learn to become passive observers of daily life rather than active members of society.

Children's play should not be limited to fifteen minutes on the playground but should come to pervade more aspects of everyday life for all of us. Playing at home and playing at the playground however should be very different kinds of experiences. At home the play has to do with playing at daily life, interacting with adults and other family members in social situations and in carrying out daily activities. This circle of interaction will extend to the immediate neighbourhood for most young children once they have learned to walk and talk. They then have the skills to carry out that urge to find out about the world outside of their home. And they want to be participants- not just onlookers to life.

Last winter we had a heavy snowfall and I was required by city by-law to clear my sidewalk of snow. It was no problem for me. I quite like shovelling snow. Just as I was dressing to go out to clear the snow, I hear Anders, who is four and lives two doors down, making motor noises as he runs down the walk and in a minute he has cleared a swath down the whole walk. He was playing at clearing snow and did it for everyone on the street. For him it was play, while for the rest of us it was a duty. Now, of course he would never have thought of clearing the snow as play if he hadn't seen adults doing it first. In his play he wanted to try out what it was like to do what adults do and much of play at home is of this aspect. This means that children need to be a part of everyday life- to see what adults do at home and at work.

The institutionalisation of childhood and the separation of work place and the home has meant that many young children have very little experience of adult work or adult everyday life for that matter. Child care centres and schools can be more child friendly by designs which involve the children in the running and everyday life in the institution. That is, the children are involved in food preparation, cleaning, laundry and maintenance of the outdoor spaces. They can be set to play at washing the playground equipment, tricycles and wagons. They love to do something worthwhile.

Childhood – a generalisation

There is no average childhood and there is no average child. All humans are unique and experience each age of live in their own unique way. There are, however, some general experiences and forms of play engaged in by children around the world.

Children have an enthusiasm about life, a joy of living that results in an ability to play with just about anything at any time. A lack on interest in playing is a sign of illness in children. They have curiosity about things and approach the world around them with the big question , "What can I do with this". It is true that children especially young children are egocentric and play often continues to be egocentric throughout a persons life time. It is a characteristic of play that it is something that comes from an inner urge.

Children, like people at all other ages, are here on earth in a physical form and therefore play often has a very strongly emphasised physical aspect. Children are on the move, they enjoy using their body and like to practise movements that "feel good". These are movements like swinging, rocking, dancing, climbing, somersaulting, balancing, hopping and running. They are exploring their body and what they can do with it. They like to practise moving and to show others what they can do. As skills develop, cycling, skating, skiing, swimming, playing with balls, skipping, tag games and sports are added to this list of physical movements enjoyed by children. Fine motoric skills develop a little later than the larger muscles and children also come to be fascinated with games that require good hand-eye co-ordination such as yo-yo, play with hoops, basketball, and other games that go in and out of fashion in various cultures.

Children approach the outdoor environment with a different view than adults. For them this is an exciting new world. Objects, like stones and events like rain, phenomena like shadows and wind, all things which we tend to take for granted as adults, to the child are curious and wonderful and they want to explore them. As adults we tend to put greater emphasis on order, organisation and the visual appearance of an environment, while for a child its potential as a resource laboratory is important. Visual appearance is important to children but they look for signals of welcome, variation in sensory experiences, and are not particularly bothered by an organisation that appears visually disorderly to us. Children have a different sense of order and organisation than do adults. They have a fine sense of what is beautiful and are attracted to things of beauty, what they find beautiful may not however be the prevailing trend that the sophisticated avant-garde adult needs to adhere to.

Children's play and their selection of spaces to play suggests that they do not find the adult organisation of planned open park spaces attractive. Children tend to spread out their play into wild lands, landscaped edges and vacant lots when they are permitted to do so. This is because children feel freer away from constant adult supervision, particularly children over 7 years old, and because these kinds of places often have a greater variety of loose material that can be used in the play. Designing for play using the children's criteria should include a greater sense of being free, less tidy, with more possibilities to play away from the adult supervisors constantly watchful eye.

Children and senses

In the first six years of life children know about the world through three sets of senses. One set are the physical senses such as seeing, tasting, smelling, hearing and touch as well as the body senses. Another set of "senses" they use are the social senses – feelings, emotions and intuition about relationships with people and things. The third set of senses are based in fantasy, imagination and beliefs. Children have many ideas about things

---

Sensing

The physical senses– touch/feel, smell, see, hear, taste, balance/gravity sense and the muscle/joint/movement sense. These are the easiest senses to discuss because we can physically experience them and our language is rich with words to describe the experiences and sensations.

The Social/ Emotive senses - emotions/feelings such as happy sad, anger, empathy, love, regret, excitement and so forth, the intuitive sense, and social senses like making friends, verbal and non verbal communication including body language. This second set of senses is a much more difficult one to discuss or design for as it has only a limited physical visibility.

The Imaginative/Fantasy senses- includes sensations such as pretending, believing, imagining, day dreaming, magic, belief in elves, having an imaginary friends, ideas and many aspects of childhood knowledge developed by the child herself. Of all the senses these are the most difficult to discuss today – we lack a tradition for taking these seriously – except in field of art and design and when sensed by adults. They are also controversial because of the close relationship between fantasy, imagination, and magic with beliefs, myths and religion.

---

based in their understanding of what they have experienced. Their fantasy world will include life in a world we no longer travel in where they have invisible friends, play with imaginary toys and fear monsters under the bed or in the closet. Together these sets of senses inform the children's aesthetic responses.

About the age of six or seven children have also developed the ability to think in terms of abstract ideas and concept and begin to also know about the world and people through theories and ideas from the adult world which in turn influence how they interpret and react to the perceptions they have from the other sense areas. Contemporary modern art which is so engrossed in the unique individual expression of the adult artist requires that the audience study the thoughts and concepts of the artist to be able to understand the message in the art and as such these works cannot evoke an informed response from children, but can and do sometimes provoke a very active, physical response. Artists seeking to give artistic insights to young children as an audience must direct their messages through the channels of perception of which the children are masters.

Children need variety

"A tree is the best way to fill the children's needs for physical movement." This statement was made by an adherent of the nature playground movement in a recent meeting of adults who were gathered to discuss renovations on a local school playground. Watching children play in a play yard where there is only a tree trunk for climbing and other physical movement activities leads me to wonder about the enormous subjectivity of the author of this statement. Children's needs for physical exploration possibilities cannot be fulfilled by any one object, and when you have a concentration of 30, 40 maybe 100 children in the play yard at one time and day after day until they are 10 or 11 years of age, such a statement becomes pure nonsense, even though well meant.

> **An exercise in landscape semiotics** – examine the outdoor landscape around the place where your city council and mayor regularly work and meet – and compare this with the landscape at the local school or child care centre. What can you read in the landscape about the communities attitudes towards the users of these spaces? Where are the works of art located?

Physical movement possibilities should be varied in terms of type of movement and should also vary so that they fit the physical size and capabilities of the players. This means that there should be some purpose-made play structures that support movements that children find interesting. Possibilities for swinging, sliding, rocking, jumping, balancing and rolling are known to be part of a traditional playground; however that is no reason to throw these movement possibilities out when trying to rethink the contemporary playground. The fact is that civilised people were enjoying these activities long before there were playgrounds and we will continue to do so; it is part of being human. To throw them off the playground because they have been done before is equivalent to eliminating all possibilities for sleeping or eating in the creation of a new form of domestic architecture. Playground design, like domestic architecture has a function and there is a need of the users that must be met. There are certain things that children like to do at play, in terms of physical movement and they have a right to demand these on their playgrounds. This doesn't mean that all possibilities have to appear in the same format on every playground, but that these needs for movement opportunities be supported in the children's play places. The challenge for the designer is to find innovative ways to provide for these movement possibilities that the children demand.

Children like to swing and to slide
Eliminating possibilities for swinging and sliding from new forms of playground design because they appear in traditional playgrounds is akin to eliminating sleeping and eating possibilities from experimental domestic architecture. New thinking is important but the new forms must continue to support the basic needs of those who use them.

Children choose to be outdoors

Current research into the brain indicates that physical activity is very important not only to our physical health but also to our brain and growth of brain cells. Physical motion stimulates the growth of brain cells. This means that people of all ages should move about – and as adults most of us are aware that we should do so more than we regularly do. Children too have too few possibilities for motion and are often expected to sit still, keep indoors and so forth, because that is more convenient for the adults. We fear dangers to the children if they go outside unaccompanied; but we, for a variety of reasons, won't go with them. When they are outside the places they have to play in are small and movements are limited to a few routine activities.

For the convenience of the adult world, urban children from an early age are trained to adapt to living and playing in very small spaces and to being outdoors for very short periods of time. To compensate we fill their bedrooms and playrooms with computers, television and toys. These are all wonderful aspects of our culture that children should have access to – as well as plenty of time and space to play outdoors.

Children whose families cannot afford to give them each a bedroom filled with equipment do play outside of the home but in their play they are seen to be problems to the adults – too much noise and running in hallways and elevators. Often their use of the immediate landscape around where they live is limited by the rules of the authority that owns the building and whose main concerns are economy and adult convenience. Often children's use of the near to home environment for playing is restricted by adult rules and signage –frequently in areas where provision of spaces for play is most limited while concentration of young children is high– in public housing estates, for example.

Children, when given the choice, will choose to be outdoors at least 50% of their waking time. And, if the adults don't transfer to them their dislike of rain and mud and such weathers, they will continue to be outside even in the weather the adults don't find comfortable. Much of the discomfort that comes with cold and wet weather can be dealt with appropriate clothing and wind shelters. The discomfort of hotter climates can be dealt with by careful siting, shade structures and planting, water and breezes.

There is an idea that children *choose* to be indoors playing with computers and watching television. That they are mostly indoors is the case for many school age children and for many girls already at a younger age. This comes about because of several factors in their earlier childhood. The main one is that the outdoor areas that the children have access to are boring and there are not enough adults out there. Where young children have regular access to interesting and sufficient outdoor space and where there are interested adults then they will choose to go outside. Children should be outside at least two hours everyday and much more whenever possible. Research has demonstrated that children who are outdoors for longer periods of time everyday in all weathers have fewer days of illness and less serious allergy reactions than their contemporaries who are indoors most of the day. When other appropriate play conditions are present outdoors the children are also in better physical condition and are more able to concentrate.

Children should be outside at least two hours everyday and much more whenever possible. Research has demonstrated that children who are outdoors for longer periods of time everyday in all weathers have fewer days of illness and less serious allergy reactions than their contemporaries who are indoors most of the day.

Girls in many western cities are very carefully watched and there is a concern about their safety outdoors and therefore they are more restricted in their movements about the city. Often their play is quieter and less physically expansive than that of the young boys, therefore they are permitted to be inside more often. The result is that they simply develop a habit of playing indoors and after time may find the out of doors uncomfortable because it is an unknown environment. Boys, on the other hand, with their noise and other boy-like behaviours can make indoor life so intolerable for adults that they are sent outside to play. Boys more often develop a competence in dealing with outdoors and come to know their outdoor surrounding better. This is a great generalisation and in small towns and rural areas there are fewer differences between genders in their competence and knowledge of their outdoor environment. In large cities however there can be a marked difference.

For the children then we need to create outdoor spaces that are interesting and secure in so that it is interesting, challenging and safe for children to play in these places for long periods of time. Originally playgrounds in most western cities were staffed with supervisors and one of the best solutions to today's problems of children's lack of fitness, and not enough time outdoors at play would be to develop a profession of play leaders, as they have in the UK and in Finland, whose work it is to enhance the play interest of the children on the public play yard. For the most these positions have been eliminated on the argument that society can't afford them. It seems that if we were to do our research well it could be shown that society can't afford NOT to have them. For the health, well being and playfulness of our children both as children and as future adults there needs to be professional play leaders in good quality spacious public playgrounds as a element of quality urban living.

Thoughtful observers see some aspects of urban planning and design to be more oriented toward protecting the environment from children rather than providing for their use of it.

A child's world is full of fantasy

Fantasy, imagination and creativity are also universal elements in children's play. Children like to make things and to make their mark on the world around them, which is the reason for the popularity of elements like building materials and blocks. The creative possibilities in a play area are affected buy the number of items available for the children to manipulate or use in the play and by the placement of these items in an appropriate setting for creative type play activities. It is not enough that there be something to

Items that suggest and support fantasy play are part of the criteria for a good place to play.

manipulate, it is also necessary that the environment support this type of play through providing sufficient ground and counter or table space for these activities. Finally, as these activities can go on for hours or even days, children prefer to play in places where there isn't a constant demand that they tidy up and put everything away after 15 to 30 minutes of play. This kind of play needs time to develop and flourish, a child's version of time, not the adults time clock. Manipulative items added on like decoration to a physical climbing structure at the playground are not sufficient for meeting the creative play needs of the child.

It is not enough that there be something to manipulate, it is also necessary that the environment support this type of play through providing sufficient ground and counter or table space for these activities.

Playhouses and toys that support the fantasy play are also part of the children's criteria for a good place to play. Not that there needs to be a lot of new, expensive toys; children often find great play in ordinary household objects like kitchen utensils, pots and pans, hammers and tools. Adults should feel their way to offering the children a balance between objects used in everyday life that children can use in their play and specially made toys for play. Giving children only objects from everyday life that adults no longer want can leave children with the feeling that their play is not important. Too many purchased toys can turn playing into a act of consuming playthings. Like all other aspects of living, finding a balance between the extremes that fits the time and personality is the best approach. This is to be done consciously by the adults as part of a broad society discussion about childhood and play. It is not good enough to say, "Well this is what the child wanted" or "This is what I had as a child so it should be good enough for my own children."

Adults are often heard to argue that just the bare necessities are essential for children to develop fantasy and creativity. They believe that giving the children more than a stick and a rock will mean that the children will not try to imagine or fantasise. These people have very little belief in the competence of the children. Bare necessities do not contribute to creativity or invention, despite the widespread folk saying "Necessity is the mother of invention". Every primitive society has proven this to be incorrect; these societies are the most rigid, unimaginative and non-progressive societies on earth. Bronowski writes of the Baktari, a nomadic tribe living in Persia:

> There is no room for innovation, because there is not time, on the move, between evening and the morning, coming and going all their lives, to develop a new device or a new thought –not even a new tune. The only habits that survive are the old habits. The only ambition of the son is to be like the father. (Bronowski, (1973) p 62).

Creative, imaginative groups of people have some resources of time and material to draw on for the acts of creation and imagination and so should it be for today's children. For fantasy to reign children need to have their basic needs met, to feel comfortable, secure and have the time and freedom to explore the possibilities of the environment. The environment should include a variety of items and objects that can be used in a variety of ways and others that signal specific elements in the culture of childhood to serve as the spark for the imaginative play. This is particularly necessary for the youngest children, whose imaginative play is supported by objects in the play yard that suggest items in real life. Trains that look like a real train, a house that looks like a house. When playing with hand held toys, the youngest children are stimulated to play "farm" if they have figures that look like cows and horses. Only at a later age, around five or six years, can elaborate, imaginative play take place with non representational shapes like sticks and stones standing in for cows and horses; and only if the children have been able to play imaginatively for some years. Imaginative play is a form of creative and imagined research into the world around them and what the child can do with it or be in it. Like all creative research environments there needs to be sufficient material and tools to carry out the research.

> **"Children's playgrounds should be renamed research laboratories."**
> **Buckminster Fuller.**

Scale is important to children

What is necessary for the children to feel comfortable to initiate fantasy play are settings at an appropriate small scale with some aspect of shelter. Playing house never takes place in a wide open lawn of grass, children instinctively set up objects to define a smaller space as part of the beginnings of the play. They like suggestions of roofs or walls for their play house and like to be able to add to the furnishings through loose materials. The very youngest children in particular are sensitive to the insecurity of the larger outdoor spaces and their comfort is increased with the creation of small subspaces with vertical objects to serve as walls and support and small enclosed spaces with low roofs for pretend play, exploration and hide and seek. Children need a variety of different size of spaces and subspaces that can be taken over for a variety of different kinds of play. Young children, before they will settle down into creative or fantasy play, will seek to place themselves near a vertical element in the outdoor landscape. Thus it is observed that children are often playing near the climbing structure or fences in a play yard. This is often because they are vertical elements that provide that sense of security of place needed to start the play.

Research has shown that young children select to place themselves near vertical elements in the play yard – and at the edges or in the corners of sandboxes. Source- author.

Children are of the earth

Children, like all people are attracted to the element of the earth – soil, water, fire, air. Outdoor playgrounds are often the first places where children are permitted to explore these aspects of planet earth and they need to have these opportunities to play with these elements in a good quality. Playing with these elements also are surrounded with risk and for this reason fire is eliminated from most play areas. It cannot be present in unsupervised play of young children, but should be present in supervised settings. Playing with soil, sand, stones, water, fire and air are all part of a healthy outdoor play experience and children need access to these possibilities. Children are of this earth and have a demand to explore it and find out about the elements.

Children need variety, variety and more variety in their play yards.

Children are much healthier when they have access to daylight for long periods everyday, artificial light is not sufficient. Play areas should be sunny places, pleasant places to be even in the most inclement season of the year. While some sun is necessary, too much sun can also be a problem so some shade provision may be necessary in accordance with the climate. Indoor play areas, no matter how well lit, are not an alternative to really being outside in the sun, in the rain, in the fresh air.

Children and animals

The elements of the earth extend also to the living things of the earth – insects, plants, and larger animals. Most public playgrounds can not include animals full time but it is very clear that children have an attraction to living things. Modern children have little access to animals other than their own pet and with the increase in allergies fewer homes have pets such as dogs and cats. Pets, however, when they are part of a family play a very important role in the emotional life of the child. Children at play should not be separated from their best friend if it is a pet. Not only is being outdoors more often a way to reduce the problem with allergies, outdoors with animals can be less likely to result in an allergic reaction. While it is likely to be sometime before we will find animals as part of the playground in every neighbourhood, public play area provision at the community level should include the possibility for children to have access to a selection of domesticated animals which are tolerant of and enjoy interaction with children. Children's Farms and Adventure Playgrounds with animals are two approaches that work. Another possibility is to have animals brought to the play area for several days and then returned to their permanent home. This requires appropriate enclosures, shelters and animal care to be designed into the play area.

In Vejen, Denmark, the major town park features a small fenced duck pond, plus a fenced goat compound and an aviary, all located nearby the playground which is visited nearly everyday by many of the children in the town. This is a relatively easily reproduced approach to ensure children have some interaction with animals in their daily life.

Playing is noisy

Much of the play of children involves sound – both as a means of communication and as something that is explored in play. Children play with sounds and words from the beginning of their interactive play – which is usually with the adult caregivers as infants. Playing outside on the playground has the advantage that children can make more and louder sounds on the playground and can make sounds that adults don't like indoors – and are often thus forbidden by adults. Playing outside is important for children because they feel freer and less restricted by adult rules when they are out of doors. This is particularly true with making sound. Outdoors, with the high ceiling of the sky is the only place where children really feel free to be as noisy as they wish. This sound making often leads to conflict with adult neighbours who value the possibility of quiet enjoyment of their garden. For the children, care should be taken in allocating spaces for play to avoid or reduce such conflict with neighbours. Children have a right to a place to play where they can make as much noise as they wish.

Space and time

One of the biggest demands children have for play is enough space. Play areas tend to be small places, just big enough for a swing set, sandbox and a climber. Like for adults whether we travel on aeroplanes, have our own office or home, the amount of space we have available for our use is an indicator of our importance and prestige. Children also know about this, they too feel the inherent need for space, perhaps even more so given their inner urge to be on the move. Most play areas are just too small. Unfortunately city living for persons without political power has meant that they are forced to adjust to living conditions that in the long term are unhealthy for human survival, and the lack of sufficient outdoor space for play is one of these problem issues. Children adjust to being indoors but in the long term it is not healthy. Time to play outdoors is connected to space. Small spaces are explored in a short period of time, small playgrounds tend to be boring to adults so they only wish to stay there a short time. For our long term health and well being we all need to be outdoors more than we are, and children are much healthier when they have much longer outdoor playtime than is currently offered in the traditional play yard. It is a need of the children to have regular access to large and well furnished play areas that are attractive places to go both for themselves and for the adults in their lives.

Play versus work

There has been many efforts made to define play over this century- some are more enlightening on the character of play than others. One I like to use is from a child: "play is when I can do what I want, work is when I have to do what an adult tells me to." Current research on play today tends to focus less on achieving an academic consensus on a definition of play and more on the character of playfulness. Brian Sutton- Smith writes:

> it is also very interesting to think of play as a lifelong simulation of the key neonatal characteristics of unrealistic optimism, egocentricity, and reactivity, all of which are guarantors of persistence in the face of adversity. (Sutton-Smith (1997), p 231).

Adults often think of playing as something linked to childhood and left behind with adulthood. Instead adults have "hobbies" and "recreation interests". These are just other labels for some adult forms of playing. Playing in all ages however has some aspect of choice and personal interest.

Children need people

One of the essential criteria for children's play is other children to play with. Not only children of the same age but also younger and older children. We are inherently social beings and being social is not something one is taught in school but is something that is practised between people. Children's play is full of practising at being social, at developing group norms, at coming to know how to use both body and spoken language to express meaning and feeling.

Adults are also important to children, and children should have access to adults who have a relationship to them other than mother, father or teacher and they should be able to interactions with various adults of both genders. When these people can play with the children a rich form of intergenerational play culture can develop. This happens most often today at special events and festivals. Children need it to happen much more often. Unfortunately playgrounds and play are seen to be childish and an adult who is not a parent of a child on the playground is not only unwelcome at the playground – they are viewed with suspicion. Children are trained at an early age not to talk to strangers and thereby early on develop a suspicion of unrelated adults. This strict division of play of children and the barriers

Is it play or is it work? It depends if you ask the children or the adult in this photo.

to adults is perhaps one of the reasons why public play provision is so weakly supported in the general adult society and why play is delegated to left over pieces of land which are often the first place to be taken over when adults need more space for parking lots or buildings. If we let the adults play there too then maybe future playgrounds will be better located and furnished.

Play provision in public spaces for children is a small chapter of the larger issue of human playfulness. In many ways it has been to the detriment of play that specific provision for children's play has been isolated on the designated playground. Children's play could be much more rich if it could be more integrated into the everyday life of the society. However, public playgrounds are a fact of urban life today and they shouldn't be eliminated until there is a better way to integrate playing into urban living.

> **"Play is when I can do what I want, work is when I have to do what an adult tells me to" - A child.**

Designing for children/with children

Children learn at a very early age what adults mean by the word "playground". They will reproduce the stereotype of a playground when asked what they want in their playground. They have been taught that this is what is in a playground. Children are very good at pleasing adults, when we ask them questions they will try to give us the answers they think we want them to give, the answers that show they know and understand the way adult's see the world. From a very early age children have been taken to places the adults call playgrounds and told that what they can do there is "play". It is not surprising therefore when we ask them what kind of play possibilities they want at their playground they ask for more of what they already know to be in playgrounds.

> Don't ask children what they want if your aren't prepared to give it to them.

Older children just ask for larger, higher and louder items than the younger ones. By the time they are nine or ten years of age, children are so used to the traditional play equipment that they ask for items that are higher, bigger and grander in every way than is appropriate for a typical public playground. They may have visited a water park or an amusement park and they will request features they enjoyed there. I saw one set of answers from children when consulted about their playground – and almost everyone of the responses included some form of large lake for fishing or a swimming pool. These requests must be refused because they are not within budget, not safe and not appropriate. Children however look for challenge and risk in their play, not safety. They don't know about budgets and don't understand the restrictions imposed on public play providers. This means that what they ask for is not what they can get and they become disappointed in the process of consultation and in the public authorities.

It is not that children aren't imaginative in their play; it is that they have been taught how to respond to the adults. They are very adaptive and will work within the adults criteria. Adults asking children about what they want at their playground will hear about higher and bigger play equipment – because adults are fixed on play equipment as the important element on a playground. It is also a case that children have never had any experience in influencing or changing their outdoor physical environment and therefore don't think that they can do so. They will ask for minor modifications in the small things and a replication of what they have seen elsewhere. This kind of involvement of children in design is a lesson in consumerism and is not really enlightening in terms of how children would like to play, nor is it meaningful to the children in terms of taking action to make changes in their environment. For an adult to find out more about children's real play needs, the adult needs to go much deeper into play and the lives of children than just to ask them what they want in their play yard.

Children have something to say about their outdoor environment beyond the playground equipment – they can tell a lot about what they like and don't like, what they use and don't use.

In the study of children in Rotterdam, it was found the children were very clear about what disturbed their use of the outdoors – things like dog's "dirt", litter and traffic. (Rotterdam, *Being a Kid*, (1987).)

In a project in Chicago, children were given cameras and asked to film things they loved and things they hated in their everyday surroundings. The things they hated included drug dealing, a teenage boy with a gun and graffiti on their buildings. The things they loved included pictures of playmates, children cleaning up garbage and playing activities. From this the landscape designers were able to conclude that children enjoy physical activities and liked settings where they can gather and see their friends without fear. (Kamin, B. "Sheltered by Design" (1995), p 11.)

For children to be equal partners in the design of their play areas they need to have experience in affecting and influencing their environment. This takes years of progressively being involved in taking decisions about events and activities in their daily lives. While modern children are very involved in and consulted about in-home family activities and often are one of the major decision makers in the purchase of the weeks groceries, they are mostly cut off from influencing decisions in the public domain. Unless children are experienced in participating in decision making around outdoor live in urban areas, involving them in the selection of the play equipment in their playground will be a frustrating experience for all. In such instances it is better that a sensitive adult who is trained in children, children's play and the potential of outdoor spaces take the lead in identifying the criteria on behalf of the children. The superficial act of consultation without any real opportunity for participation in the larger decision making can have the result that children, by the time they are teenagers develop, a very cynical attitude towards the adults in power and a feeling of helplessness and marginalisation.

References

Bettelheim, Bruno. (1980), *Surviving and Other Essays*, Vintage Books: New York.
Bronowski, J. (1973), *The Ascent of Man*, Little, Brown and Co.:Boston.
Kamin, Blair. (1995), "Sheltered by Design", *The Chicago Tribune*, special section, June 18-June 23.
Kline, Stephen. (1993), *Out of the Garden*, London:Verso.
Sutton-Smith, Brian. (1997), *The Ambiguity of Play*, Harvard University Press: Cambridge MA.
Rotterdam Municipal Health Department. (1987), *Being a Kid in a Big Town, report no 82*, The Department: Rotterdam.

7 Designer's Criteria

Designers are adult professionals who concerns themselves with the integration of art and design in practical or functional settings and objects. This group includes industrial designers, architects, landscape architects and sometimes artists such as sculptors and painters whose creative interest is attracted to setting their own personal impression on urban spaces and functional objects.

| A designer is an artist who solves a problem by creating functional art |

This chapter deals with the tools of the artist and how they can be applied to play area design. Unlike society and the child, the artist should not make personal demands on the design, in that the act of creation of a public play area is in service to the children and society.

Adults who are responsible for the provision of children's play areas in public spaces often mistake the act of designing for the act of arranging elements in the landscape. To add to the confusion this act is also sometimes called play area planning. Design and layout or organisation become confused. There are many books already published which serve as guidebooks or recipe books for how to arrange a playgrounds in terms of layout that serves the adult play-as-learning theories, where the child is seen to be in training as a future adult. In this chapter I will try to explore the act of designing for children's outdoor play as an act of creativity and artist communication. The kind of play areas I am addressing are those that serve the child as a young person with a particular approach to the world around them.

In the terminology I work with, play area planning has to do with the allocation and disposition of spaces and land areas to be used for play as learning and the celebration of childhood within the urban landscape as a whole. We will not address this issue much in this chapter, except as a side issue related to the issue of how much planning is good for or is necessary to provide quality play in city living.

Designers tend to design for designers

Design professionals, even more so than most other persons of all ages, would like to be respected and held in high regard by their colleagues. They have a tendency to design with the perhaps unconscious aim of winning the approval of their contemporaries. Designers feel the need to show that they have good taste or, if not in keeping with prevailing good taste, then that are in the avant-garde of forming a new style. This is perhaps built into the character of being a designer, but it can get in the way of being a good designer for children's play.

> For a designer, design is usually about forms – for a child, design is about activity.

Urban design in general and play area design in particular can be problematic as a design project because it is difficult to identify who "owns" the space. Public urban spaces are owned by all – and therefore all persons should be considered. To do this there is a tendency to devise an imagined impression of an average person. There is no average person in real life, though; we are all uniquely different despite our years of socialisation. Spaces for real life activities, like play, need to be created with real life people in mind.

Spaces for play are spaces where real life happens and should be designed with real people in mind.

Another designer tendency is to create outdoor spaces as a stage setting; they tend to see it as a backdrop or scenery for some kind of programmable activity and they write the script for the activity. The view taken is as one of a spectator looking at the setting. One critique of designers is that they have a tendency to treat the city as a work of art rather than as a setting for everyday life, with the result that much new design photographs well but is empty of meaning to people.

Children's play is deeply involved with the setting, with the physical environment; they use it rather than stand back and admire the view. Designing for children is about designing for play as an un-scriptable, unique event as well as for visual and other aesthetic qualities based in the children's sense of aesthetics. For children play is also about everyday life; it is life.

Children's play involves using the environment, manipulating materials and spontaneous play occurs in many places.

"Playing is living"

Designing for children sets up a challenge for the designer to train themselves to see and think like a child. There is no course for this to my knowledge and becoming a parent to a young child is not the route. Parents are all too subjective about their own parenting styles and their experiences with their child cannot be generalised to all children. I vividly recall a meeting with a male landscape architect over a play area in a small residential estate. I was acting on behalf of the social planning department in the city and the department was concerned about the children's play possibilities while the landscape architect had been responsible for the selection and placement of play equipment in the landscape on behalf of the builder. On site, I raised some doubts about the large climber being appropriate in terms of scale and function for the play of very young children who were to be using the space. The landscape architect became fired up immediately. It was the right stuff! HE had a young son and HIS SON could climb up that so all children should be able to do so too. The response was so emotional that there was no possibility for a rational discussion of the needs of the children and anything further that I said would be seen to be unimportant. Such discussions often lead to the question of "and how many children do you have?" Knowledge of children's needs does not come with bringing children into this world, even though it may lead one into a great familiarity with some aspects of children's lives.

The advantage of playing is that you can test out actions and emotions which would be too dangerous to act out in real life.

If one can't be trained to think like a child and one should not rely on their experiences as a parent, how then does a designer set themselves into the child's world? There is no clear answer to this; like with many aspects of designing, there is no simple formula or recipe. This is something one feels ones way forward. This means that one can't be an expert designer for children the first time one takes on such work. It takes years of experience and evaluation of results to be able to see the world from an approximation of a child's view of the world. It means taking a risk with one's reputation as a designer with good taste.

Designers and artist however have a head start over many other adults in that they are perhaps in personality and the way they see the world closer to children and childhood than many other adults. The designers explorative approach to materials, forms and ideas is a form of play. Like the child, the designer approaches his space and materials with the question –"what can I do with this?". The difference is the kind of answers being sought. For the designer the answer is a form, a shape, a product or outcome to be realised and perhaps displayed. For the child the answer is an activity, an action, an experience which may never be reproducible. For the child, it is the activity of playing that is the important thing, not the outcome of the play.

Playing at Designing #2
The advantage of playing is that you can test out actions and emotions that would be too dangerous to act out in real life. For a designer playing means he or she can take risks that might other wise affect their professional reputation. When we play we can take enough risk that we can actually invent something new.

Can good play areas be designed?

Good design in the adult world is equivalent to good taste. Good design is recognisable by the uninformed masses when persons who are known to have good taste give some form of recognition to the design work. Designers see themselves as taste makers and professional designers often see their role as educating an 'unsophisticated' public.

In architecture and landscape architecture good design is recognised by international and national design awards given out by juries of professional designers. Often the award is based on submissions of photographs and lengthy verbal descriptions of the project. As a result those projects that are celebrated as good design tend to be ones where there are good photo opportunities resulting in photographs that will look good in glossy professional magazines and where there are strong conceptual and theoretical arguments for the work. Designing for children's play, to do it well, usually means defying both of these aspects of professional design evaluation. Children's play when they are most engaged in it does not make good design photographs and the space may look un-designed and even downright messy to an adults eye. The theory behind children's play cannot be intellectual but should be based in the children's aesthetics. It is possible to set out concepts and theories for a good play design but it requires an expertise on children's play that most designers lack. Good design for children's outdoor play is possible – but it means challenging many of the prevailing adult ideas about outdoor landscapes. Designers find it difficult to talk or write about their plans and expectations in terms of children's behaviour at play. They are trained to work with and think about physical structures and facilities rather than about the behaviour of the user of these spaces.

> Professional designers often see their role as educating the 'unsophisticated' public.

When we look at the kind of places children choose to play in when it is possible to choose, these places tend to have an appearance of being forgotten or vacated by adults. They look somewhat unkempt. They may be places that have just grown up with little or no help from a landscape designer. Children seem to like places that look un-designed. That children choose these places is not to suggest that children prefer environments with a lower quality material or that they have a preference for nature. Children also love to play in garbage dumps if they are allowed to do so. What they like is the non-predictability of these non-designed landscapes.   Well designed landscapes for children should also include many elements of non-predictability and un-foreseeability.

> **A conversation between two landscape architects:**
> La1 "Here, you see I have just designed a landing strip for angels."
> La2 "What do you mean - a landing strip for angels – I have never seen any angels"
> La1 "Exactly, I have only just now designed their first landing strip".
> (a free translation from Danish)

Design for life

In an article in the Leisure section in *Guardian Weekly* of Aug. 4 1996, Paul Evans playful describes his reaction to a display seen during his visit to the flower show at Hampton Court palace. He writes:

> A strange thing happened at the Hampton Court palace flower show. Having struggled through the crowds looking at designer gardens, nursery displays, floristry exhibits and acres of stands selling every kind of garden nick-nackery

imaginable, I stumbled into a mirage. This is it, I thought, truly a garden-for-our-time. Here was a little muddy pond, water covered in duckweed, a few elegant reed-mace shooting from the margins, an old bicycle wheel and bits of wood sticking enigmatically from its weedy depths.

I spent some time admiring the way the pond had been undesigned, allowing Nature to overwrite the ego of the designer. It reminded me of childhood ponds, teeming with newts and beetles, long since swept away and tidied from the landscape. Here was a robust, defiant, vibrant little puddle of wildness in a world obsessed with order and instant gratification. I had of course got it all wrong. Next to the duckweed pond was another of the same size but clean and tidy, with bright red waterlillies and the fussy designer nonsense that goes with contemporary water gardens. The display was meant to be a Before and After lesson, illustrating how the designers could transform a worthless swamp into a sparkling new suburban paradise.

This experience so well described by Paul Evans clearly illustrates the difference in world views between that of the child who sees so much potential in the undesigned and the attraction is the excitement of finding "treasures" and the unknown. There are things in the untidy pond to manipulate and play with, there is living things to explore – duckweed, reeds and insects. There are pieces and wood and an old bicycle wheel –the beginnings of a cart or barrow perhaps. There is great play potential in such a place. Tidy designs too often reveal all at first glance and hold no suggestion of future surprises; they do not offer elements that can be used in play sequences or making playthings.

This description of the two ponds is a good demonstration of why children perceive the wild pond as preferable – not because they are uneducated heathens who cannot appreciate design but because there are greater possibilities for them to find and manipulate with things. Good design for children must include suggestions of potential surprises, reveal the possibilities over time, not a all at first glance – and most of all - must offer possibilities to develop further play potential. The play potential in an object or place as seen from the children's view point is what is termed affordances (Heft, H. (1988)) and it refers to the functional meaning that the child perceives in the object or environment.

The affordances in such a play area are very limited. Once the child has explored the tree trunk, balanced on it crawled under it – there isn't much else to do.

This little water source offers more affordances - water fascinates, it moves, it changes the colour of the sand, it can be manipulated, it drips. It makes noise, it can be dammed up, can channel it along the ground and much more.

Some examples of affordances in the play landscape:

Object or space	Affordance
A flat grass lawn	running, games, throwing balls, a place to build up something, a place to lay in the sun, a place to talk with friends.
Sand	Something to shape, loose material to be used in other play/can be dug/moved.
Landscape shrubs	Source of material for pretend play – twigs and leaves in food preparation in games and making toys, a place for hiding, a quiet place to get away from others, vertical objects that feel comfortable, potential source of insects, and change over seasons offering flowers, berries and different colour leaves during the passage of the year, for collecting and sorting beautiful things.
Edging – e.g. on a planting bed or to contain surfacing	A place to walk or balance, a goal in the play, a place to sit, a place to run handheld cars and trucks.
Loose stones and rocks	Things to manipulate and build up things from, can be set out as goals in the play or as bases for playing, look beautiful, for collecting, for throwing, for skipping on water, for making sound.
Playhouse	A shelter, a space of one's own, centre for role playing mother and baby, pretend play at daily life activities, something to climb on and spaces to explore, a place to hide, a place to take a nap, a dog house, a space ship, a horse to ride, a place to equip and furnish, a place to read or have a snack, a part of a village, an entry into a dream world, a goal for playing games, something to cycle around.
Swings	Signals that this is a place where children are welcome and can play. Swinging and movement possibilities, testing physical strength and how high one can swing, talking with friends, dreaming, for example about flying to the stars, twisting and twirling, flirting.

This is just a short list to give an indication of what is meant by the affordances approach to children's play environments. While this approach was first expounded by J.J. Gibson in 1979 it has not been integrated into the process of play area design to any extent. This is unfortunate, as it is a very good way for designers to gain insight into the way children perceive the world around them. One of the drawbacks has been that the work

Playhouses aren't just playhouses – for these girls this is the best horse in the world – and what a view from its back!

published to date has been very academic, laden with psychological terminology. Designers who are unfamiliar with such academic jargon have difficulty accessing such literature. Hopefully there can be some bridges created between the design profession and the environmental psychologists. Heft writes "Environmental design may be aided by the availability of a descriptive framework that focuses on the functional properties of environmental features in relation to prospective users of their designed settings" (Heft, H. 1988, p 37.).

Designers are form givers, concerned with form language, whereas children are activators, are concerned with body language and action.

Playing can be undignified

Bettelheim has written "sophisticates never understand children. (Bettelheim, B. (1980), p. 172). On the other hand, art, real *art*, is valued and takes on meaning because it suggests that those who own it have a cultural authority, a kind of sophistication. Design gives dignity to the owner as suggested by Berger (1977). This is the basis for placing a monetary value on a work of art – the status and dignity that owning such an item gives to the owner. There is a potential conflict between design which is to be taken serious by adults and designing for play of children which adults don't take seriously. Designers however who take play and playing seriously can create high quality outdoor landscapes that are both good design and good places to play. It can be done – but it is not done often enough.

Designers have difficulty dealing with children's play because of the contradictions inherent in the act of playing and in the act of owning art. But this contradiction lies only with a public that is unsure and one that sees art as a consumable item. They see art and status and dignity as poles apart from childhood and play. Art and design and play areas are not contiguous subjects unless an artist takes on a commission to design a children's play area – such as the play areas by Noguchi and Hundertwasser. These are artists who earned their reputation as artists creating works that won the approval of the adult art world. One wonders whether their play area creations have won the approval of the players.

Art that is well recognised has a high monetary value –this is already mentioned. One of the stumbling blocks to creating good design in children's play spaces is the unwillingness of society to invest public funds into play areas and designs for play areas. There are few commissions for play area design and when these are awarded the awarding is often a political decision, not a design decision. More often amateurs, gardeners or educators take on the task of drawing up a plan for the particular space to be equipped - and the approach is totally functional. As long as there is no funding to permit designers to become specialists in children's play, for them to develop an expertise, children's play area design will not advance as an art form, nor will there be new innovations. Play areas will continue to look the same as all other playgrounds.

Getting to know about daily life

Designing spaces for everyday living involves a creative and insightful approach to everyday life. A playful approach to the world brings new insights into life here on earth. Yet playing can be seen to be undignified, unprofessional. At the same time when we stop worrying about being seen to be dignified we can start enjoying life more. By "playing" with daily life, with daily routines, with conventions, the designer of everyday spaces can develop a greater insight into how people can thrive and be comfortable in their designs. This requires a balance in that it is always necessary to respect other persons and not offend (too very much) their prevailing world view. Children and children's play however is almost always offensive to some very dignified adults, and they are best advised to avoid places where children live and play. Designers who feel comfortable with children and children's play can do well by going out to a local day care or other play area and spend some time playing with the children – not just one or two children but many different children over a period of many weeks. This is the only way a designer can overcome the problem of short play episodes confirming preconceived notions about the nature of children's play. Only with greater time and experience with playing children do we come to understand that playing is very complex and also inherently defies being typecast or structured.

Children's play area design is a team process

Designing for children's play demands that designers work with other professional groups such as experts in children's play, play safety experts, and childhood specialists. As it is environmental design a landscape architect should also be involved in the process. Because play is such a complex phenomenon and knowledge about children's play is dispersed throughout many professions, a play area design benefits from having input from a variety of professions. Nevertheless it must always be kept in mind that the whole exercise is primarily a design issue and the primary user is children at play.

The tools of the designer

Play area design does not vary much from other types of spatial design projects in terms of the design tools, materials and approaches of the designer. Design elements such as forms, shapes, lines, colours, textures, light and harmony are all components of this work of artistic creation. The play area designers conundrum is – whose aesthetic should prevail in the way in which these elements are manipulated and applied in the design process? It is the designer's of course – but is it the designer as serious adult artist or the designer as playing-at-being-a child-designer. Most good play designs will be the result of input from both sides of the designer.

Designers, like most adults have learned to work in an assigned space – they may call it an office, a studio, an atelier or workshop. Nevertheless for the most design and preparation for the realisation of the end product takes place – indoors. My experience tells me that a play area designer needs to be outdoors – also at least two hours a day – while working!

Go outside into the everyday environment. If you designing for a specific site come to know the site as well as you know your face – know it in all weathers and at all times of the day. Take photographs – lots of them, from standing height – particularly from the eye view of a child – around 100 – 120 cm above the ground. Get to know about the wind and sun during the day and what happens in the neighbourhood around the site. Sketching, making models and even thinking can just as well take place outdoors in a large sandbox/sand table as indoors. If you are so fortunate as to be near a beach – go to the beach – draw and model in the sand or small stones. Take some blocks and simple shapes and strings with you to add to your creations. However you do it – develop a habit of designing out of doors. With today's telecommunication and electronic tools –the whole office can be moved out.

Rand, in his biography of Hundertwasser (Rand, 1988) tells how the artist discovered that colours shine in the rain. This is a discovery all children make but we adults forget unless we are outside in all weathers and look at the world around us with new and curious eyes. t seems to me we are much better at picking up impressions from places we visit the first time as tourist than we do when we are experiencing familiar territory. There is a Danish expression for this, meaning "home-blind". As adult designers we need to avoid home blindness and see the beauty in the familiar.

> Does it require an artist to point out to adults that colours shine in the rain? Children know this also.

Shadow patterns on the ground can be most interesting and add a beauty and texture to an otherwise ordinary environment. Young children, crawling at ground level often explore shadows and try to understand where they come from. They try to catch their shadow but they also try to discover where other shadows come from and are visually aware of and play with shadow as an element in their environment. As adults we may have forgotten about the wonder of shadows – and won't really appreciate them unless we spend a lot of timeout of doors exploring the characteristics of shadows.

The tools of the designer:

Line

Area and space

Proportion

Form and structure

The touch factor – a signal of quality

Composition

Colour and Light

Rhythm and harmony

Contrast and tension

Material

Movement

What do they mean to the child?

Nan Fairbrother writes in *The Nature of Landscape Design*, "the greatest fault of landscape design is too much planning on paper. A plan is an intellectual abstraction, not a description of the visual landscape." (p. 34). While we are mostly trained to work with the two dimensional symbols that represent the real three dimensional world, there is no substitute for the dimensional world, either in real life or in a model. Make quick and rough models with cardboard and clay or other materials you like to work with. Use a variety of materials for both your own tactile stimulation as well as for interest in the design.

"the greatest fault of landscape design is too much planning on paper" (Fairbrother, N. (1974) p 34).

Designing for birds

Computer technology has taken over much of the drudge work in the design professions and we can celebrate that. There is a tendency however to celebrate by using this tool in inappropriate ways, such as a total design tool. Like all tools from a shovel to a large bulldozer, the computer and its programmes are to be used in an appropriate way to bring about the best end result. We must be good professionals and not let what the computer can or cannot do control our ability to create and realise good design. Design magazines show designs which are very obviously created to look good on the screen and on a paper plan but in real life from the eye level of the user, the impression is a very different one. On the ground, 100 cm above the ground all the finely devised shapes are not visible, here there is

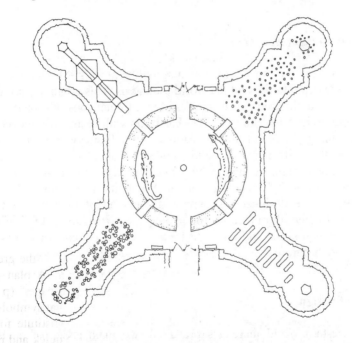

An example of a design prepared to look good on paper – no five year old player will ever perceive the place in this way. Playground in Kongens Have, Copenhagen, 1999, Drawing after playground installation by author.

a mishmash of lines and shapes. One needs to be a bird to appreciate all the details in these computer based design – and in playground design we are NOT designing views for the birds. Use computer technology to be a better designer – it is one of the tools of a designer – but so are sticks and stones.

As a good professional you will use both – according to the qualities they will bring to the design process.

Playground design is also often based in the assumption that the users are fair weather players – just like migrating birds. We tend to think of sunny summer days as the ideal times when children are out playing on the playground. However most local playgrounds and school grounds are most heavily used in the fall and spring months with less use in the high summer as holiday times means that many of the children are also on vacation and playing somewhere else. Think of an ordinary grey day, an everyday when imagining using the playground. Children have few choices of where to play and at the same time need to play outdoors in all weathers. It may be that on some sites, in some climates, it may be a good play idea to make the play area most interesting when it is raining.

The designer as researcher

To some extend the process of designing is like playing – both are creative acts of research into life and the world around us. This creativity brings the artist closer to children and to play, and is a tremendous advantage to the artist who designs for children. Play has to do with things of the everyday, ordinary things, it is not about Legolands and Disneyworlds. It is about being together with playmates and finding out about life, celebrating the joy of living through running or cycling as fast as one can, swinging high, jumping, and maybe declaring war on the adults in a snowball fight or water fight. The designer can support these kind of play by creating a design that offers the potential for playing as part of daily life, ensuring there is enough space and the right kind of spaces or outdoor rooms with appropriate furniture.

Styles of design

In the western world there has prevailed two main styles of landscape design- the romantic and the classical. In the romantic, nature is said to be set "free" with open pastures, grassed woodlands, forests, ponds and streams all designed to imitate an ideal of the natural landscape. Lines and forms are loose, curving, flowing suggesting an organic life force. In the classic style nature is tamed and trimmed and shaped with geometric forms clearly stating the human and intellectual source of the design. We continue to work within these styles or perhaps a marriage of them in modern landscapes. Trends in playground design – when a play area is designed –

show a tendency toward the more romantic style in northern European countries (See also chapter 12, Green Children). Playground design has been so little recognised as a separate art form that it is really quite difficult to talk about trends in design. The organising of playground spaces for the most has followed the functional layout model with little thought to design.

Landscape design styles that have prevailed in western cultures:

1.Romantic, nature untamed   vs   2. Classical, nature tamed, geometry

Schools of childhood development theories prevailing in western cultures:

1.The poetry of childhood – romanticism, natural play and development vs 2. The science of childhood, development is hierarchical (see Chapter 5 – Child development theories).

While today's garden designer along with their client can determine which style they will work in for a individual site – and will also bring in references to oriental garden styles, the adults attempt to lock the individual child into experiencing only one style of childhood. Childhood theories continue to be an either-or situation with many attributes of cult or belief. How well are modern children served by this?

Lines and forms in playground design

Straight lines and precise geometric shapes have been dismissed by the current generation of natural play designer and by artists like Hundertwasser who states that

> the straight line is a man-made danger. There are so many lines, millions of lines, but only one of them is deadly and that is the straight line drawn with a ruler... The straight line is completely alien to mankind, to life, to all creation (Rand, H. (1998) p 37 & 40).

Henrik Vilsbøll, a Danish proponent of the nature play movement, asserts that when we are surrounding are predominantly shapes in squares and straight lines we become aggressive, rough and frightened by it (Davidsen, T. (1996)). There is a general acceptance in the literature that organic shapes and lines are more inherently attractive to children than rigid geometric shapes. Some designers have gone so far as to suggest that the desirable forms for children are feminine shapes, meaning forms reminiscent of women's body parts. This pattern of thinking is related to the romantic notion of childhood and children as the last of the primitive tribes.

There is no doubt that lines and shapes have an effect on humans, at whatever age. It is not so simple, however as stated above. It can be that organic lines and forms suggest a more relaxed approach to nature and to the out-of-doors and therefore we can relax more in such settings. It can also be that we have learned to associate straight lines and formal shapes with serious activities. Outdoors and in large scale of open spaces, the way we perceive lines and shapes is just as important as the actual lines and shapes used. Landscape construction for play is not usually so precise that rulers are needed to create precisely straight lines on the ground, rather that it gives the impression of "straightnesss".

Some designers have gone so far as to suggest that feminine forms are the most appropriate to use in the design of children's spaces. Feminine forms have been the subject of male designer's fascination for centuries.

Good design will consider the eye level of the user and viewpoint of the use as well as the ideas inherent in the lines and shapes on the paper plans. The human eye has this trick of bending the long straight line in the landscape and large areas of perfectly flat ground don't appear flat to our eye. The use of lines and forms appropriate to playfulness in the out of doors is a part of the tools of the designer, to be used in conjunction with the other design elements. Moreover as playfulness is often expressed in the breaking of rules, in the unexpected or unforeseeable, there must be room in playground design for shapes and lines of all kinds. There can be no rigid rules.

In summary – the designers criteria

Design of children's play areas is in its infancy as a profession. This has the advantage in that there are no conventional ways of working that we need to break out from, anything is permitted. The disadvantage is that there few good role models to learn from. In this chapter I have tried to outline some measures for determining a minimal level of good professional practise where the designer balances the criteria set out by society and the demands of the children. Good design will keep these in balance, in that sense the designer is a form of referee between the society and the children. The next step is to play with designing for play.

References

Berger, John. (1972), *Ways of Seeing*, Penguin Books Ltd.: Harmondsworth.
Bettelheim, Bruno. (1980), *Surviving and other Essays*, Vintage Books: New York.
Davidsen, Thomas. (1996), "Arkitekturen savner kvindelighed" in *Samvirke*. November.
Evans, Paul. (1996), *Leisure section*. *Guardian Weekly*. Aug. 4.
Fairbrother, Nan. (1974), *The Nature of Landscape Design: As an Art Form. a Craft, a Social Necessity*, Alfred A. Knopf: New York.
Heft, Harry. (1988), "Affordances of Children's Environments: A functional approach to environmental description.", *Children's Environments Quarterly*, Vol 5, No 3, (fall) 1988.
Rand, Harry. (1998), *Hundertwasser*, Taschen: Cologne.

8 A Balancing Act – putting it all together

Playground design should be seen to be a younger sister of landscape design. Landscape design has been historically one of the fine arts, demonstrated in the creation of the Renaissance formal gardens and the English estate parks of the 18th century. During the 20th century the scope of the landscape architect's work has moved from private gardens of the wealthy to public spaces – public parks, both urban and wilderness, golf courses, zoological gardens, amusement parks, roadways, conservation areas and countryside, land reclamation, scenic values and environmental impact studies. Much of the work is at a large scale and long term. The emphasis has moved from a fine art to a practical profession where science dominates.

Children's play however is one of the aspects of landscape design where the art aspect should prevail. The designer of a play area should see themselves first and foremost as an artist creating living spaces that are aesthetically appealing and which support and nurture the playful element in human beings. A playground designer may not have training as a landscape architect but landscape architects have the advantage of having developed a skill and understanding of designing with living forms. Playground design is about working with living material, that grows, that moves. Moreover it is about designing for players, for activators that move and grow. Designing for play is about designing for living.

Playground designers are form givers and storytellers – in their work they create forms and spaces where a multitude of playful activities can take place and at the same time, through their work they are telling a story to the players about the human urge to play. The spaces are created for actors or rather activators, the playing children, who are interested in action, in making something happen, not in standing back an appreciating the work of art.

In the creation of play spaces the designer needs to be a good street performer/designer. They need to be good at juggling both the needs of society and of the children, a good storyteller to verbalise their thinking around the playing and activities and a magician to make spaces and forms that seem as if they just came out of a hat; while all involved have enjoyed the process.

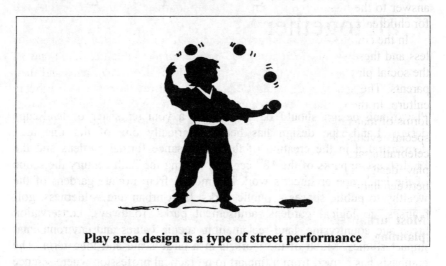

Play area design is a type of street performance

Can an adult design for children's play?

There seems to be some contradiction between the adult designers urge to shape, arrange and order forms and spaces and the children's playful urge to research, explore and take apart the environment in the making of their play. The places where children choose to play often have a quality of being unplanned, untouched by designers hands. So why design spaces for play? The answer is that, while we may not have been good enough at it in the past, we need to design spaces for play, because urban land use involves planning and design to ensure the comfort, safety, pleasure, and in the case of play- the playfulness of the area.

Urban lands set aside for children's play spaces are generally those pieces of land that can't be used for anything else. They are left-overs. These are the spaces that remain unoccupied after all the buildings have been placed in the most desirable locations, after the streets and parking lots and refuse disposal needs are taken care of – then comes the landscaping – planting up of the left over spaces and creating the playground. An adult designer's skills are desperately needed to bring children's play spaces back into focus not only in terms of design of the left over space, but even earlier on in allocating appropriate and desirable spaces for children's play.

There is a great need for adults who care about children's play to take charge of designing play areas, to replace the current efforts of engineers, gardeners and teachers who organise objects in the play spaces. So the answer to the headline question is that adults must be able to design well for children's play in urban areas.

In the countryside and wilderness the need for designated play spaces is less and these should focus on good design for the young children and on the social play and interaction between children of different ages and their parents. The spaces too should be beautiful and reflect aspects of modern culture. In the country, where humans are surrounded by nature in various forms of management, playful socialisation includes not only festivals and special events but should also include possibilities for creating and celebrating arts such as music, dance, painting sculpture and drama. Good play design is also about creating a balance or harmony for humans between nature and culture.

Most urban landscape spaces are SLAP – spaces left-over after planning

---

Play areas design is about spaces

The tools of the play areas designer as form giver, like other space designers, are primarily spaces and masses, voids and volumes. We experience spaces from within them, while we experience mass from the outside looking on. Play area design is about activities, for activators, and therefore it is the spaces that are of foremost importance. Spaces however only take on interesting character when they are defined, and in this role masses and volumes are important designer considerations. A play area designer plays with forms and masses to create spaces that can be used in a multitude of ways. They create spaces that can support specific types of movement activities and other spaces that can be used in a whole variety of ways. The spaces should be appropriate in size for the activities and comfortable for the user.

The scale of outdoors is different than the scale indoors – in our minds at least. To be good at outdoor design we need to experience out of doors. This is why I have put such an emphasis on the act of designing moving outside. What may seem to be big inside seems small outside. Things seem to shrink in the large outdoor room in its strong light.

Items for outdoor play should be proportioned larger than those for indoors and furniture, pathways and planting containers need to be bigger, more robust. Our eye also sees the landscape differently than the camera records it so it is essential that we learn to recognise what our eyes are seeing and not rely solely on the recordings on film.

Comfort in spaces has to do with the size of the space and also with the proportions between the space and the masses used to define the space. A small play area 40 m x 40 meters surrounded by open fields of grass and parking lots may feel too open and large to be attractive to the players. On the other hand a play area of the same size surrounded by high rise apartment buildings may feel too small and dominated by building to be comfortable to the user. Players in play spaces, like humans in most outdoor settings feel most comfortable in settings where there are vertical objects at a human scale. Larger trees with branches that extend out just above our head, fences and hedges, walls and planting beds, bollards, posts, sculptures, are all landscape features that create spaces and make the space comfortable for the user.

The large trees on this boulevard in Barcelona provide a sense of comfort and scale.

In the conventional playground with a combination structure set in a sea of sand, one often sees young children sitting on the ground under the structure playing at something that has nothing whatsoever to do with the play possibilities built into the structure. The children choose this location because it was near a vertical element – the most comfortable place for people out of doors. One of the unwritten rules of outdoor use by humans is that when people enter into a large open space they will always settle first near the boundary or fence or a vertical element. This is even more the case for very young children who are learning about outdoors. While they are very much attracted to the outdoors and are very interested in exploring all that is outside, they also need a sense of comfort. Young children outdoors are most often observed to enter into a play activity near a vertical element in the landscape – beside a fence, in the corner of a sandbox, under the slide or swing. Good design for outdoor play will include appropriately placed vertical elements in scale with the proportion of the space and the children to create a series of interconnected outdoor rooms. If the vertical elements can serve as frames for further construction by the children with available loose parts, blankets, sheets and so forth, so much the better.

> One of the unwritten rules of outdoor use by humans is that when people first enter into a large empty open space they will settle first near the boundary or fence or a vertical element.

Children seek spaces defined by verticals for quiet play – even when the vertical elements are so obviously intended for other uses.

The greatest need on a play space is space itself. Play structures where all types of play activities are said to be concentrated on a single combination structure, 250 cm by 350 cm in overall size, which is mostly above ground circulation space is NOT a play area, it is a series of small box-like spaces each of which can be used in only a few ways. One of the greatest errors in modern play area provision is the confusion between a play space and a play structure. A good play area may or may not include a manufactured or found "play structure". This is a matter of design choice. However a play structure does not make a playground.

Many years ago one of my planning projects included preparing an inventory of all the land used for play in a major North American city. This had never been done before in this city and the work required a great deal of footwork out on the land to locate where the children played. After a short period of time it became very clear that there was a distinct difference between the land where the children were playing and the land where there was playground equipment set up. I went back into the office and reported this situation and requested direction as to which type of land they wanted in the inventory. The answer was – those lands where there was playground equipment. The rationale is that playground equipment is set up in those urban places that adults are prepared to "sacrifice" to children's play; the

The presence of a play structure in a landscape serves as a sign that the space can be used by children.

other land could be more valuable if used for something else. The setting up of a structure, manufactured as playground equipment, is all too often seen as the way to provide for play and the structure is known as "the playground". This structure may be necessary to signal to the adults that this land has been set aside for play, but there should be enough room for playing there as well.

Playground design is not static

Designers are trained to work with forms and materials that are basically disciplined, if not dead. Stones, bricks, posts and fence panels stay where they are put and stay in their shape except for the long term effect of weathering. Nan Fairbrother writes that architects have difficulties designing with living things, "they tend to use vegetation as if it were dead"(Fairbrother (1974), p 52.). The materials of the play area designer often are living plants that grow and change, water and elements like sand that flow and move. Playground design is a discipline that involves working with design tools that change, which means that the design changes over time. Play area design is not about creating one design but about setting into growth a whole series of play areas that come about as things grow, move and change with the seasons and weather. The biggest agent for change on a playground are the players themselves; resulting in a designed space that is experienced and appreciated not by viewing it but by playing in it. The design is not static but is constantly changing with the actions of the children; with the seasons, the maturing of plantings and weathering of structures.

This may seen very chaotic to a designer who sees the activities of the player disturbing to their design efforts somewhat akin to the activities of living in a house often detracts from the efforts of an interior decorator. Those photographs of interiors in interior design magazines look like no one lives there. Imagine those designer kitchens after an afternoon of baking cookies with two young children! Playgrounds need to look like someone plays there. The designer needs to create their own style of response to this conundrum, however I have found that by establishing some strongly articulated frames for the various outdoor playrooms the play area design can withstand a great deal of the untidiness of the children's explorative play and still be an attractive place to both playing children and the adults. Plenty of space for moveable items and plenty of storage space, if loose parts are provided, are essential for both the playfulness and the attractiveness of the spaces.

The movement of the sun across the sky, rainy weather and snow can also dramatically change the play landscape. Rain and snow may seem uncomfortable to adults but they are gifts from nature to children's play. Designs should allow for maximum use of these free play items from nature. Never mind about making paving so level that there can be no "birdbaths" in them – design instead for the possibility of rain resulting in puddles in the paving. Snow play, sledding, snowball fights, making snow forts and snow angels are just a few of the play possibilities that snow offers. The landscape is also completely altered when covered with a blanket of snow.

> "But in the green environment nothing is static. The masses and spaces, the patterns and textures – the whole composition- are in a state of constant change. Landscape design is fluid four-dimensional planning with living material, with time as the fourth dimension" (Fairbrother (1974), p 53.).

Throw away design culture

The life expectancy of a play area, unless well maintained and developed according to a longer term master plan, is around 12 to 15 years. This is based in the lifetime of a play structure. Whether wood or metal, after 12 to 15 years, unless it has been regularly repaired and worn or aged parts replaced, the play items will need to be replaced. Also in 12 to 15 years there is a shift of ages of the population in neighbourhoods and a different set of demands may be set for the play area. This has resulted in a typical play area renewal programme where all landscape elements are levelled and a new playground built up from scratch. Planting are never given the chance to grow to maturity and the play area never takes on the appearance of being established or part of the landscape, it sits there like the temporary interloper it is seen to be by the adults. Playground design should be more long term where the basic frames of the play area remain over generations, including the landscape elements, while structures such as climbers, swings and shade pavilions are shifted out as the trees grow and as the age of the population shifts. That playgrounds are not static also means designing for changes, both in terms of changes in population and changes that occur as the landscaping matures.

Swings, for example are a way of playing that we never grow out of. Even if the dominant population of a neighbourhood shifts from young families to "empty nesters" in their fifties, they will want some place to go with their grandchildren. Single college students also enjoy swinging – but usually under cover of night. The play furniture can be moved or exchanged with shifts in the population, and this can be made more economical and efficient if the public authorities establish a programme of moving or circulating play items from play place to play place. This can happen when the design of the play area is focussed on the spaces and character of the place and not characterised by a play structure.

Containers for sand play can become planting beds for some time until again in demand – but be considerate, even children up to 12 –13 years of age enjoy playing in sand as long as the sand area doesn't look like a baby's sandbox. Perhaps we also need to keep large sand areas in the playgrounds so that playground designers have some place to go to practise their designs.

There is no playground design recipe book

Adults designing for play have no basic rule book to follow, they need to find their own way. Unlike designing for adult recreation activities like tennis and golf, there are no set criteria for children's play spaces. There is no established minimum size of a play area and no required equipment. Conventionally play areas have been very small, set with swings, slides and maybe a sandbox, but this is a convention; no one will say that this is the best provision for play. When we are faced with designing for tennis or golf there are organised interest groups that have written rule books on the

The nature of playing is such that it is impossible to provide a set of rules for making a good playground.

minimum requirements for such activities. Any designer who created a tennis court that was 10 meters short of the standard size and set up the net at the end, because there was not enough money for more, would be subject to great criticism and considered to be inept. Today's design for children's play can be just as inept but no one complains. There are no organised special interest lobby groups for children's play that interest themselves in good play area design. Play area design is a young design profession and the nature of playing is such that it is impossible to describe a play area in the same way as one can describe a tennis court.

Resources for play area design

The material the designer of outdoor landscapes can use are quite wide and varied, drawing upon the whole of the physical environment. Play area design is a relative of garden design in the sense that the designer needs to be very aware that the design will grow and change over time. Play areas can be seen to be a series of outdoor rooms with the sky as the roof and the ground as the floor. Space definition by vertical elements creates the "walls" and sense of enclosure.

Four categories of design resources used in a play area:

1. The hard landscaping elements or nonliving elements – bricks, wood, metal, furniture, pavilions, walls, and so forth.
2. The living elements and their support environments – plants, grass, trees, soil and water.
3. The cultural and social elements - references to our cultural treasure house of accumulated civilisation, cultures, to local history and events.
4. Loose parts that can be shifted, changed, manipulated. On public playgrounds, where what is not tied down will soon be missing, keep in mind that the most important loose part on a playground is the children.

Non living elements

The floor – the foundation of good play design

In my work with playground design I have been puzzled by the lack of interest shown in working with the shapes of the floor/ground of the outdoor play room. Indoors we assume that floors should be flat with careful designed ramps and stairs to accommodate the changes of elevation. Outdoors, at play, where one is encouraged to be physical active and alert, there is no reason that the ground should be flat – certainly not all over. Throw out assumptions about the nature of floors, walls and ceilings in the play spaces – devise new forms for these items as well.

There is now materials available for creating playful hills and mounds in all types of surface finishes. Bricks and paving stones can be laid to create wonderfully appealing ground forms that are comfortable to walk and run on. Design with play in mind however and ensure the ground forms are appropriate to support the kinds of play that the children enjoy.

A small school courtyard for young children where the floor as the main focus of the play. Photo courtesy of Notts Sport.

The artist, Friedensreich Hundertwasser, has created spaces where the floors are wonderfully playful. When you look at/ go through his creations note the playful sense that comes from designs where nothing is predictable or foreseeable. Here is an artist who, in my assessment, really plays at designing, and in his work challenges many of the preconceived notions about architecture and ways of using spaces. This is also what designing for playing at daily life can contribute to the further development of our civilisation. When we play we are most human. Playing not only serves as a continuation of old forms of human culture it is the source of innovation of new cultural forms.

God is in the details," source unknown.

Children are closer contact to the ground than we are as adults and they have a fine appreciation for details. Most adults can remember something about games around cracks in the sidewalks from their own childhood. Children improvise play in response to details in the environment – and while some just happen over time it is possible to design in surprises and interesting details into the floor. There is no reason that the same type of paving stone or surfacing be used everywhere. Like in the home the floor should reflect the kinds of activities that can take place in the room.

On the playground there should be a variety of different ground or floor surface textures which add interest as well as safety to the play. Access into play areas needs to be considered for children who use wheeled mobility devices as well as for adults who bring young children to the area in strollers or other wheeled devices.

Rolling rubber hills like these can be used in many different ways. The variation in colour adds to the quality in the play.

The activity of cycling is also an important part of play. In many cities the play area is the only place where young children can learn to ride a tricycle or cycle any distance. Cycles and cycling are also an important element in children's social play and in their developing of play groups. Where children can cycle can be designated though use of appropriate surfaces and curbs.

Walls

Walls, shelters, shade covers, benches and alternative seating, pergolas, arbours, tunnels and many other elements are part of the catalogue of non-living materials and elements that the designer can use on a play yard. Walls can also be living in the form of hills, mounds, hedges and plantings. Walls can be playful, curving and bending, not necessarily straight. Walls can become a play element in themselves with elements of fantasy, things to manipulate and with windows and doors. Low walls can also be used for seating, balancing and other playful activities.

Play items can also serve as space definers and dividers. Among the important elements are specially manufactured play items such as swings, seesaws, play houses and other social play units, climbers and slides. There are some adults who feel the necessity to design their own play structures – this urge should be for the most resisted –it has more to do with the desire of the adult to play at the child's expense. There is no need to design a new slide but perhaps there is a need to breed a new Platanus tree with good strong branches low to the ground for climbing. When have you heard of a play area designer designing new plants for playing?

The living resources

Grass in the playground

Open space for running, games, laying in the sun or shade and many other things is an important element in play area design. Design so that the grass is a positive form in the design; consider the shape, size and location of the grass as an essential element in the design form language. The size and shape of the grass should be useful for the play. All too often grass is seen to be the background or filler for those left over spaces after the play equipment and its safer surfacing is located. For ease of maintenance create only grass areas of a size that can be cut with a motorised mower – find out what size is used by the maintaining authority.

Don't place a grass area in deep shade, and do select grass types that can withstand the wear and tear of play. To be durable on a playground, not only does the grass need to be tough, there needs to be enough space to play so that the grass doesn't need to bear all the activities. In small, high density urban spaces where there are many children grass may not be able to survive – many little feet going over the soil everyday can result in the ground being so compacted very quickly that the roots are choked out.

Nature in the playground

Children, like all other humans are innately attracted to nature. Yet, children in modern western cities are restricted in their access to the natural world by the way in which the adults have organised daily urban life. It is therefore the responsibility of adults who design outdoor spaces for children to replicate the most interesting, attractive and child friendly aspects of the natural world in the children's environments.

Plants should be introduced right into the play area, not fenced off, and selected to withstand the playful use by the children. Sand, mud, stones, water, and soil are also materials that the designer can work with to create interesting play experiences. There has been a recent trend to throw playground equipment off of the small play areas in cities and make "nature playgrounds", where tree trunks and pieces of relatively unworked wood, stones, earth, sand and water are offered for play. This is an "either-or" declaration to the children; an adult censoring of what children are permitted to play with and how they should play. These nature elements in

Heavy play use would soon wear away these grassy hills and wood figures- they are more for visual display than real play.

a play yard can be very good play possibilities for the children, if they are well designed and of high quality. They must not be, however, the only play possibilities offered to the children. A good play area design will also balance the elements to include some from nature as appropriate, some specifically produced items to support movement and challenging play and some aspects of culture and local society. For a further discussion of the nature playground movement see chapter 12.

Cultural and social elements

Children are as cut off from access to many aspects of human culture and civilisation as they are from nature. The spaces where they play should include possibilities to research both contemporary childhood and adult cultures. Designers of play spaces should also introduce positive aspects from civilisation and culture. Researchers have pointed out that there are many aspects of traditional childhood that actually are remnants of adult cultures of the past. Possibility to engage in traditional games, skipping, and rhyming games should be provided. Artistic motifs, sculptures and relief artwork can all be part of the aesthetics of the area. The entry to the play yard can make a declaration about the kind of space one is entering though a specially designed portal which is thematically linked to the history of the neighbourhood or is just good art.

Music, dancing and singing take on a whole different dimension outdoors and are a wonderful addition to the play possibilities. To allow

Dancing and music outdoors – especially with adults- can be a highlight of children's outdoor cultural play.

for this possibility the designer should include a space where it is possible to dance and provision for power and amplifying music and sound should be available. Dance pavilions and formal structures are not necessary, just a multi-use space.

I was thrilled when walking through Zizhuyuan (purple Bamboo) park in Beijing to hear music – good music- but not too loud, coming from the speakers throughout the park for a period of time in the afternoon. It was just so wonderful to walk through this tremendously well landscaped setting, listening to the music and enjoying the late autumn sun. The next morning I awoke to music outdoors again, this time it was livelier music coming from speakers in the parking lot next to my hotel. Here people were dancing- western waltzes and jigs- as their morning exercise. In Beijing people have very small indoor living spaces, they live much more outside and they make their outdoor spaces part of their cultural and social experiences in many ways.

Loose parts

Things that children can manipulate, built with, dig with, use to make sand castles, dam up water, make little sailboats – all require that there be loose parts to add to the quality of the play. The availability of loose parts however is the most problematic aspect of public play area design, as in many cities, objects loose in the playground soon disappear from the area. A partial solution can be to provide a storage space for loose parts, which is equipped by the local play authority. The storage is locked up except for set play times during the week when an adult worker or volunteer takes responsibility for opening and later locking up of supplies. These can be supplemented by a "play pack" specially prepared in the family for trips to the park and can include sticks and small pieces of wood, sand and water play toys, balls, skipping ropes, frisbees, and dress-up clothes for dramatic play. If all this is kept in a backpack the trip to the playground can be so much richer.

The best answer to the need for loose parts on the playground is a play leader or supervisor supported by a fully stocked loose parts depot. For school age children the adventure playground or building playground is an excellent service, unfortunately they are not made available to children to the extent they should be. Play leaders on public playgrounds were part of the original playground concept, however in many countries staffing was eliminated in the round of service cutting already in the 1970's. The issue of eliminating services for children is not that there is less money in city budgets, it is that the politicians find it very easy to allocate proportionately less money to children and play as there is no strong lobby group working politically on behalf of children's play. It is also the case that, when faced with the need to cut budget or agitate the taxpayers to agree to a tax increase, crafty politicians throughout the world know that if they cut budgets for services to children, to the sick and to the elderly they can strong arm the population to eventually accept a tax increase to improve these services again. If, however they cut allocations to their offices and executive assistants, their salaries and pensions, travel to conventions and participation in international delegations and other "hidden" activities that do not directly service the taxpayers, only the politicians and their friends would be inconvenienced. In most western societies children compose 18 to 20% of the population yet they have access to far less than 20% of land and resources.

Design and safety

In chapter 5 Society's Criteria, there is an discussion about current safety standards and guidelines for public playgrounds. Play area designers, approaching safety issues for the first time often see the standards as barriers to creativity in their design. This is not the case. The standards do set some limitations on the design possibilities for playground equipment but do not create any unnecessary limitations on the play space designer. The problem in the standards for playground equipment is that it does not permit the creation of play items that are challenging enough for older children. Play equipment design for movement and challenge however is a very specialised field of play design and should be left to experts working within experienced production companies.

The play area designer should use only those manufactured play structures that are certified as complying with a safety standard as part of the furnishings of the public play area. If the play area is one which is supervised by adults or where the play is part of a care institution or therapy then the standards do not apply. The standards however are intended as a definition of the minimum level of good professional practise in designing for play and working outside of these standards is professionally irresponsible except where the special needs of the children in the institution demand some deviation from the standard.

In general, research indicates that playground safety is directly related to the quality of the play area design and the amount of play interest the children find there. Play spaces which are attractive and offer plenty of varied and challenging play possibilities are found to be safer than those where children have little choice in how to play and which are found unattractive. Play area designers need to focus on creating spaces that are attractive to children and where there is a variety of interesting play possibilities. When they do so, they will have done their best for the children at play.

Plants and safety

Some playground safety experts and guidelines devote a great deal of time and space to the issue of eliminating poisonous plants from the play areas. This has resulted in a great deal of unnecessary worry and in the destruction of many beautiful landscapes. There are very few reported incidents of deaths of children from poisoning from plants on the playground. Plant poisonings that do occur, most often occur indoors in the home and it is crawling infants who are at greatest risk. Landscaping of play areas should include a wide variety of plant materials that are durable in the play yard but are not all full of prickly spears. There are a few plants whose seeds if eaten in very small quantities could cause problems, like the laburnum tree (Laburnum anagyroides), daphne (Daphne mezereum), holly (Ilex aquifolium) and euonymous (Euonymous europa) and these can be avoided (as listed in DIN18034). Most other landscape plants can be freely used.

Children are attracted to plants and love to learn about their scents- they can quickly learn which plants they can use in play and which to avoid.

The best way to ensure children and adults are protected from potential plant poisonings is to ensure that people of all ages know which plant parts can be eaten, which plants are a good source for branches and wood for fires and for grilling food, for whistles and so forth. It is today's population of urban adults who have an uninformed relation with nature that fear poisonous plants and other "threats" from nature. We can not eliminate nature from our surroundings and the best way to ensure that people are able to deal with the negative potential in nature is through a sound familiarity with nature and how to interact with it. This interaction starts in childhood at the playground and park.

Playing with fire

Fire and water – two of the basic elements of the earth and two that are so attractive and fascinating to humans. Access to both are symbols of luxury in modern urban adult life, yet both are almost totally absent in children's play. Why? Some adults perceive that these elements are too dangerous for the children and that children are too irresponsible to be let near these elements. When children are permitted to explore the fascinating characters of water and fire they also come to know about the dangerous ones. Under supervision young children can and should be able to discover the qualities of fire and water and they should be on every play area where there is supervision. Unsupervised public play areas should also offer possibilities for water play in the form of sprays, shallow streams and fountains and places for fires and grills which the parents can oversee.

Snow is one of nature's best gifts to children.

While safety is an issue in the design of play areas so are challenge and risk as well as developing a competence in dealing with elements of the earth. This means we need to provide children with access to elements of the earth and nature within the playground setting. While adult society may find it most convenient to deny these things to the children, the good play area designer will find ways in which children can experience the joys of exploring these aspects of life on this planet. Children's safety at play is an issue of providing well for their play interests so they can become familiar and competent in their interactions, not in cutting them off and keeping them isolated from dangers.

Other aspects of water play that are related to safety are the use of water collected when it rains for water play and the recycling of water in play. These ideas are popular ones, particularly where water consumption is metered and taxed. The quality of the water however is often not sufficient for the health/hygiene requirements of clean drinking water. Children not only play with the water, they also will use it in their role play and they will drink it – therefore the water for water play must be of a drinkable standard. Rain water and play water can be collected and used to water the landscape and children can be part of that process – they often enjoy watering the garden. Small mud puddles that children splash in are quite safe as is playing in the rain or snow.

Play area design is not about reinventing the swing

It is not necessary each time for the designer to invent a new form of climber or multi-platform play structure, anymore than an interior designer needs to design their own furniture for every interior they create. Work with well designed and well made play furniture available on the market as well as plantings, open spaces and other landscape elements to create unique and interesting spaces. The designer of play spaces needs to be well informed about what materials and resources are available in the market and work imaginatively with these items. Often it is possible to have representatives from the manufacturers or suppliers provide information on using the items, be they swings or brick paving, and the play area designer is well advised to take advantage of these offers and learn as much as possible about these elements. Keep in mind however that there is an element of a sales pitch in the information from the supplier. Ask for reference sites and observe the children playing there as a part of your research in play area design. Select furniture that has a design quality appropriate with the play signals you wish to communicate to the children and which complements the other elements in your total play space design.

The total effect of the design is influenced both by the ground forms and shapes and by the design qualities of the structures and furniture placed in the spaces. Unfortunately there has been far too much focus on the design form of the all dominating multi-platform play structure on play spaces that are organised by gardeners and teachers. One result of this has been a great criticism of manufactured play structures and the complaint that all playgrounds are the same. The play area designer is thus tempted to set their mark on the playground by trying to manipulate with a new look for the structure. This has happened because these structures often were the only object in the space that had any form or shape, so all attention was focussed there. This however is not a genuine effort at play area design any more than selecting a white automobile over a blue automobile has anything to do with car design. Work with the ground, with the vertical elements, with variety in spaces and with planting, and then the select the multi-platform structure with appropriate visual and play qualities to fit in as just one element of many; redirecting attention to the play area design and away from the structure.

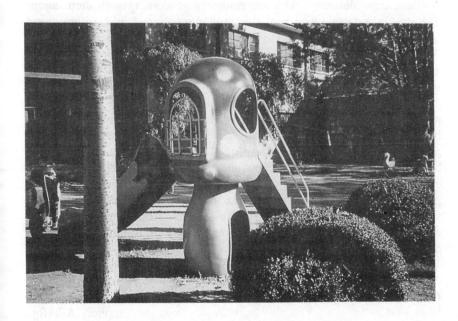

Play equipment is but one part of the furniture in a play space.

Linking and unifying elements in playground design

Play areas with so many different things happening and the demand for variety of all kinds also demands that there be some unifying or linking elements in the design. These can be walkways or circulation spaces within the play yard, plantings, lines of trees, ground forms, edge treatment, repetition of decorative motifs. Good quality furniture, fencing and detailing are also unifying in their quality, as is quality maintenance.

There has been a tendency in some playground organisers to see a type of colour co-ordinating of the play structures as the unifying element in the design. Some go so far as to colour the play items the same colour as the colours used in the logo of the owner. This is a very silly approach to design and to unifying elements. Colour can be a unifying element but it is also a signal giver for the children, their way of reading the playground. It makes good design sense that those playthings for young children are visually different than those for older children. Colour coding so the children can understand the environment is a good design idea, colour matching of everything is not.

Landscape designers who are comfortable working with earth forms and plantings can unify the playscape through use of landforms and plantings.. To do this these forms must be visually attractive and dominant. Be bold with plantings that are to enclose or to unify. In that way the design unity is carried by the landscape and not overwhelmed by the play structure.

Pathways are not just a means to get from place to place but can be a play feature in themselves. In addition they can be strong visual lines that can link together the whole design. They also serve to invite the player to move, to explore, to see what happens next. Selection of surfacing should be based on playfulness, and accessibility. When using pathways as linking elements the temptation may be to use the same material throughout the path. For the play of the children use subtle or not so subtle patches of varied texture at intersections or where something different happens. Not only is this playful it is a very important type of information giver to children at play and to those who may be visually impaired.

Colours in the play area

Colours have association despite the misuse of colour in modern commercialism. Colours have meaning to young children, meanings that are different than the adult meanings. And colours have social and local culture associations. Globally, the use of bright colours on flags and banners and so forth signal amusement, a festival a party. They send a message that now is the time to be imaginative and playful. Similarly careful use of bright colours in the play yard can signal to the children that they are welcome here.

Designers untrained in children's play and the child's view of the world focus on functional and organisational issues – and they have a tendency to organise by shapes and use colour in the same way as they arrange the colours in their wardrobe. They are not able to address the children's issues. They are not aware that to children a variety of colours signals a place of interest, a healthy varied environment. Some adherents of the nature movement claim that nature is all about greens and browns and children's play places should blend in with nature. Such a statement shows these people really have little understanding or sympathy for nature. Nature is wonderfully multi-coloured, and was even more so before human beings killed off so many species of plants and animals and transformed the landscape around them to monoculture of plants for profit.

This does not mean that every playground should take on the haphazard appearance of a child's crayon box – there is a demand that children's play spaces be beautiful, not condescending. Good design for children administered by a good adult designer can combine elements of the natural world, local culture and geography, with aspects of childhood and children's play to create unique play environments. This always involves that the designer will make decisions about colours, forms, textures and other visual qualities. These decisions are to be made with the knowledge of how children use colour to read the landscape and to understand how spaces and objects are arranged in the landscape.

> Hunderwasser has stated "a colourful world is always a synonym for paradise. A grey or monocoloured world is always a synonym for purgatory or hell"(Rand, H. (1998) p 107.).

Colours children prefer

There are studies that claim to prove that children prefer certain colours over others. There are also experts who claim that children find bright colours disturbing, while others show that children are attracted to full saturation colours. The fact is that we know very little about children's response to colours out of doors. It is very difficult to design any kind of research methodology involving children and their response for colour where the impulses learned from the adult culture are not a dominant influence. Young children adopt responses they observe from those around them – and this also applies to how children respond to objects. It would seem very reasonable to assume that, for young children, there is no differentiation between an object and the colour of an object, rather the colour is a characteristic of the object. That is to say, for a young child when you change the colour of an item it is a different item. It is with the acquisition of language that children learn words for colours and come to understand that in today's technological consumer times, colours have meanings in the prevailing adult culture and that colours and objects are not consistently the same. By the age of six or seven they can understand the concept that objects can be the same when the colour has changed, but still have hesitations about it in daily life, and don't change the colour of their favourite food.

This means that by the time children can verbalise or otherwise communicate with adults about colours they have already been very much inundated with local adult values regarding colour. Their responses will be formed by what they have experienced, as are everyone's. Children from infancy are receiving impressions of responses to colour. While many of the toys they are given to play with are brightly coloured, their parents may choose to dress them in colours that clearly signal their gender. Blue for boys and pink for girls has been a standard formula throughout the past century at least. Almost from birth on this message is sent to the child – and by the time they are five most modern girls are very experienced at shopping for and selecting their own clothes and they know that colours like pink, and light shades of purple are for them whereas blues and blue greens are for boys. Very early on colours come to be identified with fashion and clothing and throughout our life many of us continue to see colour as nothing more than an element of style and fashion that signals something about our adult good taste.

How we see colour and what we recognise when we see a colour can be two very different worlds. We receive the sensation of light in our eyes but it is our brain that recognises the colour. And while our eye can distinguish hundred of varies hues and shades as distinct from each other we have words for only a few colours and a great deal of disagreement between people about which is the real one of these colours, i.e. the one that the label can be applied to. This becomes even more problematic when we are exposed to a series of colours such as the rainbow or spectrum in the outdoor landscape.

Colour is in the mind of the beholder

Young children's ideas about colours are not the same as adults ideas about colours even though their eyes are equally able to perceive the sensations of light. There is a saying that "beauty is in the eye of the beholder". With colour one perhaps should say "colour is in the mind of the beholder".

> In some European and Oriental cultures moreover, a disdain for colour has been seen as a mark of refinement and distinction. The taste for black in clothing, for example, was a prerogative of wealth and nobility in the Renaissance, but in succeeding centuries it spread in Europe to all levels of society, and black still forms part of our dress-code for many occasions (Gage, (1993) pp 188-9).

Even today, black is the preferred choice when serious adult activities are on the agenda and has been fashionable with young adults in the mid to late nineties. This association of colour in clothing with sophisticated taste which signals wealth and superior status means that designers who want to be seen to have these attributes will slavishly follow the prevailing colour codes. Such codes however are meaningless in the world of children's play

Outdoor play areas are the only spaces in the city where childhood culture is celebrated, where the public institutions signal to the children that they too are important citizens in their right as young people. The colours of the area, as well as all other aspects of the design, should reflect this and signal that children are important. Public play areas are no place to show off sophisticated adult tastes, but to sensitively reflect the tastes and values of childhood.

Boys colours and girls colours

One quick survey of the shelves in a toy shop makes it very clear that toys for children over the age of three are clearly gender differentiated by colour as well as function. Dolls, doll houses, horses, cycles, soft toys for girls are all in pastel hues with a predominance of pinks, light reds, rose colours and warmer colours on the whole. For boys pastels are replaced with darker shades, blue, black, grey green, brown-green and so forth. Colours are taken from the world of male heroes – soldiers, police, guns, tractors, dinosaurs, jungle beasts and so forth. Why are these colours chosen for these toys by the producer? Partly because they are the colours associated with the object in the real world and partly because they are the colours the buyer prefers.

Who buys toys?

Research shows that most of the elaborate cute baby dolls in their tulle dresses and all their accessories are bought by grandparents for their young granddaughters. Young girls are taught that this is what a real dolly doll is like, and from experience learn to ask for more of this because it so pleases the adults to give them these toys.

Toys for boys over three are more problematic for grandparents partly because the main shopper is often the grandmother who finds boys toys unappealing and maybe even for moral reasons will not buy them toy guns or weapons. So, after the toy train, boy children are more frequently given money or are participants in the choice of toys as gifts. Toys of wood, without applied colour, are seen by adults to be classical good taste, but these are hardly ever chosen by the children. Children will choose the plastic with the "right" colours.

What does this means at the playground? Actually it means very little. Play with hand held toys and the large movement play in the big outdoor room should be very different experiences. Outdoor play in a playhouse can be something of interest to both boys and girls which means that one needs to avoid use of colours that children have already learned to associate with the girl gender. While girls can easily and without much comment from their peers cross the bounds of gender play and play with boys, boys are very sensitive to peer pressure around "girly issues". A colour scheme that means something on the playground but does not reflect current trends in consumer toys is the best approach. Playgrounds have a life time of ten to fifteen years and throughout the life of the playground it should reflect the world of childhood in a timeless way. The replication of figures and colours from a certain popular media toy will only serve to make the play area seem outdated very quickly.

Designing child life habitats

Designing for children's play is a legitimate design activity and should be undertaken by experienced and well trained designers. When society plans zoological gardens they engage a whole team of highly trained and experienced experts to ensure that the environments created for the animals are sufficient and appropriate for the health and well being of the animals who will live there. Zoo design is a highly respected profession.

Playground design should be like zoo design – with a team of highly trained and experienced experts who will ensure that the play spaces for children are appropriate and sufficient for children's play. It is in these places where children experience living and where they can explore what it means to be alive on this planet. Playgrounds are child-life habitats and designers of play areas should bring to the work both a design competence and a knowledge of children's play behaviours. In this chapter I have discussed some of the aspects of designing for children's play, however every designer will need to develop his or her own style, as well as undertake on going research and enquiry into the nature of human playfulness.

References

Fairbrother, Nan. (1974), *The Nature of Landscape Design: As an Art Form, a Craft, a Social Necessity*, Alfred A. Knopf: New York.

Gage, John. (1993), *Colour & Culture*, Thames and Hudson: Singapore.

Rand, Harry. (1998), *Hundertwasser*, Taschen: Cologne.

9 Play Yards with Early Childhood Institutions

Children do not engage in the same kind of play in all places. The quality of the environment, the time for play, playmates and the child's personality all influence the kind of play that takes place at various locations. As play is not the same, play areas should not be designed to be alike even though there is a tradition for this approach. In this chapter I will look at the factors that make a difference in play area design depending on the type of location of the play space. The design criteria for the children and the adult criteria discussed in previous chapters apply to all sites, but the form of response to the criteria should be different in each location. In the daily life of a young child it may be that there are three play areas within visiting distance – one at the kindergarten where they go everyday, a park near the home they visit often when out for a walk with the family and on an outing with the kindergarten and, thirdly, a school yard that also serves as a neighbourhood play space that is located on the way to the corner store. When designing for young children it is important to take into consideration what kinds of play opportunities are available in the daily world of the child and not repeat the same play structures at every site.

One exception to the non-repeat rule is swinging. Possibilities for swinging in city life should be set up wherever and whenever there is space for them. Children seem to always be tempted by the possibility of a quick tour on a swing on the way to somewhere else. And children never grow out of the love for swinging – even at eighty swinging is a wonderfully stimulation experience.

The design of a play space will be influenced by where that play space is located – is it attached to a pre-school child care facility, is it part of a school yard or is it in a public park. Perhaps these kinds of spaces do look alike all to often, but they should be very different kinds of spaces. Play spaces that are part of institutions like child care, kindergarten, play-schools and schools have the characteristic that there are adults present when the children play. Adults whose role is play leader or play "enabler" can use their knowledge of play to transform these spaces into a wide range

133

of play possibilities. This means that it should be possible to include more manipulative play possibilities, loose parts and play opportunities with nature and elements of this earth. There is great play potential in these types of play yards, however most traditional play areas do not take advantage of the potential.

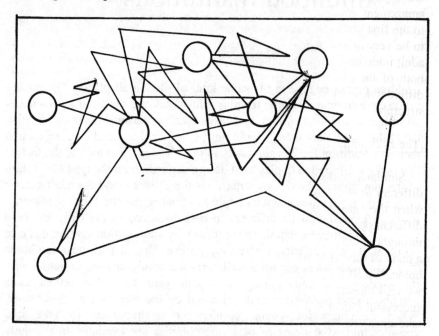

Young children's play involves a lot of movement and spatial exploration. This drawing shows the movement patterns of an 18 month old child over a period of seven minutes in a space with 8 play stations.

Environment and environmental personality

In the opening paragraph I have referred to the child's personality as a factor that influenced they type of play. By personality I mean the child's environmental personality – that aspect of the personality that changes when we change environments. Children learn very quickly what they can do and how they can act in specific environments, and will approach a new play environment with already pre-formed notions of how they should play there. After a period of time playing with the other children they may change their environmental personality to match behaviour with that of the other children. For example a child who has been able to play freely in an outdoor environment will approach a playground slide structure with a lively imagination and very soon slide down head first, climb up the slide or organise other play activities around the slide such as investigating sliding down on various types of materials. A second child, from another environment where there are sliding rules such as they are only permitted to use a slide for sliding down feet first while sitting up, will watch in amazement at what this first child is doing. This second child will explain to the first child that one is not permitted to slide that way and will appear to be very unimaginative in the way they use the structure. However if no adult intervenes it is quite likely that after several days of playing together both of the children will be freely using the sliding structure for many different ways to play – researching the affordances for them in such a structure.

The environmental personality -a different place, a different person

Similarly, children learn quickly that one may be required to behave different at grandmother house, that they can't do what they do at home when they are in the kindergarten. In other words – a different place, a different person. The environmental aspect of personality continues with us throughout our life – we all know people who are very different persons at a party of their peers than they are when they visit their family in the family home. We all feel a little bit, or a great deal, the effects of the change when we visit our elementary school again as adults. We may be parents with a successful career but, back in the environment of the school, we start to take on some aspects of ourselves as we were when we went to school there.

Play spaces for pre-school children attached to child care institutions have the advantage that there are adults who are potential play leaders present. Whether these adults act as play leaders or "play police" depends on how they see their role and the role of play in the institution. When the institution is a child care and is seen to be a "parking place" for children until their parents come to take them home then the adults are likely to be relatively disengaged in what happens outside except to ensure that the child is not injured in any way. These "day care" institutions place emphasis on delivering the child back to the parents in the same condition they arrived in. In some countries, child care for pre-school children involves an organised early educational curriculum and children are indoors in a classroom-like setting much of the day. In these institutions, play outside is seen to be an outlet for energy for a short period of time so that when the children are back inside they are quieter and easier to teach.

In other institutions the approach is that everyday in the life of the young child should be a quality experience based on play in a community of caring adults and other children. In these places what happens outside on the play yard is an important part of the day. While such issues directly influence the form of the physical design of the play yard, they are aspects of the culture or social organisation. The designer however can ask leading questions to find out what kind of institution it is.

The most frequently encountered barriers to good design of pre-school children's institutional play yards are lack of space and lack of funding. Despite these critical problems it is necessary to provide good designs for outdoor spaces for young children. In my experience these kinds of play yards are the most rewarding to work with as they can have a huge potential for fascinating play possibilities. When a good play area designer and a team of determined institution staff members set out to create a good play area it will happen; the funding will be obtained, even if it requires a staged development programme that stretches over many years. Sometimes it is necessary to dare to dream on behalf of the children and not be too bound the immediate appearance of limited resources. Resources to provide well for children are only limited in our wealthy western societies because we do not put priority on good public provision for children. It is a matter of will not a matter of a lack of resources.

For too long it has been possible to operate child care facilities with painfully inadequate outdoor play opportunities – and one of the aims of quality services for young children must include upgrading the quality of outdoor spaces where young children play. Designers can aid in these efforts to improve conditions for children through interesting themselves as a profession in children's use of the landscape, by creating great designs for small design projects and by developing within the landscape profession minimal space and quality standards for children's play spaces.

How much space is minimal?

In my experience there is a minimum space of 2000 square meters necessary to create a well rounded and balanced play environment for an institution for young pre-school children. This is the minimum size that will support the growth of nature as well as the more active exploration of the children. This size area will serve a small day institution with around 20 children. This space is to be use exclusively for children's play – not parking, not garbage collection, and not buffer shrubbery unless the children can play in it. Where there are more children the play area should be increased at the rate of 50 square meters per child. There are many long established institutions with much smaller play yards – which are inadequate. In some instances these child care institutions use the local neighbourhood park on regular outings, however this is not a sufficient alternative – children are always visitors at a public park and they cannot move or change much there, there are few loose parts and so on. Space is a critical element of quality when we talk about children's outdoor exploration and we need to provide children and the adults in these institutions with sufficient space that they can experience a fine quality garden like environment.

> A minimum space of 2000 square meters is necessary to create a well rounded and balanced play environment for an institution for young pre-school children.

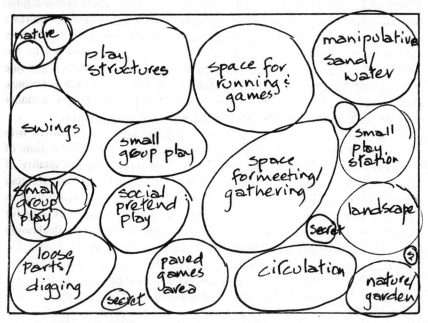

Suggested allocation of space in a pre-school play yard

This minimal space is far more than is usually set aside for play spaces in children's institutions, but the usual practise has proven to be insufficient. One need only look at the problems of the indoor climate, noise pollution, increasing rate of allergies and asthma in young children, concentration problems and learning difficulties to see that children need to be outdoors playing more often when they are young – and they will only go out if the adults who care for them also go out. Adults and children will go out if they have attractive, interesting and comfortable outdoor spaces near at hand – that is right outside the door. Arranging an outing is feasible once a week, but will not happen everyday- it requires too much organising and packing to move 20 children from the centre down the block to the park. Playing outside should happen everyday – and for many hours everyday. Stephen Kline writes – "A civilised society is one which struggles to make the world better for its children" (Kline, (1993)). How civilised are we? We can do better – and we can live much healthier with fewer car parks and more playgrounds.

Space and subspaces

Young children tend to play in small play groups except when organised by the adults into co-operative and group games –which they also enjoy very much. A play yard should be subdivided into a series of subspaces of various sizes – some no bigger than 200 to 300 cm in diameter for the "secret" play of two or three children to the larger spaces needed for running and ball games, for group gatherings and games and space for everyone to socialise and eat together outside. Much of the play time when children are permitted to play freely occurs in small playgroups of 2, 3 or 4 children. An institution with 60 children requires not only an open space where all 60 children can play together they also need 20 to 30 small subspaces where groups of children in twos and threes can play out their own play. For example it is typical that a child's birthday is celebrated in the institution with some form of traditional birthday treat and singing. This can and should take place outside – and there needs to be space enough with appropriate furnishing for this to happen. In Denmark there is also always a flag pole on the play yard – and the national flag is hoisted on children's birthdays along with the other days that are marked by flagging. There needs to be space where grass can grow – a sunny space so the grass will thrive but one that is not constantly walked on as part of the circulation, and there needs to be paved spaces for cycling, jumping and ball play among other activities. Different kinds of play happens in different sizes of play groups and requires different kinds of spaces.

All of the outdoor space is the playground

There is a tendency among adults to think of that place where there is fixed playground equipment as "the playground". In general adults are far to fixated on playground equipment as the playground. In a pre-school institution the whole of the outdoor space is the playground or play garden and children should have free access to the whole. Playground equipment can be part of the furnishing of one or more of the subspaces and provision for movement activities that the children like so much, like swinging, sliding, climbing and rocking should be provided in some form which will result in a quality experience for the children. On a play area used by 60 children there should be a number of places where the children can find such interesting movement possibilities. It is a great mistake, however to set up a play structure that a manufacturer or designer describes as accommodating 60 children and expect that the children's play needs have now been met. Although this is frequently the usual practise in a number of western countries that are otherwise quite civilised – it is not a civilised way to deal with children's play. Play structures, when well designed, are wonderful elements on a playground – they just shouldn't be the only thing the children have to play with. Physical play facilities and structures including their safety spaces should never occupy more than 25 % of the total open space available for children – and on a minimal play yard of 2000 sq. m this means never more than 500 sq. meters. Rarely would the constructed physical play items occupy more than 250 to 300 sq. meters, not including water and sand play and the role play structures. A two seat swing will occupy from 50 to 70 sq. meters depending on the local requirement for safety space around the swing and the height of the swing. There should be a minimum of four swings, more if possible. Other physical play structures and their required minimal space would take another 150 sq. meters. This leaves 200 to 250 sq. meters for open space for physical games such as a small grass soccer/football game field or a paved enclosure for cycling, mooncars, roller skating and street hockey.

> Physical play facilities and structures including their safety spaces should never occupy more than 25 % of the total open space available for children.

Just as it is ill advised to set up a single large play structure as **the** answer to all the children's play needs, it is wrong to throw out all of the built physical play structures and offer the child only "nature". Children need to have a balance of nature and built things, of spaces for making their own play, for creating for socialising. There is no one type of thing – nature or a climbing structure, that is sufficient. Sufficiency is determined by the number of different kinds of play possibilities. Good play yards require variety – variety in spaces, in materials, in movement possibilities, in ways to play. Children's play is deeply dependent of the environment in which they play and children are very much influenced by the character of the space or micro environment.

> Sufficiency is determined by the number of different kinds of play possibilities.

A view of the world from 90 cm

Tables and desk surfaces tend to be at around 80 cm over the floor while kitchen and workroom countertops accessed while standing tend to be at around 90 cm. Many old fashioned keyholes are also at that height –it is a comfortable hand height for an adult. For a three year old child it is approximately eye height – this is the height from which they view the world when standing – it is lower when they are sitting, bending, and other play movements. Children live closer to the ground in a number of ways than we do – first their eye level is closer to the ground and secondly they spend a lot more time sitting on it or kneeling on it than we do as adults. When we design for young children's play yard we should squat down so our eyes are at 90 cm above the ground and view the site from this point – and work with the child's scale in mind. For a three year old child a fence or solid barrier at 100 cm is impenetrable – and if they want to see over they will try to climb up or pull themselves up. If you want to create barriers to prevent children's access – make sure they can still see through

A low enclosure is sufficient to define the play space – and young children should be able to see through the fence so they can see what is happening.

them at strategic view points or viewing holes. It is particularly important that young children can see through to where the adults enter into the institution – so they can keep an eye on who is coming and going.

Being up high means standing higher than your head is usually when you stand upright on the ground. For most adults standing up on a ladder at a height of over 200 cm feels like they are high up. So too for children – being up high means standing on a surface higher than one's head usually is. Many adult designers make the mistake of offering young children play climbing structures that are much too high in the belief that the greater the height the greater the thrill. This is not so for a three year old – although it is the case within limits for a 12 year old. Vertical elements in the play yard for young children need not be so very high – fences, hedges and other elements set up to define shapes and boundaries need be no higher than 80 to 90 cm.

This 90 cm height creates a problem for the designer who is trying to get a good sense of proportion – as these large open spaces also require higher vertical elements to be kept in scale and to create subspaces. A 90 cm high hedge will create a sense of enclosure on a space approximately 350 cm across but will appear to be a fussy frill on a space 10 meters across. Small spaces at 200 to 400 cm however are just right for cosy play such as role play corners, reading and story telling circles, places to play in the sun or play with dolls and so forth. There should be many of them spaced throughout the yard.

Proportional vertical scale for the larger open spaces can be brought in through shade pavilions, summer houses for adult staff, barbecue and grills, pergolas and tunnel and sculptures. The very best scale givers are large mature trees like linden, oak, maple, and plane trees. These trees with their wide spreading branches seem to invite and embrace the children at play. It is necessary to have enough space for a large tree to thrive yet not shade the whole play area.

These higher scale giving elements should not completely cut off views. A play area however is more interesting if not all the space can be seen at one time and if there are places where groups of playing children can get away from the eyes of others. In terms of the playability of the environment it is also important that some of the play area that supports messy type play be screened off from adult views – as it is vital that children at play here be allowed to finish their play and be required to clean up and put everything away as the day ends. Messy digging and construction plots should be enclosed and separated from other play uses so that the children's world order established here can be maintained until they have decided to establish another pattern.

Play yards at pre-school institutions should take full advantage of the fact that there are caring adults present to interact with the children and to support their play. This means that these yards can include many more possibilities for loose parts, for construction play, for elements like fire, water, and elements to be part of the daily outdoor experience of the children. That these institutions are supervised also means it is possible to include garden areas where fruit and vegetables are grown, where there are flowers and herbs to please the senses, where there is singing and dancing to express the joy of life. In play area design it is not just an issue of having all these kinds of spaces but the relationship of spaces and how they are used by the adults determines whether and how they will be used by the children.

Location determines use – another environmental behaviour factor

There was a time when I was designing play areas when I worked with a theory of zoning the institutional play area into a series of spaces such as social, physical structure, physical open space, nature, garden, manipulative/creative, construction and so forth. In one yard where I was working with the staff to redesign an existing space to make it more varied and stimulating to the senses there was an existing group seesaw placed in the middle of what we had zoned as the social gathering area which was a lovely sunny place just in front of the main door where two of the kindergarten group came out to the play yard. In my way of thinking I saw the item as a physical play item so it was relocated away from this space and into the physical play zone further away from the building. Some months later I came back to observe how the children and the staff were using their yard – and while the work had been carried out well, there was something missing. In discussion with the staff they expressed how they missed the group ride, and they stated that it wasn't used nearly so much now as it had been in its previous location. Then I realised I had seen that they used this structure as a gathering point –one complete kindergarten group of 20 children would get up on it and sing and tell stories while moving it rhythmically. This was an institution where the every child was out at least two hours everyday and they could choose to be out longer. While the children were out it was a tradition for the staff to bring out small treats and freshly baked bread for the children to snack on – and it often was served to the children while on the ride. I had seen this but I hadn't noted consciously that here was a social gathering tradition focussing on what I had seen to be a physical play item. We moved the ride back to the first placement and everyone felt much better served and satisfied. I add these comments here as a lesson in the importance of paying attention to behaviour patterns of the staff and children and their play traditions out on the yard. Play things and spaces need not be used in only one way and staff behaviour patterns and movements out in the play yard are incredibly important in influencing where the children will play. If staff do not move away from the building into the far corners of the play yard, many of the children will not as well.

Infants play yards

> **"Play is children's way of perceiving the world they have been called upon to change"** Maxim Gorki.

Play areas for infants and toddlers (children from birth to three years of age) should communicate the joy of discovery of the outdoor world and the elements of this planet. These children approach each day with great enthusiasm – "Look out world – here I come" they seem to say. It is a self centred world view, not in any negative sense, but it simply is that the child and their body are the base from which they are learning about this new world. These children use their bodies to explore; they don't stand on the

Toddlers have a fantastic enthusiasm for exploring the outdoor world

sidelines and look. If they were made to experience the world only though windows of houses and cars, they would never develop to be able to function in the real world, they would always need to be protected, guided and helped.

The long childhood of human beings is part of our evolution – and it is necessary to give us time to develop the tremendous brain potential we are born with before we enter into a routine of raising our own children and providing for (and defending) a family and a society. During this long childhood, the early years are crucial in terms of establishing the basic frames of good health, mental and social and emotional well being. During this time the young children enjoy and benefit from close contact both with caring adults and with other children – of all ages.

> Very young children are uncomfortable with wide open spaces, they prefer small scale spaces, and they want to be near an adult caregiver.

Very young children are uncomfortable with wide open spaces, they prefer small scale spaces, and they want to be near an adult caregiver. Outdoor play spaces for these children need to be designed with care so that they are comfortable for both the child and the adult who plays with the child. For this age, adults as play mates and as play enablers are very important. At this age the child finds the residential scale to be the most comfortable, with lower ceilings – even outdoors in terms of shade awnings and tree branches. An infants play yard can take on the qualities of a big home garden, with plenty of interesting spaces.

These children are not so mobile and do not require as much space as the older children but they should have at sufficient space for a quality sand and water play area in a sunny location, some grassy space in another sunny place, some plantings with trees, shrubs and flowers, a shady space for play in the summer and room for physical movement possibilities – a swing, some way to slide or roll down, something to climb up, something for rocking. Places where the adults can sit with the children on their lap and play quietly, read and tell stories are also important. Places to dance around and sing should also be provided. Adding all these spaces together along with circulation and seating for the adults results in a minimal space of around 300 sq. meters not including storage space or outdoor sleeping spaces. Even more than any other age these children thrive in a varied and well designed outdoor play space. They need to move, to explore, to discover the fascinating aspects of the weather, to discover and chase their own shadow, to feel raindrops and bugs and to enjoy the company of other children and adults.

Infants and toddlers are close to the ground, often sitting and crawling on it and details on a small scale are very important. When learning to walk, the ground is a very important surface. Marks and details in the ground are researched with eye, fingers and feet. Here ground details are incredibly important. The children see them, feel them, use them as points to walk to, move to, play with them by hopping over or onto them and so forth.

The ultimate success of an infant play yard depends on the willingness of the adults to be outside with the children and therefore the design of these areas needs to take great consideration of the comfort of the adult – usually an adult woman. It is not sufficient just to set out a regular garden bench. There should be comfortable seating in both winter sun and summer shade where adults can sit with infants and play with them. This requires big arm chair type of seating, preferable with backs. Places to plug in for music and sound can also make the outdoors more attractive to the adults. And while mobile phones now free up the adult from having to sit at a desk indoors it can also be possible to create a portable office furniture on wheels so that the adults can do their necessary administrative work out in full view of the children. I know one very successful day care director who is outside most of the time with a portable phone strapped to the waist of her blue jeans. Outside she plays with the children, holds short staff meetings, arranges for deliveries and works in the garden. Children like to see adults at work – don't hide it away.

Adults outdoors are necessary for the successful outdoor experience of very young children.

Young children appear to have short attention spans in many ways. Outdoors they like to buzz from one play piece to another – this may be just because they love the feeling of moving freely on their own. For whatever reason they spend much of their physical play time moving from one place to another, looking and manipulating for a short time and then on the move again. They want to move around and touch everything in the yard and to see what is on the other side of everything. This is very important experience for the child's developing sense of space, distance and size as well as for their recognition of objects and structures in the landscape. They need to experience the outdoor world with all their senses so they can come to know it. Play areas for infants and toddlers therefore should include a whole range of small scale and varied spaces and play furniture. In such a play space it is inappropriate to use any kind of combination play structure, rather the play items should be dispersed, here a slide, there a play tunnel and in a third place a small swinging or rocking device. On the way from one to the other, the ground should be gently undulating and should be of varied surface textures. It is the moving *from* place *to* place that is just as important as the activity in the place itself. If all activities are concentrated onto one structure than much of the play interest is lost and the children will not get the play stimulation that they need.

> In general adults are far too fixated on playground equipment as equal to the playground.

Toddlers love playing with sand and dirt –they prefer to sit in a corner or at an edge while playing with the sand – and they need some kind of flat surface or counter to play with the sand and their small toys they use to make patterns, to measure, to sift and to pour and shape these materials. Sandboxes for these children should be small spaces with lots of corners; it is better to offer two small sandboxes than one big one.

Nearby should be a convenient storage for all the loose parts, or even better there should be storage carts on wheels to be moved in and out. Sandboxes should be located so that they are in a sunny situation in winter, spring and fall and can be outfitted with sun protection where there are hot summers. There is usually some demand for covering sandboxes for hygiene reasons – to keep dogs, foxes and cats from using them as toilets. The best disinfecting method for a sand box is fresh air and sunshine, so the preferable type of cover is one which lets the air circulate and lets the sunlight in on the sand. Sand in sand boxes should be completely shifted at least once a year in infant and toddlers area, local health regulations may require this more often. In the design of the play area, location and design of the sand boxes should include consideration for ease in this type of maintenance.

Accessibility and play for children with special needs

Pre-school institutional play yard entries should be designed so that there is access out to the yard for both children and adults who may be using mobility devices, crutches or other movement aids. In infant yards they will likely be using strollers of some kind. This means that changes in elevation between the building and the entry to the play yard are either to avoided or ramped appropriately. Near by the door or doors there should be a nicely landscaped paved area where all can be together. Furnishing here can include special provision for a wheelchair pull up to the table.

Much of young children's play has to do with the joy of being out of doors and the joy of moving. Children with special needs often do not have the possibility to be outside as much as other children either because of illness or because it is too awkward for the adults to prepare them to go outside. One of the biggest barriers to access out of doors is the architectural tendency to place ground floors of building above the grade level of the outside ground – and using stairs to connect the different levels. Young children's institutions should be built at ground level or with only a slight ramping to the ground – ideally the transition from being outside to being inside should be as easy as possible.

Once outside, there should be a well surfaced pathway wide enough for mobility device users leading to at least part of the play area. Children using wheelchairs should be encouraged to be out of the chair as often as possible when outside – and they will enjoy laying out on the grass, and participating in the play with the other children, crawling, rolling, sliding and so forth.

In general designing for accessibility and for play for children with special needs starts with eliminating barriers to access to the outdoors and to interesting play spaces. While some specially adjusted furniture in the form of wheelchair accessible tables, raised sand and water play do add to the play possibilities for these children what they really need are to be able to play with the other children and play like other children to the greatest extent possible. Provision for children with special needs should not result in less challenging and interesting play for the children in general. Never should the level of physical challenge in the play provision be limited to that of the least physically competent, but a well designed landscape should allow all to practise and extend physical and social competences.

Often children with disabilities have greater sensitivity to sun and cold wind and shade provision and wind protection needs to be examined so that there are comfortable places to play for these children as well, not just on a sunny spring day , but every day of the year. In these cases the pavilions and arbours again should be designed so there is no barrier to access and should be large enough for both wheelchair uses and other children to be together.

"I can do it myself"

Children in pre-school facilities are actually at home away from home. In the outdoor play yard they should be able to do most things for themselves, although the youngest ones may need some assistance from the older children. This means that internal gates, if any, should be designed so that the children can open and close them, water taps once the water is turned on from a central control are operable by the children, portable furniture is moveable by the adults and children. Play movement activities are activated by the children, with swings that can be made to move by the youngest children so adults don't need to stand and swing them all the time, just sometimes! There will be some things that the children will try to do that are not acceptable, such as cycle through a flower bed or climb on the roof of a playhouse; in this case it is best that the adults and the children talk through the rules of acceptable behaviours so that the children develop an environmental personality that is in keeping with the concepts of the institution.

> We grow, we find meaning in life and security in ourselves by having understood and solved personal problems on our own, not by having them explained to us by others (Bettelheim, B. (1989), p 19.).

Storage sheds should be designed so the children can put the cycles away and get them out – no high door threshold or barrier. The same with the garden tools and wheelbarrows. This is the children's place and they will be most happy to be part of the everyday rhythms of working and cultivating the gardens, preparing food and other aspects of their institutional home.

The Design Process

Designing play areas is a co-operative project. This is not something an adult designer does while sitting in his or her design studio. At least, successful designs do not come about this way. Good pre-school institutional play yard design must involve the staff of the centre – the adults who actually work there on a daily basis. If this is a new institution, then the play yard design should not happen until the staff are hired and they have defined a pedagogical concept and developed a philosophy for the centre. Once the basic adult considerations are in place than the design of the outdoor play spaces can begin. This does not mean however that because the play area is one of the last construction projects that the available funding is to be whatever is left over after everything else is done. From day one a fast and sufficient sum of money must be set aside for the play area – for example around 10% of the total budget amount – and it must not be used for anything other than the play yard.

> From day one a fast and sufficient sum of money must be set aside for the play area – for example around 10% of the total budget amount – and it must not be used for anything other than the play yard.

One of the big challenges for the designer of an institutional play yard is to work as a team member with early childhood educators and pedagogues. These are the people who have a sense of proprietary ownership over issues related to children and play.

They know what children need – they think. It sometimes requires diplomatic skill on the part of the designer to bring these people to think beyond the usual or the current trends when addressing play area design. Often early childhood specialists, like all other adults, see the outdoor play space as functional spaces. Designers need to find ways to appeal to the inner soul of the adults, to get them to understand or remember the importance of beauty and aesthetics in the play yard. Too often when it comes to an issue of functional activities over beauty the adult educator will choose the functional because they think they are getting "more " for their money and they won't be challenged to justify the use of the money. This is too bad, it is the impressions of that which is beautiful or the absence of beauty that the child will carry with them throughout the rest of their lives.

The process of play area design is also a process of learning and understanding the interrelationship between people's behaviour, their professional pride and their sense of ownership over the place where they work. For a play area to be successful the adults who work there must feel that it is a good space, find it comfortable to work in and feel that the designer has reflected their wishes and criteria. For the designer it is a balance between good design and being a play advocate while leading the adults to want what the children need. In the end it should be the adults who work there who have the final decision about the play space. This is often to the detriment of the design, however design must never be seen to be an end in itself. Playground design is the creation of beautiful spaces that are enjoyed by those who play there and that meet the needs of the users.

A designer is an artist who solves a problem by creating functional art.

Making a culture of daily life

Play areas at children's institutions can be the major focus of the children's daily life in the institution – and it can be a quality life if there is quality in the outdoor spaces. Adults are an important element in the lives of the children in these places and play yards should be attractive places to be for both the children and the adults. Early childhood institutions are cultural institutions in the sense that the children and adults create a culture – a form of environmental culture which is partly unique to the place but includes also seeds of a wider culture. In the end the success of a pre-school play yard depends on how successful the design is at enticing the adults to be playful out of doors, to be out of doors for long periods of time and in all weathers and to spend time in all spaces throughout the yard –not just by the door or gate.

A play yard at a pre-school institution may include many of these kinds of things:

- a welcoming and beautiful entry.
- art work and sculptures.
- fountains, the sound of falling water.
- paved areas for social/gathering and for games. One which catches the morning sun and one with afternoon shade.
- Good circulation space and pathways.
- Social play facilities and loose parts- play school, play ship, play houses and so forth.
- Several types of sand and water play possibilities – good quality clean, play sand.

- Messy, dirty play in the mud and construction materials, digging tools, storage to put order in materials, fenced or otherwise screened.
- A "dangerous place" where the pretend crocodiles and dragons live – like under a bridge.
- A special place where the fairies or *Nisse* live.
- Comfortable seating for adults in several locations.
- Sunning places for adults and children, good comfortable sun lounging chairs.
- Story telling corners or circles/ amphitheatre. Comfortable seating. In infant areas seating that is comfortable for an adult to sit with child on their lap.
- Play hills and sledding and rolling slopes.
- Landscaping of all types – big and little trees, fruit trees, nut trees, trees for craft activities, kitchen garden, herb garden, flowering shrubs, grass and low plantings, wild nature areas, wet boggy area.
- Compost and recycling.
- Garden tool shed, wheelbarrows and gardening tools.
- Animal pens.
- Bird feeding stations and nesting places.
- Fire place with cooking surface and/or raised grill area, outdoor wood burning stove.
- Physical play structures for climbing, sliding and other challenging movements.
- Swings – both single seaters and a big group swing or rocking device. For infants little low "learn to swing" devices.
- Open grass space for ball games and group co-operative games.
- Small enclosed spaces for hiding and secret play.
- Good quality outdoor tables and seating for eating out of doors.
- Outdoor water source with water hose. In colder countries it can be a good idea to arrange that it is possible to have warm water on tap outside near a door to wash hands etc without having to go indoors to do so.
- A pavilion or arbour, wired with electricity for music, an administrative work station and working tools.
- Outdoor lighting in some areas of the playground to extend winter time play.
- An outdoor sleeping hut/cave/tent.
- Cycle path, Moon car racing track, roller skating area, street hockey.
- Stage for dancing/music and theatre performances.
- Music, music making instruments.
- Tunnel.
- Arts and crafts area with drying lines/shelves.

- Snow play.
- Rain water collectors to water plants.
- Rounded stones for sitting and exploring.
- Logs and stumps either as part of the play landscape or as enclosures.
- Good perimeter and buffer landscaping.
- Peepholes and vantage points to watch what the adults are doing outside the play yard.
- A flag pole.
- Shade canopies, stable shade umbrellas and pergolas.
- Litter bins.
- Cycles, scooters and all sorts of wheels, and storage place for them.
- Covered construction area.
- Winter wind shelter belts of planting or straw bales etc.
- Good drainage in grass play areas and under play structures, poor drainage in muddy messy play areas and other areas where rainwater can be played with and channelled.
- Clothes line – for drying wet clothes and to hang blankets and towels as room dividers for play and for shade. Can hang art work to dry, sound makers to blow in the wind and so forth.
- Fences around garden areas and to define special outdoor rooms.

What should NOT be in pre-school institutional play yards

- Large, high, complex play structures in a sea of sand, occupying most of the play space as the only place for physical play and sand play.
- Just a paved yard.
- Only "dead" nature in form of stumps and stones.
- Used, real life vehicles like old cars, trucks, tractors or war tanks or other "cast offs" from the adult world.
- Real life boats.
- Adults who don't like playing with children.
- A lot of rules on how and when to play.
- High solid fences or fences that look like fences around high security institutions and jails.
- Sand play under or near physical play structures.
- Polluted soil, sand or water.
- Things of poor quality, broken furniture or poorly maintained landscapes.

Playing is living

For children in their younger years playing is living. The outdoor spaces we design for their play should be like outdoor living rooms – places where they can relax, find comfort and challenge and enjoy the company of other people, both children and adults. Places where they can discover ideas, listen to stories, create fantasy worlds, dream and repeatedly enjoy the pleasures of physical movements, the joy of moving their bodies. The institutions where young children spend the day away from home should not be places where they simply wait until their parent returns to pick them up at the end of the working day – they should be places where the children can discover the wonderful aspects of life on earth and participate as young and learn to be responsible and competent beings in the creation of culture and the organisation their own daily life.

References:

Bettelheim, Bruno. (1989), *The Uses of Enchantment, The Meaning and Importance of Fairy Tales*, Vintage Books: New York.
Kline, Stephen. (1993), *Out of the Garden*, London: Verso.

10 Play Areas at Public Parks – unsupervised

The only urban space devoted to childhood

Public parks often lack the presence of adult play supervisors although parental supervision is necessary for young pre-school age children. Unsupervised playgrounds in public parks are, in general, the public space with the most limited play potential. This does not need to be the case but it is a reality in most of the western world. The current interpretations and implementations of the demand for accessibility and play for all children in public parks threatens to make these areas even more boring.

While this chapter focuses on the designated play area inside a public park it must be kept in mind that no one play space can fulfil all the play needs of children – children need access to a variety of different landscapes to come to know about living and the place where they live. In fact, the use of public park play areas takes up a small fraction of the total of children's play time today. When play areas are better designed and more interesting they will occupy a larger role in children's play life but they must never be seen to fill all the children's play needs, nor should they be the only places children are permitted to play in the city. They are of interest here because they are the only public space in the city where the space is solely devoted to childhood and playing and where the design should be based in the child's view of the world. The rest of the spaces the children play in are spaces designed for adult purposes, where the play is a secondary use.

> No one play space can fulfil all the play needs of children – children need access to a variety of different landscapes to come to know about life.

The environmental personality in a public park playground

Play is active interaction with the surroundings. How we play is dependent on the environment we find ourselves in. Architects and landscape

155

architects know how to design to send signals to the users of their spaces – for example to say "this is serious business", as in a bank headquarters, or "here, one is to be humble" as in the head offices of a large corporations, or "focus your attention this way". Often the message is something like "the person who lives here has power and money", or "an important man works here", and so on and so on. We don't need written signs to tell us these things, the environment does and we have learned appropriate reactions in such settings.

It is the same with public parks and playgrounds. The design will signal to us if this is a place where we are welcome and are valued visitors, where we can find comfort and refreshment. The environment will also tell us if and how we can play. Typical playgrounds with swings and slides and teeter totters signal to children and adults that this is a space where children can play. Further, we have learned from experience that this is a place where the children play with or on a play item. There is very little social interaction between the adults and the children in these places, in fact adults are assigned the role of by-standers. Adults are not so comfortable in these places and so want to move on. Visits to typical playgrounds are often very short duration and this is built into the design message.

The environmental personality and role play

One of the puzzles of play environment design relates to the provision of play possibilities for social and role play. It seems that even though the roles of modern parents have changed enormously, with mothers having full careers and fathers taking more time to care for children, the family role play of children is still very much the old stereotype of mommy nurturing a baby and preparing food while the father is absent from the home, away at work. Perhaps the explanation or part of it is to be found in Judith Rich's work, *The Nurture Assumption*, where she notes that children are driven to keep their own personal home life private and are trying to find out what is a normal, acceptable public version of family life through role play in public spaces. They do not dare to use their own experience as the pattern for what is average, they do not wish to reveal private family matters to the world.

This urge on the part of children to keep family life private along with lack of time to develop complex play routines often results in very little role play taking place in public parks. Yet role play is perhaps the most vital play expression for children in modern times. Through this type of play they can test out ideas, interpret meanings and emotions and form their own thoughts and attitudes. Role play and socialising with other children to develop norms of behaviour that promote social interaction is vital to children's success with peer groups and these are skills acquired only through playing with others. Support facilities and play items for role play in public parks should perhaps focus less on family life and home and more on public life –not playhouses, but play vehicles, play castles, fire stations, schools and other structures that are not part of private life. They should focus on the possibility to practise ideas and emotions and not focus so

Facilities to support social play in public play areas should suggest aspects of public life – such as public transport or public places.

much on representing the external world. Such a play settings may stimulate the environmental personality to engage in playful activities they could not at home, and allows them to play with unrelated children without fear of revealing home secrets.

> "If you want to do something good for a child…give him an environment where he can touch things as much as he wants" Buckminster Fuller, *Letter to Children of Earth.*

Communicating playfulness and welcome

Good quality playgrounds in public parks should, on first sight, signal that here is a place for children to play – and that adults are also very welcome to find joy and refreshment here. Play spaces in public playgrounds should celebrate the joy of living in this time and this place. They should uplift the soul and make one smile and feel happy. They can be seen to have the same effect on our spirit as spring flowers when they break out in bloom through the snow – a wonderful aesthetic experience that talks to that which is most human in us – our playfulness and our culture. Playgrounds should not visually "blend" in with the rest of the park environment, they should clearly tell their own story, but should be in harmony with the total experience of the park environment. There is a big difference between blending in something and being in harmony with something. To illustrate this let us go into the kitchen. When we plan and prepare a good meal to celebrate a special occasion we select wines that will complement and increase our appreciation of the flavours of the foods being served, we don't put it in a blender with the salad and the main course and serve up a well blended mush that is unrecognisable. That would be most unappetising. The same with spaces in a public parks. The park experience should consist of a series of well planned and varied "courses" of spaces where each space has its own unique flavour or atmosphere, and where each subspace complements the other spaces and elements in the park to fully satisfy the appetites for refreshment and relaxation of the residents.

Public parks, like their precedents, the royal pleasure gardens, are intended to be places where the residents can find refreshment and positive energy through activities and experiences in fresh air and well designed park or garden-like atmospheres. The word recreation in itself suggests the intent – re creation. Through interaction with a high quality outdoor environment the human spirit is renewed and uplifted. Those in sorrow find solace and comfort in the living nature and the closeness with people, while those who are exhausted and stressed are re-energised. Public parks are also spaces for maintenance of mental and physical health. Research today tells us how important natural daylight and sunshine are for maintaining good health, especially for avoiding depression.

For children, parks however are places where they discover and play with aspects of the physical world. Play is what healthy children do. Children's play is not a juvenile version of recreation, play is celebration and discovery. One could perhaps say more accurately that many typical adult recreation activities are aged versions of playing. For adults the sight of children at play is also important. Playing children and play places in parks, when of good quality, communicate the pleasure of living to the adults in a way that nothing else can.

Playing in public parks and established play areas in parks may not always occur in the same space. Ideally children should be able to use and play in most if not all of the park spaces while there will be play items in only a portion of these spaces. Where there are pleasant green grass open spaces of the right scale surrounded by shrubs and trees, spaces that the children can use for running, informal ball play, rolling and sunning, then there is no need for more grass space as part of the play area. In fact in a public park the boundaries of the play area are quite fluid and it should not be that children are permitted to play only within the fenced compound where there are play structures. The furniture and items provided to support the play activities of the children should be set in a well landscaped setting, where the furniture and structures are used as one of the elements to define subspaces. When children play much of the play takes place in the spaces between play items, and the play space designers should focus on the creation of playful spaces furnished by playful items and not just on the organisation of play equipment itself. All to often the spaces between equipment is treated as left over space after equipping. It is not a matter of finding room for play equipment; it is a matter of using play equipment to define and create rooms. To give a well designed character to the play area make these spaces with strong playful qualities and forms that harmonise. Spaces should have simple but clearly defined shapes with well finished edging.

There should be several spaces or subspaces within a public park play area. There would be at least one space where children can play with materials of the earth, like sand and water, and one or more spaces where children can gather and socialise while moving their bodies. The second types of spaces in particular need to be furnished and defined with care to ensure that the physical challenges are appropriate for the skill level of the user. It is not recommended that there be only one physical play structure for all, nor should the several structures be placed in the same space. It should be clear to both parents of young children and to the older children which kinds of play items are appropriate for which age and skill. Children benefit from and enjoy playing with children of other ages and the neighbourhood park is one of the few places where age segregation is not imposed on the children – so children should be permitted to play together, however inter-age play is best when it is playing with sand and water, social play, hiding and chasing games or ball games. Physical skills required to enjoy the challenge in the physical movement equipment are often so different that the best way to provide for these opportunities is with separate play movement items.

There should also be a space with well selected play furniture where adults and children can play together – like swinging and seesawing. In many instances it is the weekend parent or grandparents who goes for a tour to the park with their child and they can all enjoy playing together if the space is appropriately designed. There should be places for comfortable sitting for adults and parking provision for strollers and baby carriages. Hard surface areas for roller skating, riding a trike or cycle, bouncing balls and skipping are also features that can be part of a play area.

Out of the sandbox and into the city

Public parks often also include separate playing facilities for children of the middle years where they are very physically active. This may include spaces specially designed for skate board and roller skating, challenging cycling paths or circuits. These should be located so that older children on bikes or other wheels do not need to go through the younger children's play area to reach their spaces. It should be possible and comfortable however for the younger children to watch the older children – they love to do so. Some of the play interests of older school age children seem to the adults to

Once on wheels children can explore the whole of the local environment. Most often it is boys in smaller towns and villages who have the most freedom to explore.

be just too dangerous to be provided for in public parks. Children of this age, when asked about playing, say they want more challenge. They find the types of movement possibilities provided just too tame and boring, especially many boys.

By the age of ten many boys want to climb higher, go faster, make louder noises, construct forts, go carts and wage "war" to protect their own territory. Not war, in the negative sense of gang wars, but playful games of attack and defence that has always been a healthy part of children's play. Such activities should not be seen as anti social or inappropriate – they are also an important element in children learning how to socialise, the use of appropriate body language, to care for others and to deal with negative emotions. It is when children are not permitted to play out this aspect of humanity that problems of real aggression and violence occur. Bruno Bettelheim says it well when he describes the children's right to play with toy guns as an appropriate right for a child just as an appropriate adult right is to be able to read in peace (Bettelheim, 1980).

Spaces for these kinds of activities for older children should take on the appearance of almost being un-designed, like they just happened or that the adults have forgotten that the space was there. These children seem to prefer to play in spaces that are somewhat removed or enclosed from adult overview – playing in the shrubberies, and wild areas. They prefer informal spaces and don't particularly want to thought of as a "little" kid who still plays in the sandbox. Designs for this age of children should include some space of wilder, natural-appearing landscaping, away from where the adults frequent. If the ground is a bit hilly so much the better, and trees and bushes for hiding in are a requirement. Such a space appears to be in conflict with our western image of an urban park being very much tidied up nature. It goes also against the trend in western urban planning for more structuring of the land, more formalisation of land use. To deal with these adults concerns keep the adults out of it, surround the space with high shrubs or hedging. This is working on the basis of "what the adults don't know won't upset them". Children learn this rule early, designers of spaces for school age children's play should remember it.

If there is a documented basis to any fear that the space with be used for criminal activities in the night, one solution might be to fence it and close the gates at night fall. What is important for the children's play is that the negative uses of the spaces by others should be dealt with without removing the play possibility for the children. Our children should not be the ones who bear the burden of the older generations mistakes and crimes.

> **"Playgrounds should be renamed research laboratories"** Buckminster Fuller'

Older children still like playing in sand and water – as long as it doesn't look like a place where the babies play. Watch them at the beach – nature's supreme sand and water play area. Even adults are attracted to these places.

Sand play for older children can be a large sand pool with flat stones and wide raised surfaces like garden tables. The very best are high piles of sand – unfortunately the children's enthusiasm for playing with sand mounds means that the sand isn't in a mound very long. They also like all the engineering aspects of mechanically moving sand and water.

These are some of the types of play spaces that can appear in public parks, however I will repeat –no one play place should be seen to serve all of the children's play needs. This means that other places in the neighbourhood should also be open to children's play. But it also means that one public play ground does NOT need to fill all of the children's play needs. More than anything it needs to be a place where the children feel welcome and where childhood is inspiration to the design to the proportion and to the aesthetics. That children are found playing elsewhere in the neighbourhood is not necessarily a criticism of the quality of the playground – children as resident of the neighbourhood should be welcome throughout the whole area.

A sunny exposure

Play areas in public parks should be located in a sunny exposure and be well drained so that they can also be enjoyed in all seasons. Many designers imagine the play area as being used in perpetual summer time. In fact summer time may be the season when public parks are least used – many people go away out of the city on holidays in that season or it may be too hot in the city to go outside. Heaviest use of parks is in early spring and early autumn in many parts of the northern hemisphere, while good park design can also result in residents enjoying the parks also throughout the winter season.

Some characteristics of successful public playgrounds

- Enough space to allow a variety of subspaces, some big open spaces and many smaller, enclosed spaces.
- Includes spaces that are sunny and some shady places.
- An aesthetic that allows an immediate sensory response touch, taste, smell, sound.
- Is visually linked with childhood culture and signal free play in forms of colour and symbols.
- Visual contrast with the surrounding allows the child to read the play
- environment and understand its organisation.

- Invites exploration – by touching and manipulation and or exploration all over and throughout.
- Offers interesting movement possibilities like swinging, rocking, sliding, climbing and rolling. As children of a variety of ages and skills use public playgrounds it is necessary that these play possibilities be provided in several sizes and levels of challenge.
- Child friendly semiotics – a visual language of welcome and quality, things that are beautiful to the aesthetics of the children.
- Curving lines, flowing, waving or serpentine forms in correct proportion are both pleasant to the eye and invite play. Horizontals, verticals and straight lines predominate in the adult built world and have a more serious intellectual appeal.
- Allows children the freedom to choose a variety of ways to play and places to play.
- Enough space for a rich variety of play possibilities and still room for nature and good quality landscaping. Good play yards are first and foremost gardens for children's play. There should be living things – plants of various sizes and heights, bugs, worms and small animals like birds and moles. Living nature should be inside of the fence in a public playground, as well as in the rest of the park.
- Places that are comfortable and pleasant for the adults. Ideally there should be possibilities for adults and children to play together.
- Variations in elevation in the ground and a wide variety of different textures and materials in ground surfacing.
- Surprise and mystery. Good hiding/secret places.

The sameness of public park playgrounds

In 1971 Albert J Rutledge wrote in *Anatomy of a Park*:

> An example of standardisation run amuck is the "typical" playground. Always the same swings, the same teeter totters, the same slides. Sameness dulls visual appetites, including those of adults who are there to supervise the kids or who pass alongside everyday (Rutledge, (1971) p. 21).

This sameness was also criticised by Thomas Burton (1976) and many others over the past thirty years who have concerned themselves with the quality of public parks, nevertheless this sameness is still apparent in public playgrounds of today. One of the things I have found fascinating in the critiques of urban playgrounds is that while this critique has been

Some Essential Ingredients in a Neighbourhood Park That Will be Used /some or maybe all elements to appear in some form.

- Plaza/square
- Bar/kiosk
- Exercise area
- Dancing
- Seniors gardens
- Children's gardens
- Game tables
- Grills
- Music/power source/speakers
- Demonstration garden
- Day care mothers meeting place
- Play supervisors base
- Play with nature sand/water/soil/fire
- Fire ring
- Water feature
- Service facility/ toilets
- Park-like landscaping furnished for quiet activities such as reading /writing and thinking

- "nature"/wild lands
- Open grass/green
- Landscaping • Playhills
- Sports areas – ball, basketball,
- Amphitheatre/ neighbourhood gathering
- Picnic
- Pavilion
- Pet play/exercise (fenced)
- Play equipment
- Storage
- Teen activity space
- Play space for wheels
- Hard surface games area
- Soft surface games – rubber
- Bocce/petang/bowling
- Entry
- Art
- Lighting
- Bulletin board

publicised frequently over the past thirty or forty years, the quality of public parks and playgrounds seems to have declined into greater sameness and dullness even further during this same time period.

Those who have reacted to Rutledge and company's critique of play areas have tried to redesign the swing, the teeter totter or slide – or just change the colour. In my analysis the problem is not that there are swings, slides and teeter-totters on playgrounds – the problem is that there is nothing else. If these play items were set within a uniquely designed and well landscaped setting there would be no problem of the visual sameness in the same way that few people pick up that the same lamp post, bench and litter bin reappear again and again on urban landscapes around the world. Similarly many urban parks use a very limited palette of landscape plants and these are repeated in city after city. I have yet to hear anyone complain that only green shade trees are used throughout urban parks.

> **Let's stop this nonsense about criticising playgrounds for having swings and slides and teeter –totters.**

Let's stop this nonsense about criticising playgrounds for having swings and slides and teeter–totters, these are the movement possibilities the children like. Let us face the fact that playground designs, in general are too boring and do not include enough landscaping and variety in spaces. They are not welcoming to either adults or children. Innovative playground design does not mean throwing out the well loved play items or disguising them, it means making better quality play landscapes. In fact the absence of play items is confusing to the children – they don't know if they can play there. For the past two years now I have carried out routine observations at a so called "nature playground" in a public park where there are some very rustic assemblages for playful exploration and on the side they have set up several swing sets and some spring seesaws. When the children and the parents come to play in this space, the children run immediately to the swings, they ride on the swings, may or may not use the seesaw but only go on the other items if an adult takes them by the hand and leads them though or over the structures. When the adults tire of that the children try to play with the sand/gravel surfacing. Visits at the playground are short duration, not because there is the same old swing and seesaw but because there is little else to do and the adults are bored.

> **In general adults are far too fixated on playground equipment as being the playground.**

There is another reason for this fixation of the sameness of swings and slides, this has to do with the minimal budgets and imaginations that most adult park administrators have when they approach the subject of playground design. Making better quality playgrounds demands more space and sufficient budgets. To date it has all too often been more convenient for the adults to criticise the typical playground as being too boring - and there after do very little to improve the play landscape. Economy rules, and

This rustic structure is seen by some adults as a better play item that a teeter totter or swing. However observations of the play area suggest that it used mostly by adults and rarely by children.

results in the substitution of dead tree trunks and rocks for well designed play equipment. These dead trees and stones, when they are seen everywhere as the only elements of the typical playground are just as visually boring to the adults as the typical swings, slides and teeter-totters of the more traditional parks and unappealing to the children. Sameness is a problem and is boring only when it is of poor quality.

This critique of the sameness must also be balanced with the fact that children have limited geographic mobility. They do not know that the same swing and slide are used everywhere – what they like is the swinging and sliding possibilities in their playground. We, as adults, must be very, very careful not to infringe on the children's needs just to satisfy our adult sophisticated tastes. There is no doubt that most urban landscapes are boring and it is true that sameness does dull the appetite as Rutledge has stated. There are many ways to bring variety and interest into the urban landscape by improving the quality of both the spaces for adults as well as those for the children. The typical urban park is a boring, functional landscape where ease and economy of maintenance has resulted in the removal of much of the shrub layer of the landscape and often there are few trees of any age left as well. Parks far too often are dull, boring places of flat level grass to be used by men for playing ball games or to exercise the dog. When the quality of the total park landscape is improved and made more varied, than we will no longer find a boring sameness in the swings and slides in the children's play areas. Our eyes will be enjoying the beauty of the rest of the landscape.

Each play area should be unique

Each and every playground should be designed as if it were unique in that it has a unique geographical setting and population. The character, and perhaps history of the area should be reflected in the spaces, in the landscaping and in the furniture. Dramatic or prevailing natural features should be included. For example in northern Scandinavian and in the mountains everywhere – stone outcroppings can be a wonderful feature in a play area. Use native plants and trees rather than exotic grasses and landscape trees. This can be difficult to do in some places as landscape nurseries carry only the most sold landscape species. It is possible however, and a contact with forestry associations can lead to sources of native plants.

The urban park creates challenges for the design in terms of creating a comfortable scale and proportion for the children within the play area. These wide open spaces demand vertical elements but unless there are mature trees this is often difficult to obtain. Use of entry portals that one goes through into the play area can be one small contribution. Similarly sculptures and shade pavilions can help with the issue of scale and serve as space definers. Other space makers can be low, playful panels and fences, shrubberies and hedges, hills and mounds. Play structures should be scaled to the child – where there are role play furniture such as a play train or ship, the spaces within should be no bigger than will accommodate two or three children and with roofs not much higher than the height of children. But they should have roofs.

The issue of enclosure is a emotional one with adults who fear that children can come to harm by nasty adults who hide in the bushes and in enclosed spaces. To prevent this they remove all of the potential hiding places. While crimes against children are heinous, they are not as prevalent as the media makes them seem and there are actually few attacks on children by persons not known to the child. To keep our children safe at play does not mean denying them comfortable and quality play spaces, it means we need to make these places attractive enough that many adults are there – eliminating the possibility of the criminal taking over. We need to change the attitude of adults towards who goes to the playground – adults must go also.

When you want to change how people use a landscape you need to change their perception of that space. Play areas should be seen to be places for play and for playful people of all ages, not just for children. Today it is the opposite, an adult who goes into the playground without a child in hand is immediately suspect. That is often because they are the only adult there. This absence of adults also creates problems for those of us who want to study children's play behaviours and their use of the play landscape, our interest in the children is often misread. Children have been warned about talking to "strangers" so that it is nearly impossible for a researcher to find out from children what they think of a playground. This is not a design problem but a problem of the socially acceptable use of the urban landscape – another form of environmental personality one could say.

Fear reduces children's access to play possibilities

The fear of crime or violence to children not only influences the landscape of the play yard it also directly affects who can play there and when they are permitted to do so. The children's needs to use the outdoor public space is counteracted by the adults perception of dangers in these places. Parents find it easier to limit the child's access to outdoor public space than to do something about the perceived danger in these spaces. They have grown up themselves without little or no experience of being involved in the decisions around public space use and now feel quite helpless to deal with issues like drug dealing and crimes against children. Traffic is another threat to the movement of children and parents are often the perpetrators of this threat.

One study in Denmark showed that the majority of drivers who exceeded the speed limit in the vicinity of a elementary school were parents whose children attended the school. Being a car driver is another one of those many environmental personalities that people have; and often the speeder in traffic is irreconcilable with the responsible parent. The consequence is that the child is limited in where they can go in the neighbourhood and the lack of time on the part of parents reduces the children's visits to the public playground to one or two short visits per week.

Children like to play where things happen and often like to place themselves near or on the street if vehicle use is controlled.

Designated playground spaces in public parks are not well used in many countries. This is partly because they are boring and partly because children's use of outdoor spaces is restricted by adult fears of crime and traffic. There has been a marked decrease in the use of neighbourhood parks while at the same time an increased mobility of the family. Today when they have time to go on a outing with the children the parents will choose to go to some destination park, the zoo, an amusement park or perhaps one of the new indoor playlands. When at home the children are referred to home based activities such as television and computer games. This is not doing today's children any favours. They need to be able to move freely and unsupervised about their own neighbourhood. They need to come to know for themselves about the good places to play, the secret places, the places with special meaning for them and their friends. The insulation of the children that is occurring in large urban areas is another form of isolation – it keeps the children from knowing how a neighbourhood is built up. Children on their way to adulthood and in their role as future adults need to observe adults living a daily life and exploring all aspects of the adult world. Children who cannot experience at first hand neighbourhood life will not know what citizenship is nor have any skills in participating in local society as adults.

Play areas where all ages enjoy playing together such as at this playground give children opportunities to play outside with their neighbours and come to know their neighbourhood.

It is therefore imperative that we find ways to ensure that children can and do freely use the local outdoor spaces, including the playgrounds. One solution is to find ways to make quality public parks spaces that are well used by people of all ages and interests so that there is the security of numbers, permitting parents to allow their children to go there to play more often. Parks should not just be outdoor facilities for sports jocks. Rutledge writes " Parks... should be developed to serve as exemplars of what is possible in terms of soul-satisfying environment and catalysts for promoting higher works in other types of developments, towards the day when everything which man builds contributes to a positive physical surroundings"(Rutledge (1971) p 8.). Wise words written nearly thirty years ago yet still so rarely put in practise. Dare to imagine what our western urban centres could look like if for the past thirty years everything that was built was a positive contribution.

Traffic reduction and control in residential areas such as this permit children to play in spaces near to home.

Another strategy is to get serious about traffic controls and introducing more traffic calming measures in the residential areas. With the threat of traffic injuries reduced children can and do take up use of their immediate outdoor surroundings and are outdoors for longer periods of time. In this time the children come to know their neighbours, develop stronger social ties, and become more physically competent. This can only happen however if the fears of the parents are allayed.

Children who cannot experience at first hand neighbourhood life will not know what citizenship is nor have any skills in participating in local society as adults.

Boys and girls at play

Whether we like it or not there seems to be some influence of gender in the way in which children play. And during middle school years there also appears to be a tendency to prefer playmates of the same gender – at least in public spaces. This has really very little influence on good play area design – other than there should be sufficient spacer for a number of different groups to be able to play without interrupting the play of others while they can keep an eye on what the others are doing. This is another argument against the single large multi-play combination as the only element in a playground. There simply is not enough room for different groups to find their own space. Such structures tend to be taken over by the dominant group – and the others may as well go home again. This dominant group is often a group of older boys but not always.

If there are possibilities for playing in less organised lands within the neighbourhood it is most often the boys who will take over this land – with the occasional girl joining these groups. This leaves the rest of the girls to use the designated play area. Boys are often permitted to travel further away from home – and when they have the freedom of their cycles or skateboard they may go at long distances from the home to specific play sites. Girls however tend to be more restricted in how far and where they

Girls in cities are often more restricted in their movements about the city play in or near the home most of the time.

can go without an adult and do tend to rely on the local neighbourhood playground as the main source of their play possibilities. On the other hand boys are outside more and many girls stay very close to home for much of their free time.

These kinds of variation in usage can be confusing to the researcher who is trying to map the children's use of the environment. To do so requires a longer period of time to come to know the children and their play habits – it is not enough to set oneself in the play area and observe usage over a matter of weeks – it is necessary to identify who isn't coming to the play area and find out why they are not. Typically because public lands are for all, play design criteria will include some demand such as appropriate play opportunities for all ages. On the other hand is can be very misplaced to be politically correct and design a play area for all if only one special sector will use the area.

Generalities can be misleading and research in one community on who plays where cannot be applied to other communities. Children's use of outdoor spaces varies much with the nature of the community and with the established play patterns within the family. The only general statement that applies to almost all western cities is that children are not outside and playing as much as they should be. Other generalities we read often include that children today are less fit than previous generations of children and that today's children are more often overweight and more show symptoms of beginning heart disease. All of these problem would disappear if children played outside more.

Dogs and children at play

Children today live for the most in small, nuclear families. After the age of ten they may often be the first to come home after school – to an empty house. Or an almost empty house. Many families are now being extended to include a family dog, often for the sake of the child or children. After school it may be the child's responsibility to walk the dog – or at the least let it out to run.

Children in small nuclear families have indicated that their dog or other pet is often the family member that they tell their secrets. Pets are a major centre for the emotional life of many children from 8 to 15, and play a bigger role than previously known.(Morrow, V. March 1999). While the dog may be the child's best friend, children are not permitted to take their best friend to the playground.

Think about creating a in every neighbourhood where children could go with their pets – to walk them, to play with them, train with them and to meet with other children. "I walk my dog on a long cycle ride. In that way we're away from those that are always telling us what to do. We can decide for our selves." says one 13 year old boy. At 13, this boy has the freedom to move around the city at a great distance. But children, both boys and girls, at 10 or 11 years of age will also enjoy walking/running their dog, playing with them and maybe exercising with them on established exercise courses, if they within easy access from the home.

Fashionable trends in public park designs

Water

In their search to make playgrounds different from the usual swings and slides some larger projects have included elements such as mazes or water spray pools. In some designs these are successful additional play features that add visual pleasure, signal playfulness and, for the children, hours of fun. In the hands of others, such features have been a means of rewarding business associates with a profitable contract but very little given to the community of any lasting value.

Among the best of the best of the water play designers to my knowledge are the staff of the Parks Department in the City of New Westminster, Canada. Not only have these people created fun and attractive water play areas, they have solved many of the problems of water on an unsupervised public park and have developed techniques to reduce maintenance of the water spray features. They were doing this already in the late 1970's. This parks department has demonstrated how very important a group of well informed and dedicated staff are in the making of good quality park play areas. They have shown again that where there is a will to do a good job in terms of offering attractive play spaces it does happen.

Water play in public parks needs to meet requirements for safety and health but is by no means difficult or necessarily expensive. Simple sprays that are quickly drained away so there is no depth to the collected water add a liveliness and human quality to a park that attracts all of us. The sound of water falling can soothe the crying baby and the cranky director. Water is such a fascinating element and humans value outdoor places where there is water, to such an extent that lakes, ponds, fountains and pools signal prestige, wealth and power. Arrivals at prestige sites like Buckingham Palace, other European Palaces are tame and disappointing when the fountains are not turned on. But what an impression when they are in full display. It isn't surprising that tourists travel halfway around the world to visit the most awe-inspiring waterfalls or that native peoples have attributed such sites with special powers. Today's children living in urban centres also need contact with water in playful ways, even if it is in a shallow pan.

Water features and water sculptures commissioned by artists can be attractive elements, if they are child friendly and it is easy for people to enter into and interact with the water. The modern art movements of massive stone, metal and cement surfaces in rectilinear shapes can repel even the strongest urge to play. Most important is the transition from the ground to the water – if this is soft and easily accessible the children will

Such water play areas are well used when the water is on in warm weather. Even when there is no water the area is a fun space.

find a way to get in contact with the water. Features like the water play area at the World's Fair in Vancouver in 1986 show how a very attractive and well designed and playful sculpture can draw the whole family into playing.

Mazes

Another trend in play area design has been to commission artists to create mazes within the play area. While mazes have had a history which includes amusement for the wealthy, and later became features in public parks, offering them as play features on playgrounds for children is a new idea. On playgrounds these mazes are often formed in wood palisades or poles standing upright creating narrow passageways. To my mind they always look like very complex livestock loading pens used when animals are on their way to the slaughterhouse and therefore I am uncomfortable with this visual image on a playground. For urban children however it is unlikely they will make such associations although after several tours through them labyrinths and mazes cease to be of interest. In my opinion such play features can be appropriate as part of a larger play garden or amusement park which children visit once or twice a year but has no place on a playground that children use everyday – it looses all mystery or sense of being special.

Pavement mazes and ones in low rounded stones, when integrated into walking areas and plazas add a playful touch to what otherwise might appear to be a serious space, however such features should not take up any of the precious little space allocated to children's play. The most playful hedge to my knowledge is the one at Sofiero in Sweden where the designer has created low, rolling earth walls where long grass grows. These serve as both walls and pathways in themselves. Children love rolling around on the grassy banks. Usage and erosion however are concerns in such a design and cannot be part of a heavily used everyday playground.

Children live in the here and now

A small maze of rustic material is a popular idea amongst adults but little used by children. Mazes for children to enjoy need some sense of magic, mystery and challenge.

Designers of mazes are too often artists or architects who are fascinated with plan view complexities and patterns and have little or no understanding of growing things or how growing things change over time and with the movement of the sun. They treat the design of a labyrinth as a paper exercise that is then inflicted on a piece of land – and afterwards the children can use it. Garden designers who have little understanding of children's play have also imposed long corridors and seemingly meaningless barriers to children gaining access to the play feature set in the centre. Pre-school age children do not appreciate the intellectual challenge of a maze and unless the process of moving through the maze is a series of playful activities that is not uni-directional, a maze simply becomes a hurdle to the children's access to play spaces. In general mazes have been more of an adult imposition on children's play than an interesting play opportunity for the children. Let the children build their own mazes in the sand box or digging patch for their small animals and cars, for the most fun in mazes is in the making of them.

Adults can continue to write treatises about the mysteries of mazes and the journey of life, children however look for wonder of life and mystery in more physically active and less controlled settings. Children live in the here and now. They have no concept of life ending or even of going on for a long time, and persons over thirty are "the oldest beings on earth". Items and spaces in children's play areas should be there because they signal play or have some value to childhood, not placed there for the sake of some adult fascination with a historical relic. Let us hope that there will soon be found another trendy designer object and leave mazes and labyrinth to find their place in garden history.

> Designing play areas requires a playful approach to designing, to taking risks, to testing the boundaries of trends in design, it means to risk being seen as not serious.

Accessibility and play for children with special needs

All children play. When a child doesn't play it is a sign that there is something wrong. Play is such an important feature in children's lives that it is now being used by adults both as part of therapy to heal children and as part of education to train children. These forms of "play- training" are not however what we are addressing at a public playground – here the play must be child initiated and child directed. It must be play for childhood's sake not play as a tool of the adults. These must be play places where all children can and do come to play.

The basic consideration in terms of creating public play spaces for all children is access from the home to the park play area. This trip must not be so very difficult that it is almost never embarked upon. There must be no physical access barriers such as long staircases, narrow entry gates or very steep slopes. Children who use mobility devices or are ill often also take medication and may need to have access to clean and useable toilet facilities and drinking water. If these are not present at the playground then it is not likely they will come very often. Items like shade protection from hot summer sun and protection from strong winds must also be considered. A comfortable and attractive outdoor space is the primary drawing feature to motivate a tour to the playground even though it involves some organisation and some difficulty. The design of a play area with an attractive landscaped setting is essential to the families which include children with special needs as they often rely on other children at the playground as play mates.

It is of utmost importance that there be other children at the playground with whom they can play. A child in a wheelchair taken to a park to wheel up a ramp or sit on a wheelchair carousel and then be wheeled home has really not played. Children need other children to play with – this is the primary ingredient to playing, the swinging, going up and coming down are secondary. When the child's abilities mean that there is little possibility to experience the joy in playful movement of one's body, it shouldn't be so that play at the playground consists of artificial replacement of movement possibilities such being wheeled up onto a platform and so forth. This only serves to highlight the child's disabilities while limiting the play possibilities of those children who can enjoy challenging physical movements. Being wheeled about in a mobility device happens to children who use wheelchairs everywhere – play at the playground should be something different. The joys of playing are many and children who have disabilities can and do still find much to explore, discover and wonder about.

When I watch children at play I often see that the play has become a pile of young children laying on the ground, giggling and laughing. A child using a wheelchair can very likely also be part of such a group without any difficulty. But only if they are not isolated from the other children, sitting up on a raised platform in their wheelchair. Much of children's play takes places in the spaces defined by the play equipment – and this is where the children should be able to move freely.

Not all children who are specially challenged use mobility devices, yet most effort in public parks has been focussed on making them useable by this group. There is consensus amongst many experts that the demands for equal access to play opportunities for children using wheelchairs has and will continue to result in a reduction in challenging physical play possibilities for the children who do not use such devices, both able bodied children and children with other needs – visually impaired, learning and social difficulties and so forth. This is true only so long as playgrounds are outfitted as places for solely physical play possibilities. In such cases, and particularly in the case where the combination structure is *the* playground, then there is little physical challenge left after these structures are made wheelchair accessible. However as already stated, such an approach to designing for play doesn't really serve any children's real play needs. Combinations structures – smaller ones as part of a larger play facility have their place and are enjoyed by children, but must never be all there is for playing.

Good play designs offer a wider variety of play possibilities.

Where there are sand and water play, good fantasy and social play possibilities, open grass, sunny spaces for talking and socialising, then the possibility of a tour on a swing or a climb to the top of the roof is but one of the play possibilities that the children will engage in after ability and choice. However, to serve all children is not the same as to meet a specified level of ability. Able bodied children will seek out physical challenges and they need these at the play area – otherwise they will not be there when the children with special needs come to play. Integration of playing children is much more of an important goal than making access to all things for the least able to move bout freely. Only though contact with a whole variety of children will a child come to understand the competences of all the children and the many nuances in their play world. All children love to play, and the most important play things we can offer them are other children to play with. All children need the social and emotion interaction with others. Children of all abilities can play together if they share time and space. Play is about fun, enjoying each other company, about exploring the world around them, not about going up a ramp and turning around and coming back down again. That is just " Ho Hum".

Community participation in playground design

More than any other force it is the process of involving the local adult community in playground design that has perpetuated the sameness and lack of innovation in public playgrounds. As adult advocates for children and children's play, the adult community has failed completely. This is not really their fault. The fault lies back with the city government that has side-tracked both local democracy and quality provision for children's play needs through this process. The politicians have cynically allowed the adults in the community to make decisions about some things that they the politicians don't think is very important. They would never let the local community decide over roads, over economic support to businesses, or over the location of a shopping centre. The result has been the appearance of local involvement in government but what is really a distancing of the local community from making decisions about things that really matter. These local groups can't decide anything other than what brand of swing slide or teeter totter – and often they have to work hard to raise some or all of the funds – and they even spend time on weekends to install it. All this is done with the best intentions of doing something for the children. The planners who have designated the amount of space, its location and relationship to other elements in the community, and allocated funds for development have already made the big decisions that have pre-determined a low quality outcome for the children. There is never enough space, funding or expertise to permit the idea of a playground to be expanded to a beautifully landscaped play garden. It is an exercise in repeating the old mistakes and pulling the citizens into the problem so the results can't be criticised. "It is what the community wanted" is what is said when one questions such boring and minimal provision. It is not the communities fault, but a weakness in local government, it is formulaic urban planning magnified by low political priorities for children and play.

Sophisticates never understand children Bettelheim, B.

Manufacturers of play products as designers of playgrounds

Much the same as the process of community involvement, the custom of asking playground equipment suppliers to provide a free design service as a prerequisite to obtaining a contract to supply is one of the main reasons for the poor quality and sameness of public playgrounds today. This is like asking the producer of sofas and arm chairs to design your house for you.

No city would ever ask the supplier of asphalt to design their traffic system yet somehow responsible authorities in many cities in the western world have taken to the idea that it is okay to do so when the issue is children's play. This is another signal from adult authorities of how very little importance they place on providing well for children's play. A playground equipment manufacturer is only interested in one thing – making the most profit on the order. This is not negatively meant, it simply is a necessity of business life. The staff set to prepare the proposal have no expertise in space design and probably not even in layout, most often they are computer technicians. They can arrange space so their product fits into the flat 2 dimension space allocated – and that is all they can do. They can try to impress then with a flashy computer generated impression of what their product will look like in the space. These companies are specialists in the manufacturing of a set array of products for profit, they have engineering and technical expertise but have no knowledge of designing play spaces, no play advocacy, no ability to highlight the unique character of the site, they have no outdoor spatial design skills. There is no concern for making well balanced spaces for play. There is no design. This is a process that has resulted in sameness and boredom and an emphasis on low cost.

When one combines the demand for low cost to the buyer and the maximising of profit for the producer with a user who has no power to influence the product it always results in poorer quality. Public playgrounds stand as a clear testimonial to the failure of this trend in play provision. Manufacturers of play items have a role to play in society, as do the producers of asphalt and sofas but it is NOT as designers of public spaces.

In playground design, like with any other commodity on the market – you get what you pay for. Like with the process of community participation the problem is not the producers need for profits; the problem is the unwillingness of society – of all of us – to invest in our children and in quality public spaces. As we begin the twenty first century we seem to have no vision for a quality community life. It should be a matter of course that there is sufficient funding for a well trained and competent designer to prepare designs for children's play spaces. There is a market economy rule that says "you get what you pay for." When you pay nothing, as in the case of designs for children's outdoor play spaces, the children get nothing.

Playgrounds as charity cases

Children's public play provision has always been coloured with aspects of charity in a way that public roadways and policing has not. This century just past was predicted to be the century of the child. While life in cities today for western children is a good one it is good for them because it is good for adults, the children benefit from the spin-offs of the good life of the adults. They also suffer from the negative back side of this same good life. We cannot take credit for any special efforts to improve the quality of child life in cities or outdoor spaces for children during the twentieth century. There has been a tremendous increase in the number of adults who earn a living off of childhood however. In the twenty first century we should perhaps try to be known as the century of play. If the adults play well and demand access to good play then the children too will benefit.

Can we do better?

This chapter has been very critical of much of the status quo of public park playgrounds. It is not the first time these places have been criticised –they have been under the gun since the 1970's. Yet every decade brings new versions of cutbacks in government spending and somehow it always goes over children and play. It seems that all the arguments for children's development through play, all the statements of what children do need will never move the adults in power to provide well for children's play. What is necessary is not to *make* them provide well but to get them to WANT to do it.

Public play spaces in older cities are often very small spaces squeezed in between building and street, with little regard for the playfulness of the space in contrast with the character of the building. Play spaces are charity cases – in this taking up a small garden attached to a church.

We can if we want to!

A long time ago, when I was a little child I loved to help my parents with taking care of the farm animals. At that time we had a team of work horses to do some of the heavy work on the land. One thing I liked to do was to take this team of wonderful gentle animals out of the stalls and down to the little stream so they could get a drink of fresh water. I was far too little and too weak to make them follow me – but always the temptation and appeal of fresh water made them willingly follow down to the water. It is the same with politicians and provision for children's play. The advocates for children's play are far too few and have too little power to make the politicians and the powerful do their duty to the children – based in arguments of what children need. The dismal results of the twentieth century have demonstrate that. In the twenty first century we need to find ways where there is pleasure, prestige and appeal to be a political leader who is known to provide well for children's play. Places where children and children's play are prioritised would become the preferred places to live, the best addresses. Community leaders in such places would be highly respected as wise leaders. The communities would be exciting examples of new democratic processes and ideas.

Creating childhood habitats

It is easy to find consensus that public playgrounds are not in good shape. It is much more difficult to find examples of well designed public playgrounds. To improve play provision we are inspired by good examples, not by criticism of bad ones. We need to create and celebrate good playgrounds. There is good political value in creating high quality public parks. Communities are held together, generation after generation by sharing public spaces that all enjoy and value. There is good citizenship in places with high affection value. One need only refer to some of London's central parks, Central Park in New York and to Vancouver's Stanley Park. Not only are these places aspects of civic pride they also unite the residents in common experiences of space and affection for the space.

> "A civilised society is one which struggles to make the world better for its children"(Kline , 1993).

There should be a Nobel prize awarded each year to the city who has made the best contribution to children's play and an Academy awards programme for such play areas. But more than the publicity and the media attention, the real rewards would be the warm regard of local respect, and the joy and satisfaction that comes from having struggled to make things just a little better for the next generation and for future developments of our culture.

Again and again, as I write this chapter I have been faced with the realisation that good design will not solve all the problems of public playgrounds nor do away with all the criticism. Good design of landscaped spaces with high quality furnishings and items specially to support children's play are essential physical features of a good public park playground. To make public playgrounds successful in the hearts and minds of both the design oriented adults and the citizens of all ages and abilities means we also need to change the perception of what a public playground is. Buckminster Fuller has said that playgrounds should be renamed research laboratories. I love that idea – every time I remember his words I think of playgrounds as a different place – a research laboratory conjures up images of a space or spaces filled with interesting tools and equipment for measuring and weighing, materials to make magic potions and special machines to see into the heart of an object in a way we can't see with our bare eye. Playgrounds should include these kinds of possibilities.

I would also like to add a new way of talking about playgrounds. To paraphrase Fuller I would say that playgrounds should be renamed *open air refreshment bars*. Playgrounds should be places where all who live in the area can come to celebrate the joy of living, to find pleasure in the company of their fellow citizen while enjoying the harmony of nature and living things. A playground should be a strong life reinforcing element, where one can drink in the wonders of this planet and the mysteries of life.

References

Bettelheim, Bruno.(1980), *Surviving*, Vintage Books: New York.
Burton, Thomas L. (1976), *Making Man's Environment :Leisure*, Van Nostrand Reinhold Ltd.: Toronto.
Kline, Stephen. (1993), *Out of the Garden: Toys and Culture's Culture in the Age of TV Marketing*, Verso: London.
Morrow, Virginia. (1999), *Anthrozoos*, March 1999.
Rich Harris, Judith. (1998), *The Nurture Assumption*, The Free Press: New York.
Rutledge, Albert J. (1971), *Anatomy of a Park*, McGraw-Hill Book Co.: New York.

11 Designing for Play at School

School is children's work

Children's working contribution to society is their participation in schooling. In this way they are preparing to take on their responsibilities as adults. Most of school life is controlled by adults and promotes an adult view of the world. There have been great advancements in education systems which are becoming more children friendly and children have more involvement in daily organisation, nevertheless the orientation is the adult world. In school, children are adults-in-training.

Training to become something, training to develop a skill, and more importantly training for future roles in life not only requires practising at the subject under study but also requires time out so the person can work out what they have just learned. The brain and the body need time to find out how to accommodate this new information or skill. Learning also requires a mind and body that is free and open to learn. For these reasons there is a need to pay attention to the amount and quality of time outside of the classroom as well as what goes on in the classroom during class time.

> If we want children to grow up with a zest for living we need to give them living spaces that express that life is a grand experience.

For too long now the public educational systems have been seen to be training workers rather than citizens. Routines, sitting still, paying attention, regular attendance, homework and other procedural aspects of training are highly valued. Academic progress is measured and a child's future professional possibilities in adult life are often determined by the time they are age 12 or 14, based on the school systems evaluation of their abilities. But has the school system and the adult society provided adequate conditions for the children to fully explore, expand, practise and demonstrate their abilities? Despite all the grand efforts of many good teachers, the environment of the school and its potential influence has been neglected and as a result children have not been provided with the best conditions for starting life as adults. The social environment with the focus

185

on making workers who fit into a routine work day and will accept management does not lead to generations of young adults who are filled with enthusiasm for working life or for taking up the challenge to further develop civilisation. Rather, they concern themselves with consumption and outward signs of prestige and position – roles they have learned well from previous generations.

"**If children only learned what the adults can teach them, the human race would have died out long ago – perhaps after the first generation**" Source unknown.

Schools are places where children go to work to learn to become adults. School environments should represent the best and most attractive aspects of the adult world. Here is where the adult in training will develop attitudes toward adult life and society that they will carry through for the rests of their life. If we want joyful, enthusiastic, engaged adults who feel empowered to take on life's challenges, who have the strength to endure life's sorrows and go through life with a strong passion for living and life on earth we should make schools places where life is celebrated and enjoyed.

School yards should be a microcosm of culture and nature where the children can explore the world around them, come to know other children, come to know about their neighbourhood. Out on the yard there can also be school festivals and celebrations – as many positive and happy experiences as possible. If we want children to grow up with a jest for living we need to give them living spaces that express that life is a grand experience.

Design and schooling

Design is about expressing ideas and feelings. Design of functional objects and spaces involves not only making spaces or things that do the work well but which also express some idea or feeling, which communicate some fantasy or fleeting expression to the user. Design of children's outdoor play spaces involves making spaces that can be useful for play and which at the same time have elements of design and aesthetics that express the joy of living, the playfulness of the human spirit. The design can suggest dreams and fantasies and the possibilities of magic. Play area design should appeal to the inner child in everyone, talk directly to our dreams and imagination. Well designed play spaces make all who enter them smile deep inside. Good quality play areas not only touch the children, they affect and improve the quality of life for everyone in the society who lives near them.

While the physical environment is not all-determining and the social and psychological environment for the child is much more important, a good physical environment can add immensely to the child's feelings of self worth and confidence. In school surroundings the children can come in contact with a more public or societal wide view of design and aesthetics. School yards, like kindergarten yards and public parks, have not been a serious subject of the design profession, but work has been left to whoever wants to take it on. For that reason there is a very weak base of design experience and knowledge to guide a designer in their work. School yards have the additional challenge of being places under the supervision of teachers – people who "own" the knowledge of childhood – and it is often difficult for a designer to move or widen the teachers view of what should happen on the school yard. The overseeing committee will select to work with a designer who sees the world the way they do. In fact most work on school yards today is not "design" but arrangement and fitting in of functional facilities. Fortunately there are also exceptions.

There are some fine examples of good school yards that work for both the teachers and children and these can be the starting point for future school yard re-developments that are of good quality. In the physical design field a good example in real life proves to be far, far more influential than thousands of words. Designers can look to other good works to start the teachers and parents committees discussion about good outdoor spaces. Designers of school play yards must dare to be advocates for children's life and children's play to balance the teachers and parents advocacy for the adult in training side of child life. It is surprising how often this approach will also quickly meet with sympathy and acceptance from some if not many of the teachers as well. To design well for children's outdoor life at schools means developing a visual quality that captures the joys of living and the excitement of learning. It means emphasising elements of social life, of friendships, of community groups and community life. Designing for school yards requires that designers invent new ways of looking at school life and push their design skills to communicate with children, to signal to the user/the children that they are important and what they are doing on the schoolyard is highly valued.

> **Playing at Designing #3**
>
> **The advantage of playing is that you can test out actions and emotions that would be too dangerous to act out in real life. For a designer playing means he or she can take risks that might other wise affect their professional reputation. When we play we can take enough risk that we can actually invent something new. When we risk enough we learn and make this new knowledge our own.**

Children as future adults also need time to be children as young people. They need time to play to be themselves, to "digest" the formal education aspects and get ready for more. Play time out of doors is where children can do this. Playing at school should be seen to be not lost or wasted teaching time but important support time to the actual formal education periods. The quality of what happens out on the school yard is also an important influence on what the children learn and if they are ready and able to learn.

This school yard emphasises community and opens to the neighbourhood. It is a meeting place for all residents. Tree branches are trained to create green walls but at ground level the yard opens onto the street. School in Amsterdam.

Architects and other designers who specialise in education facilities focus on buildings – because that is what architects are trained to make. Yet it is perfectly possible to make good learning environments without walls – the "Landscapes for Learning" movement in the UK has shown this. The formal education system is moving outside as well as using the indoor spaces and there are new demands placed on the school yard. Hopefully this will mean a renewed emphasis on the quantity and quality of outdoor spaces for children on lands administered by the education authorities.

School yards, like other play areas, suffer from being "designed" without the benefit of design. As discussed in previous chapters it happens far too often that the act of arranging functional equipment and sports facilities is labelled *playground design*. In Chapter 8 we stated "Designers are adult professionals who concerns themselves with the integration of art and design in practical or functional settings and objects." Design then is the outcome of the designers activities and a designed space is one where art and design are integrated into practical spaces. A balance of aesthetics and functionality is the main characteristic of good design.

A balance of aesthetics and functionality is the main characteristic of good design.

It is an established western, protestant attitude that effectiveness and efficiency should dominate in the public service sector and that elements like art and design are reserved for special places to express civic pride or to show that the governing elite have good taste. With the changing societal attitude toward children, the design of spaces that society allocates to children need to be rethought and revised. Children's outdoor spaces can and do show the real inner values of a society. If the city governments really want to show that they are enlightened and have good taste – then the school yard and the playground are the places to begin to promote good design and quality landscaping.

Design in school yards can and should recognise that when children have reached the age of formal education they are also thinkers and capable of increasing abstract thought. They perceive conceptual ideas and move away from their reliance on information about the world coming in through the physical senses. Now they come to know about the adult knowledge of the world and are fascinated with ideas, thoughts, symbols, theories and so forth. Rules and organisation become interesting. Social relationships and social structures form a dominant part of their emotional and social worlds. Good design for these children in school yards can communicate ideas about the world, about friendships and family, about concepts and abstract ideas, using a language that is accessible to these children. The insights need not be so very obvious, it should be that there are new ways to understand and see the design elements at the age of ten understanding that the child did not have at seven. One of the many advantages to good art is that it allows people over time to find new meaning and inspiration from the art.

School yards and playground spaces in school yards

The school yard is not necessarily the same place as the playground, and many school yards may not include a playground – or do they? Children play in the yard –so isn't it a playground? A playground is hard to define and in the chapter on playgrounds in parks I raised the question about calling that place where there was playground equipment a "playground". On a school yard, the playground would be the place where children are free to engage in playful activities of their choice without adult organisation and which are not sports or rule games. The playground on the school yard is that place or those places where the children's world prevails, which is designed to support the way the children see the world, with designs that reflect the childhood culture, it is primarily a place where children can play as children. It is likely in well designed school yards that much of the yard will serve the children as the playground during free play time. If, however the whole of the useable outdoor space is set aside for sports – then there is no playground, just sports grounds. And if the drive to use the outdoors as an extension of the formal education system has so taken over that all the outdoor space is now developed to be part of the curriculum and the children have no space to play freely, there is no playground, just outdoor classrooms.

Are playgrounds all those places where play happens?

In daily life, children have such an inner urge to play that they will play wherever they are and there is some play happening on every school yard. So, in a way it is possible to argue that school yards are playgrounds, which is in fact how most city planners would label these spaces. Schoolyards then could be said to be places where play happens. Play happens on streets and shopping malls as well – would we call them playgrounds? Are playgrounds all those places where play happens – or are they places where the primary intent of the space is children's free play?

There is a great deal of difficulty defining what is a playground, when there is no playground equipment to signal the adult intended use. The kinds of play that is supported by most playground equipment are seen to be physical movements like swinging, sliding, climbing, rocking, twirling, rolling and other interesting movement possibilities. The social needs of the children are met when they can do these things in the company of friends and playmates. This is a limited listing of what play is about, not so much because that is all that the children do with traditional playground equipment but because that is all that the adult can imagine the children will do. It is no solution to criticise and then eliminate the equipment and offer nothing in their place. It is necessary for adults to design play spaces for children which include some physical signals as to the intended uses of the space. There must be some signals that stimulate the children's playful fantasies and that tell them they are welcome to play here. Traditional playground equipment may be boring for adults to look at but they serve an important signal function telling the story of a place to be a child. When the traditional signal givers are not present or even if they are – there should be other carefully selected and well designed signals that the children will understand to mean that they are welcome to play on their own terms.

"**The play of the young child flourishes best when the adult world is shut out**" (Bengtsson, A. 1970).

Open, empty spaces in a school yard too often are taken over by running and ball games, leaving no space for children who wish to play in other ways.

School yards and barren grounds

School yards around the world have a reputation for being dismal, barren lands. Schoolyards share the same design approach as do prison yards – grim and punishing. Both places tell the story that the people who use these spaces are not important.

This is a generalisation – and fortunately there are some good exceptions. School yards originated as exercise yards early on in the development of education institutions. They took their form as functional spaces, much like small military exercise yards, and throughout the history of education have retained this aspect. Even as we see a revolution in the position of children and education methods there is a great time lag in the re-evaluation of the school yard. But now the time is in.

School yards are changing – and there are many new ideas about what should happen on a school yard. There are many new organisations and agencies proposing new roles – as neighbourhood parks, as nature study centres, as outdoor classrooms, urban campuses and so forth. All adult ideas these – and in all this adult enthusiasm about renewal of school yards let us take a stand that play must not be lost. School yards, more than any other of the open spaces where children play, are dominated by the values of the adult world – because school is where the adult world forms children into adults. Designers of school spaces are given a set of criteria from the adult world to meet and it is hard for the children's needs to be heard in this forum. However in the same way as educators have discovered that a playful approach to learning is very effective so to has it been shown that children who play well and for long periods are better at learning in the formal school setting. Free play and formal learning are two sides of the same coin and a well designed school yard with varied and challenging free play opportunities is just as important an educational element as are good teachers and well equipped classrooms. The children's need for free play must stand as one of the primary purposes for the outdoor spaces – even in schools where there are middle school and older children. We must trust children and not over-organise their free play spaces – otherwise they will never find out how to use their free time without a calendar or time manager.

Outdoor spaces and climate

Designers of buildings take care to create a pleasant indoor climate for the users, outdoors this rarely happens. Playing outside on the school yard happens everyday of the school year and therefore it is important that the outdoor climate be modified so that it is as pleasant as possible even in weather extremes. Landscape design techniques in shade provision, sun exposure and wind protection need to be employed to create spaces that can be used in most kinds of weather. The very location and shape of the building is a major influence in the creation of micro-climates on the yard – yet all too often this is ignored, with the architect selecting placement and shape of the building to impress and ensure a good profile for his building rather than for good outdoor liveable spaces.

School yards tend to be SLOAB – spaces left over after building!

The ground as a playground

Schoolyards experience a great deal of wear over the course of a year. They have periods of intensive use and then periods when no one is using them. The times of intensive use means that the surfacing of much of the ground needs to be able to stand up to heavy use in all weathers. For this reason asphalt has become the number one surfacing in school yards, followed by some form of gravel or shingle. Reactions to boring school grounds have focussed on digging up the asphalt – such as the "greening of the school yard movement" in the 1970s and the Landscapes for Learning movement of the 1990s. While a whole yard of asphalt is not appropriate because there is not enough variation in surfacing, asphalt is a useful and playful surface and can be a part of many school yards.

The grounds of a schoolyard are often left without plantings because in the experience of staff nothing is left alone to grow, plants are tramped on and killed and so forth. Also all too often it is the physical education teacher who takes on the responsibility for the outdoors – and for them more functional space for movement activities is first priority. It is unknown how many lovely old trees have had to be cut down to make way for another sports area at the demand of some physical education teacher whose narrow view of the world was left unbalanced by the absence of a lobby group on behalf of well designed quality outdoor environments for children. We should not blame the physical education teacher too much for this situation – we should blame the absence of interest on the part of the rest of society.

The grounds of the school yard – the outdoor floor – has been neglected even while it is heavily used. The lack of design imagination and the adults unquestioning repetition of usual forms of outdoor spaces for children has meant that school grounds are almost always bulldozed flat – even when the original landscape may have had many fine contours. Only when costs are too prohibitive has the bulldozing been limited to part of the yard. There is no reason why the grounds need to be flat- in fact they can be much more attractive and playful if some areas are not flat. The ground can roll up and down, fall away in steps and rise up in walls. Playful design with the floor element can create a whole new way to use the space and give new meaning to the words "play ground". Asphalt and cement are very pliable surfaces and can be used in making playful ground but the subsurface must be well prepared. Other materials for grounds for play can include a variety of synthetic materials chosen for specific qualities such as softness, impact absorbing and sound reduction. Use of colour and light reflection also can affect the microclimate.

Patterns on the ground can be created through use of paving tiles – visual character should be best when seen from standing height of a child.

Even where the ground is flat and heavily used it is not necessary that it all be asphalt. There are new surfacing materials that create better microclimates than asphalt-materials like the sand filled carpeting invented by Notts Sport which not only is visually more attractive than asphalt, it is also cooler in summer and reduces transmission of sound.

On a school ground in Copenhagen I watched children playing card games laying on the newly established rubber surfacing. Before the whole yard had been hard paving. The new surfacing was put in to serve as an impact absorbing surface for a new climbing net. While some children were enjoying playing on the net, others were exploring what they could do with this new surface. In one corner a small group of young girls were putting their dolls to bed and in a larger space a group of boys were playing cards and the cards were laid out over the floor. By changing the feel of the ground – the ground became a more comfortable place to play and there was a huge increase in the amount of playing while sitting or using the ground.

A school yard where the ground has been designed for playful activity. The surfacing Notts sport ChildsPlay™, is hard wearing but pleasant to touch – colour changes give life and playfulness. Photo courtesy of Notts Sport.

Playing in the corners

Large open spaces are the most characteristic aspect of school yards – based in the historic concept of these spaces as exercise yards – with an aspect of adults acting as "police" to ensure all behave appropriately. While there is a new attitude towards children and education inside the school, the old patterns of blank, empty outdoor spaces overseen by adult "guards" remains all too prevalent. Research studies have shown that much of the play of young children takes place at the edges of these open space and in the corners. When the outdoor space is reorganised to include series of smaller spaces for quieter play and chatting in warm sunny settings, spaces for active play with friends on fun movement structures, varied elevations in open ground, and well sited spaces for skipping and ball bouncing games, then the school yard appears to take on the character of a well used plaza or town centre with groups of people in all sections engaged in various playful activities. A small school yard with many well landscaped and furnished corners will actually be more attractive and better serve a larger number of children and teachers than will a very large open empty space.

The adult concern for surveillance often has served as a barrier to development of well landscaped yards. As in earlier discussions we must balance the adult perception that the world is a place filled with criminals and potential danger with the children's need to experience the world as a place full of wonders and joy. There are other methods to deal with danger and criminals – and it may mean that the school yard needs to be secured with entry only to legitimate users – however as in many other public situations – the presence of many people is the best deterrent to many crimes. The issue of antisocial behaviour within the child population is not solved by eliminating all elements of quality from the play yard, but is a social issue to be solved by the parents, teachers and children. A poor quality outdoor environment serves to reinforce the message that children are not to be trusted. If we do not trust them – how can we expect them to become adults who can function in today's society. Children are actually just as trustworthy as adults and feel strongly their responsibilities to others. Being children however they should be given time to practise and gradually take on more responsibility.

Children and adults outside together

School yards and school playgrounds have the advantage over public park playgrounds in that there are adults who can widen and enrich the play possibilities. With adults present it is possible to provide loose parts for play, including but not limited to balls for various kinds of ball games. The presence of adults permits other manipulative elements to made available, such as construction materials and tools, running water, sand moving tools, troughs and so forth. Caring and dedicated adults also can plan for special events and activities on the yard so that, both with the children and for the children. Children also have a great curiosity about what it is like to be adults – and school teachers who go out on the yard during outdoor play time and join in the play with the children can be a important role model in the life of the children.

There is also the advantage that schools still have maintenance staff and it should be a highly emphasised and valued part of their work to keep the out of doors in good clean condition. Design and materials chosen for the outside should be based in playfulness and quality, not in low maintenance. Necessary maintenance services must be provided and carried out just as in city hall and the art gallery. The attitude of staff toward the play area and children's play is as vital to the success as is good design. Poor maintenance or an anti-child attitude from the maintenance staff can quickly erase all efforts of good design to make the children feel welcome.

The outdoors should also be a pleasant place for the adults who work at the school, with quiet corners for sitting and enjoying their coffee break, places for refreshment and inspiration. Teacher and other staff under the stress of working with large classes and demanding course schedules can benefit greatly from a short break out in the fresh air in pleasant landscaped surrounding under open skies, a quick run around the yard or even five minutes on a swing. Schoolyard design should also include some refreshment for the adults who work there.

Community and children's involvement in school yard design

Should the community be involved in the design or improvement of the school yard? In many countries it is an accepted practise to leave such efforts to the local parent teachers committee. This approach, while adding facilities that seemingly would otherwise not be there on the school yard, is one of the prime reasons why school yards are so poorly designed. As with public park playgrounds, the message is that decisions about the condition and quality of schoolyards is so unimportant and uninteresting to men and women of power and authority that they willingly delegate such things to local residents to let the residents believe they are participating in a democratic process. Such a poor democracy, and such a poor attitude toward outdoor spaces for children. Community participation should not happen because these spaces are unimportant, but community involvement can happen when these spaces are highly valued in society.

> "When one has been in school for 6 years – one can do many things" 12 year old child.

In the absence of a highly involved community it is much better that the school yard be designed by a qualified designer who works with the teachers and children in the school – after all it is their living space. While involving children in the process is important it must be done in such a manner that it serves more to give children a feeling of being able to change something, to have some influence. If children are simply asked what they want and then the adults decide what can be done- the children end up disillusioned about their ability to influence the form of their public spaces. While to date the process of involvement has not been much in focus in my opinion this is the most important aspect of the design decision making process in a setting where children are in practise for adulthood. It is vital that children, through real involvement in decision making at school, develop an understanding of how they can be part of influencing and changing their environment for the better of all. It is critical for future cultures that they don't learn to be disengaged and uninvolved- which happens when they are superficially involved in the process – they understand quickly if it is a real process or if it is one where they are used as window dressing.

> The process of involving the children is a time consuming one – it doesn't work if they are set to list what they want or to draw pictures of the playground they would like.

The process of involving the children is a time consuming one – it doesn't work if they are set to list what they want or to draw pictures of the play equipment they would like. There needs to be time to study and talk though what should happen outside including looking at other types of spaces and other school yards. The process should include time and opportunities to identify what the children like to do outside now and where they do it, and what they do not like. The children need to be encouraged to think broadly – beyond just asking for more of the same – daring to dream of asking for sunny environments, wind protection, shade pavilions, fountains, trees and gardens rather than just the usual higher and longer slide. Children's involvement must move them from being a consumer of play things to a participant in creating good quality public spaces. John Berger writes, "publicity turns consumption into a substitute for democracy. The choice of what one consumes takes the places of significant political choice" (Berger, 1977, p 150). It should not be that children learn this as their first lesson in local democracy.

This courtyard at a high school in Germany, with volleyball, seating and places to do homework as well as chat with friends and open space for movement activities clearly signals that the students who use this space are respected by the society.

School yards should complement the school curriculum

School yard play spaces have the potential to be spaces filled with the excitement of discovery and the wonderful joy of living on planet earth. They should complement the work of the educational system in the most positive way by acting as an intermediary between the child's world and the adult world – a place where children are respected as children and as persons in training to be responsible adults. Play spaces may include manufactured play structures and independent play things, then again they may not. However the space is furnished, it must be intended primarily for the free play of the children and must communicate to the children that they are important citizens.

References

Bengtsson, Arvid. (1970), *Environmental Planning for Children's Play*, Praeger Publishers: New York.

Berger, John. (1977), *Ways of Seeing*, Penguin Books Ltd: Harmondsworth. p.150. reproduced by permission of Penguin Books Ltd.

12 Green Children and other Trends in Playgrounds

Trends in playground design at the end of the twentieth century

At the end of the twentieth century public play spaces for children have an appearance that has changed little from the beginning of the twentieth century. It is also the case that facilities for specific sports have also retained their character – a tennis court, a golf course, a football field from one hundred years ago is very like those of today. On the other hand there have been changes in recreation provision – such as the new type of swimming centres and water parks, replacing the baths and spas of previous centuries.

The amusement park

There has been a tremendous increase in private amusement parks, integrating the latest in technology with entertainment. This trend has been spearheaded by financial interests. Shopping centres – unheard of in the beginning of last century- are changing as well into entertainment centres, based in the argument that consumers want more for their money than just a product; they demand that the act of consuming or buying be a unique experience in itself. In response, shopping centres and the shops are taking on aspects of amusement parks. Most shopping centres and streets now include the mandatory coin operated ride for the children. Much of this amusement takes places under cover with little or no opportunity for the child to play freely out of doors. There is a tendency in all this hoopla over amusement to mistakenly confuse amusement parks activities with the kind of play that should take place daily in the life of a young child. Amusement is good medicine for the spirit and soul, as is humour and play – however it is not the same as children's play.

Playful cities

Other trends we see is the focus on city centres as people places. This trend is led by city planners, architects as well as commercial interests. Here the emphasis is on culture and social and cultural activities, often with a large element of consumerism. The spaces are the outdoor public spaces in older city centres, those places that are the store-houses of our cultural heritage. Visual character and materials of the outdoor spaces is of a high quality and demonstrates sophisticated tastes. Here all is culture, children's play is not sophisticated enough to be suggested; however children will often find the fountains and open spaces pleasant places to play with friends and family. They could be much more people-friendly spaces if more playful elements were included in the design. This trend is very much oriented toward visual values of the sophisticates, however if the society really wants to make cities attractive places to socialise with fellow citizens the planners will do well to focus more on creating better climates – both in terms of microclimates and social climates by improving spaces to make them attractive places to be in, not just to look at. One of the strangest outcomes of modern town planning is seen in many public gathering spaces today. After decades of architects and planners ignoring the issue of microclimate and neglecting to ensure that there are sunny warm places at street level for people to sit out and enjoy each others company, we see the proliferation of outdoor gas heaters to warm up the outdoor spaces so people can sit out in comfort.

Nature playgrounds

The third trend in western cultures is the "Nature" playground. This is a new idea specifically addressing how some adults think young children should play. The nature playground idea is based in the environmental movement, the green cities organisations and in a pedagogical concept that nature is the best for children. This movement is spearheaded by teachers, gardeners and landscape architects, beginning in the late 1980s. It has some carryovers from the 1970s recycled playground movement and the handcrafted playgrounds of local carpenters and gardeners in Germany. The nature playground takes many forms and may be difficult to recognise as a playground because its main premise is that all traditional forms of playground equipment made by established manufacturers are banned. Application of colour is limited to a very small palette of dull shades, intended to resemble the paint used before the invention of synthetic pigments. The emphasis visually is on rusticity, crudely finished wood elements, revival of medieval peasant craft traditions, stones, sand, earth and a very limited selection of plant materials. In some cases the children are bussed out to wood-lot plantations for the day – this is known as a forest kindergarten. In other instances small working farms are renovated to include a child care aspect, with the interaction with the farm land and animals forming a large part of the children's daily experience.

The nature playground, in a whole variety of physical forms, as a trend so far, has been most popular in northern European countries. In a way this is understandable. The modern northern European cultures have a very caring and considerate attitude toward children as future adults and during the twentieth century have been the leading countries in the world showing the way to improved living conditions for children. Within these cultures there is a search for better ways to deal with childhood and to provide children with the conditions for a good child life. These societies, such as in Sweden, Norway, Denmark, Germany and Holland, have striven to study and improve the professionalism of adults involved in children's lives and have established academic centres and government departments to address children's issues. In these countries you can find the best of modern western culture funnelled into developing new thinking about childhood and children's position in society. Nevertheless when searching for new ways to form the children's outdoor play spaces, the new age playground movements in these cultures more than any others have chosen to focus on nature as the prominent element to the exclusion of modern day culture.

> The lack of funding for play made it tempting for those working on new playgrounds try to obtain some of the funding set aside for nature experiences.

This happened partly because simultaneous with the urge to develop new play spaces for children, governing bodies became aware that children growing up in cities had too little contact with nature. To improve this situation government organisations made available special funding for the development of spaces where children would have access to nature. The lack of funding for play made it tempting for those working on new playgrounds try to obtain some of the funding set aside for nature experiences. Unfortunately the results have not been particularly good at giving children quality experiences with nature nor developing quality play environments for children. Part of the problem also lies with the fact that the generation of adults who are planning these play areas for children have too little understanding of nature in the city, play and the outdoors themselves to be able to create something dynamic out of this combination. This is one of these culturally informed responses that demonstrates the complexities of human responses to environmental issues and further shows that our culturally formed responses draw on many deeply entrenched roots and beliefs.

There is a idea that Nature playgrounds develop healthier children who are better at educational tasks when entering the school system. This belief is supported by several studies often quoted by pedagogues and teachers at colleges for early childhood specialists. One of the most frequently quoted studies is the one in Sweden undertaken by a team of researchers, headed by Patrick Grahn, and published in *Ute paa Dagis*. While this report is often quoted as having proven that nature playgrounds are better for children than conventional playgrounds, a careful reading of the research

A nature playground like this cannot give children quality experiences in nature, nor does it offer quality play possibilities.

shows that such a conclusion is not supported. The two play areas had so many other variables present that it is not possible to conclude that it was the presence of "nature" that influenced the better test results of the children in the centre that is classed as a nature kindergarten. Among the significant variables was the amount of time the children could play outside, the amount of space the children had to play in, the time of day the children were outdoors and the position of the sun at that time, and the frequency with which the adults interrupted the children's play. A well designed, spacious urban playground with manufactured play items and well trained play leaders can also be a healthy and happy place to play. There is not nearly enough research done on children's reactions to various play environments and it is a dis-service when the work that is done is affected by adult bias and not carried out following good researching principles.

A similar study has been carried out in Norway by Ingunn Fjørtoft at Telemark College in Norway. The study's results were presented at the ICC World Play Conference in Oslo in Sept 1999. The conclusions were the same as the Swedish study – that playing in nature was better for children's motoric development. While the study report was well prepared and well presented, the results were pre-determined by the selection of sites for the study and the kinds of adult manipulation of the "nature" site during the study. It was the intention, perhaps unconscious, to prove that the nature site was better. The variables outside of the presence of nature were not controlled for, with the exception of living conditions and ages of the children. That the one group of children played 1 – 2 hours everyday while the other group only visited the play area occasional in itself can point to the outcome.

The play garden movement

The fourth trend is relatively new and young and could be seen to be a refinement and improvement over the nature playground. To date it has had little media attention and until now it hasn't been given a name as a movement. It is led by pedagogues supported by a small group of play environment designers. I will call this movement the *Play Gardens* movement. In the Play Gardens movement the emphasis is on both the playful nature of children and their drive to explore the elements of this planet. This is complemented with spaces for children to enjoy aspects of gardening, appreciate the beauties of nature, including flowers, plants, water and animals. Culture is brought in with outdoor art, music, children's painting and drawing, group games, well designed play items and facilities for garden parties such as grills, patios, group seating and garden houses/pavilions. Play gardens require professional adults working with the children and as designers of the garden and demand sufficient space for the nature to survive the children's play activities. They appear most often as the outdoor spaces in a pre-school children's institution, although some school yards also come close to this concept. There are also a few public parks where the play area takes on a similar character.

Green children

Human beings of all ages have an affinity for elements of nature and young children feel the attraction to nature very strongly, but not more so than the attractions to be with people or to elements of our culture. Nature is part of us; we evolved from and in nature, and we sometimes seek out nature when we look for renewal and inspiration for life. Nature, in western thinking, is often associated with purity and innocence. In today's culturally informed understanding of nature it is often seen to be the polar opposite to culture. Nature and culture are seen to stand at two opposite ends of a spectrum and somewhere in between stands mankind. Where we stand along this line depends on our attitude towards the natural environment as a feature of our civilisation.

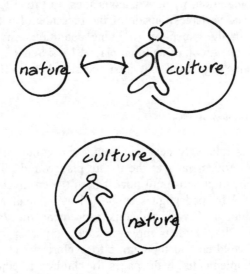

One can see nature and culture as opposing elements or consider the concept of nature to be a cultural constructed idea.

Those who see mankind as the ultimate master over the earth will see that man and nature are opposing elements while those who see man as an integral part of an large global ecosystems will place man and nature closer together. Children are often seen to be closer to nature than adults based in a cultural belief that children are born innocent and pure. Children are seen to be modern day primitives – inherently in harmony with nature but uncultured. The implied message in some of the nature playground movement debate is that children are inherently "greener" and if the adults can only keep them away from the evils of consumer culture in public spaces they will grow to be better/purer adults.

> Young children feel the attraction to nature very strongly, but not more so than the attractions to be with people or to elements of our culture.

Northern European cultures are based in myths and legends based in Nature, nature worship and forests as places where the gods live. Along with the magnificent civilisation developed in these countries based in Humanism, the Renaissance and western religious values, the old pre-Christian beliefs still are embedded within the culture. Remnants of this come out in the attitudes and ideas towards children and childhood and in particular in the play of children and in the forms of play provision for the children. It is therefore popular to believe that "nature is the best we can give our children", an approach that parents in many other cultures would find shocking and unacceptable.

What is nature?

Nature is the eternal politician – she is anything and everything the person wants her to be. Therefore nature has many different disguises but we must accept the fact that nature is a cultural invention and that our culture forms our attitudes toward nature. Our early impressions and knowledge of nature are part of those memories from childhood that inform many of our opinions and attitudes throughout adult life. For those older persons who grew up with summers out on the farm with grandparents or relatives, there is a warm, nostalgic attitude toward childhood farming and animals.

In many lands the countryside is equated with farming and agricultural organisation of land uses, where even forest are worked as wood-lots. This type of countryside, while it has been dominated by the work of mankind for centuries, with many species of plants and animals becoming extinct long ago, exemplifies to urban dweller the best of nature. This is a very prevalent attitude in those generations who when young moved to the city in the mid twentieth century to be educated and to take up professional careers.

In other countries and cultures the division between town and country and between nature and culture have slightly different connotations. For example compare the experience of a middle-aged western Canadian and a middle-aged Dane. The Canadian, growing up in the wilderness in Western Canada which was settled during the first half of the twentieth century had a childhood experience of nature of a kind that has been unknown in western Europe for centuries. As a child, the Canadian still had opportunities to meet native peoples who walked or rode over traditional native pathways from winter to spring to summer living quarters. Right outside the child's front door were thousand of hectares of forest land that had never felt the footsteps of a European; was inhabited by birds, deer, moose, bears and a very few wolves along with numerous other small animals, insects and other living creatures. This was a "nature playground", and as the child walked across the ground they wondered if any person had ever walked on this piece of ground before them and if they would ever stand in that place again. There were hills to climb and run down, moss beds to sleep in, perfect settings for games of hide and seek, and the best was a gentle stream filled with fish and beautiful stones. In places the stream forked around small gravel beds creating island that the children claimed as their land. In this landscape children could and did play all day and at night. Yet with all this nature, these children loved their swings and dolls, their music and dancing as well.

In this wilderness, farming and ranching activities represented the invading culture and were never seen to be part of nature but rather seen as disrupting to the nature. Forest harvesting practised were even more anti-nature. With an attitude formed in this cultural setting, the Canadian will find it disturbing to learn that a Danish colleague classes factory-like agricultural land use as "nature". In the western Canadian cultural reference it is the very opposite of nature. It is unlikely that the nature playground movement will find much foothold in western Canada in the form that it is practised in Denmark for example.

This landscape while appearing "natural" has been considerably affected by human activity – so is it nature?

The awareness that our concept of nature is formed during childhood and that our feelings toward nature throughout our life are coloured by our childhood experiences in nature are the prime factors that have influenced the play providers to develop the idea of the Nature playground. Young children growing up in cities have too little opportunity for contact with nature and this lack of contact when young could result in an alienation, fear and rejection of nature later in life. The environmental awareness and scientific knowledge that we have today informs us that for the well being of this planet and human life on earth in the future we need to change some our cultural oriented activities to permit the continuation of healthy ecosystems. There is an element of urgency in turning around human behaviour to be more in balance with the other systems of this planet. This sense of urgency has been transferred to childhood with demands that children learn early on about nature, environmental issues and pollution. Nature and nature preservation has become a fashionable campaign and is a respectable object for charitable good works with the nobility and kings and queens as Protectors.

> There is a desire to transmit to the children that they need to take up the burden of saving the earth and adults are prepared to manipulate with children's play and play places to achieve this goal.

Nature playground provision in many countries is further ensured by the availability of grants and funding for nature playgrounds, support which is not available for traditional play facilities. There is a desire to transmit to the children that they need to take up the burden of saving the earth and adults are prepared to manipulate with children's play and play places to achieve this goal. Bettelheim writes " I think the danger to middle class children is that they are sacrificed by their parents not to the past but to the future...Children are sacrificed by parents who burden them with the future by telling them from early childhood on of their obligation to correct the evils of the world" (Bettelheim, (1980) p 178). In manipulating children's play in this way the adult's sense of urgency and perhaps their guilt drive their desire to have the children make good what the older generation neglected to do.

> If we want today's children to feel strongly enough about nature and planet earth that they, when adults, will suffer inconvenience to improve conditions for nature we must provide them early on with opportunities to fall in love with nature.

Not only are we needlessly sacrificing childhood to the future, this is not the path to the creation of an appreciation and affection for nature and natural elements. If we want today's children to feel strongly enough about nature and planet earth that they, when adults, will suffer inconvenience to improve conditions for nature, we must provide them early on with opportunities to fall in love with nature. Children should not see nature as a problem but as a wonder, children should be permitted to play and explore in the most beautiful and exciting natural and cultural setting that humans can possible provide. They must be permitted to play freely and with the playmates they are fond of. After years of happy experiences in and surrounded by nature and culture then children develop such a strong attachment to nature that they will work to preserve and improve conditions for nature.

What does nature mean to children?

Children's concept of nature seems to be different than that of adults, although adults also hold many different ideas of what is nature depending on their cultural and educational backgrounds. A study carried out in Denmark in 1994 with both children and adults responding, shows that

While adults may focus on the obvious urban setting, for children this is an area with real "nature". Nature is living things for young children.

adults have a far wider spectrum of associations and meanings for nature than do young children. Young children predominantly associate nature with plants, the elements of the earth such as sun and water and with animals but they also placed more emphasis on people as nature than did the adults. Adults on the other hand more often associated nature with a place such as forest or beach and with experiences such as vacation and with environmental issues. (Hendricks, B. (1995)). Nature to children has something to do with living things. To young pre-school children all things that move are living and they cannot distinguish that while a hopping rabbit is alive, a bouncing ball or running water are dead. Such fine distinctions, which depend on an understanding of what make things move, come later on in childhood along with the understanding of other abstract concepts. When we think of nature and children we should be careful to think of children's nature and not some adult concept of nature.

> You see Merry Phillis, that dear little maid,
> Has invited Belinda to tea;
> Her nice little garden is shaded by trees,-
> What pleasanter place could there be?
> (Kate Greenaway)

Children's nature is a nature of activity and life, of children's knowledge, not abstract adult theories or scientific information. Once, on a visit to a kindergarten, I was walking in a sand area when I was approached by a young girl who told me that I shouldn't walk in the sand box with my shoes on. When I asked "Why not?" she explained that the sand would get between my shoes and my feet and it wouldn't feel good. She was right. Children have a good knowledge of their world - it is a child's knowledge that we leave behind in the adult world.

In their work with children, Piaget and his researchers asked children questions about elements we as adults consider to be nature. When asked about the origins of sun and moon, Piaget writes of one child named Roy at the age of six

> there are in fact three tendencies in Roy's thought: (1) an artificialist tendency, the sun and the moon have been made by man. Their origins lies in the flame of a match; (2) an animist tendency; the sun and moon are alive, they know when it is day time, and what we are doing, etc.; (3) a tendency to establish participations between themselves and ourselves, they grow because we grow, they begin to live 'because we were made' etc. (Piaget, 1977, p 291).

Playing is living for children. What is life for children? After many hours of discussions about life with young children Piaget concluded " The impression these children give is that the assimilation of life to movement is evidently simply a matter of words. That is to say, the word 'life' means simply movement, but this movement has none of the characteristics with which we should define life, such as spontaneity, purpose, etc. The child says that a stream is alive just as a physicist would say that a movement has been 'imparted to it', that it 'has acceleration', etc." Piaget goes on to note that it is around the age of eleven or twelve when children make a distinct between spontaneous and imparted movement and until then continue to relate movement with life (Piaget, (1977) p 229-30). Life and movement are interchangeable for children, nature is living things, nature is moving, playing is moving. Playing is nature?

Nature and design

Nature has always been a source of aesthetic experiences for mankind and of inspiration to artists. Nature has also provided mankind with a temporary place of refuge from world's worries and sorrows. Nature has been the source and support of human life, however unaware we may be of that fact.

Design and art are creative and expressive acts. Modern art movements have attempted to be free of the shackles of restrictions imposed by the more tradition ideas of what was a painting, a symphony or a ballet dance. Artists create individual expressions and the act of creation is as important or more important than the result. In some instances there is a blurring of the boundaries between the basic primitive creative instincts in all persons and the harnessing of these creative instincts with skill, discipline and artist inspiration. Creativity is muddled in with that which is primitive and instinctual. We may have difficulty distinguishing between children's art, icons created by primitive peoples and art creations of modern western civilisation for all are expressive and creative, informed by basic instincts.

Good modern design in play spaces, using nature as a source of inspiration should also communicate some modern interpretation about life and the human condition and include a strong element of playfulness. They should celebrate nature as a source of life, of beauty and wonder. Nature playgrounds, however, like traditional playgrounds, are rarely approached as a subject of design, and like traditional playgrounds are seen as functional spaces where young children are to learn the lessons the adults have chosen for them. There is very little difference in theory between nature playgrounds and traditional playgrounds, just in the type of lesson to be learned.

The "Nature" playground as a place for play

Adult provision of public outdoor spaces for children's play is based in arguments for children's development. The rationale is that the kinds of play experiences provided are for the children's benefit so they will grow up and be good adults. The values of the adult culture and the skills and abilities that the adults think children should learn dominate as features in playgrounds. This is the case in both the conventional types of play areas and also in the experimental, new lifestyle movements that have influenced the objects placed in the play space. While playgrounds should be the places where childhood and children's values dominate, it rarely happens. The adults in all good intentions are so focussed on children as human "becomings" that they completely ignore the importance of childhood culture and the benefits to all to celebrate playing and living in the child's way.

While traditional playgrounds have been the subject of much criticism and very little praise from the adult world, in learned articles as well as in the daily media, the "Nature" playground movement has obtained a lot of media coverage and in most cases the coverage is complimentary and positive. Some newspapers have gone so far as to use headlines that predict the end of swings and slides on the playgrounds. None have done an evaluation of the play possibilities from the children's play viewpoint, all the journalists and writers evaluate the play area according to adult values, most often those values shared by a small group of new-age environmentally oriented adults who are concerned that our society has lost contact with nature. While many adults who support the nature playground movement have not really much changed their consumer life styles they are prepared to support the idea that the next generation must do more this planet and for nature. And they are prepared to sacrifice children's play to this end. The movement has a large element of new-romanticism and it is not surprising that it has arisen in cultures where there has always been a tendency towards romanticism and viewing nature as good and pure. The nature playground movement has been taken up because it fits in with the adult ideas about what children should learn to take on their role as the next generation of responsible adults. However, more than the traditional playground, it has betrayed the children's world and culture and neglected the importance of playfulness in and with quality spaces and materials. One of the other reasons why the nature playground movement in its lowest common denominator has become so popular in some countries is that these places can be constructed at very little cost to the community.

The nature playground with its rationale in producing more environmentally aware adults in the next generation, and the possibility of reducing the amount of money and space to be allocated to children's play fits in well with some current thinking in the adult culture. That these play areas blend in with the surrounding greenness of a park also is an advantage in the adult value system. Therefore it has received a tremendous amount of positive media coverage and quickly been adopted by communities and child institutions. Its popularity and wide spread use is quite undeserved when one looks at this movement in terms of serving childhood culture and children's play. In terms of spatial design these places clearly show the hand of amateur play designers who emphasises adult values of economy and use of rustic and found materials that have some connection with adult ideas of romantic nature. Design and creation of a mood of playfulness are missing.

Designing for play is about expressing ideas and feelings, about communicating playfulness and joy of living. In the typical approach to nature playground there is no attempt to create a mood, it just happens and it expresses barrenness and sameness. Rather than celebrate the many complexities and wonders of nature these places with their dead tree trunks, piles of dirt, poorly maintained grass and low quality willow plantings express a disdain for children's aesthetics and a strong adult desire to control the children's experiences. At the same time there is a very heavy dose of anti-consumerism in this movement, where the adults have mistakenly equated traditional playground equipment with consumerism. It is another version of more of the same but with a cheapness of spirit that shows the adult society in a poor light.

> Design of functional objects and spaces involves not only making spaces or things that do the work well but which also express some idea or feeling, which communicate some fantasy or fleeting expression to the user.

Design of functional objects and spaces involves not only making spaces or things that do the work well but which also express some idea or feeling, which communicate some fantasy or fleeting expression to the user. Nature play areas are either purely functional spaces with no design or the designer has been so caught up with the adult values that they have neglected to communicate aspects of play to the user – that is the children. In summary in my opinion the nature playground movement has been well intended but the forms of play spaces that have resulted have shown a lack of respect for both children as young citizens and a rather frightening aspect of new age movement adults forcing their opinions on others. Neill has written "Every opinion forced on a child is a sin against that child. A child is not a little adult and a child cannot possibly see the adult's point of view." (Bettelheim, (1980), p 179). In school, in religion and in politics we respect the children's need to come to understand the world in their own way and to form their own opinions – yet in the one space dedicated to childhood, to the celebration of the children's world we see a popularisation of a movement which represents a huge intrusion of adult values into childhood and in the way in which the children can explore the world around them.

Nature epitomises innocence and purity

In the thinking of the new romantics there is a strong relationship between the innocence of nature and the purity and innocence of children. Children are seen to be closer to nature than are educated adults and in to some extent seen as modern day primitives. Culture is seen to be the antithesis of nature and objects created by culture are rejected unless they have some appearance of rusticity or a primitive handcraft. This view is restricted very much to the physical objects and spaces in the public forum and is undermined by the very culturally influenced aspects of the theories of nature and innocence. The idea of the nature playground is not well thought through nor is it based in any well grounded theories of nature or children's play. In practise it has become a movement and at time taking on some aspects of being a "cult" where reason is dismissed and belief prevails. Non-believers and non-practitioners are derided and excluded from the group. It is so that in 1999 many highly qualified and soundly trained pedagogues in Denmark were afraid of collegial disapproval if they choose to install traditional play equipment in their yards, even though they are convinced of many good arguments for such facilities. This situation will of course change and the change is already underway and we can only hope that not too much space and play opportunities have been lost during this return to the dark ages of play. There will be a more reasoned approach to play provision in the Northern European countries but it may be some time before they again take the a strong leadership role in trends in public play provision.

Nature playgrounds as a movement has been quite dominant in the "new thinking" of pedagogues and child specialists in Northern European countries during the 1990s. The result is that most new playground or playgrounds under renovation in these countries have some or many elements taken from the nature playground movement. The movement has become so entrenched that there are even playground equipment manufacturers offering catalogues filled with "Nature playgrounds"! The Landscapes for Learning movement has brought more focus on the greening of school yards and much available funding for improving children's play opportunities is channelled into re-landscaping of previously barren spaces. In North America these movement have been combined in early childhood yards where more nature is being introduced both as an element for play and as an element of a more formalised playful learning curriculum.

The Playground of the Future –Kongen's Have (The King's Garden), Copenhagen

In March 1997 the State Fund for Art in Denmark announced a competition for the design of "The Playground of the Future" with three specific sites located in three centres across the land, one of which was in The King's Garden in Copenhagen. The criteria set out for the competition made it very clear that a conventional playground would not be a winner and that any suggestions of swings, slides and seesaws would be rejected. In the Copenhagen site the emphasis was on the adult values of the historic nature of the garden, with play provision for children from ages 0 to 6. It was clear from the design brief that no element of children's play should intrude into the serious adult world. Working out from these criteria, the judges selected an entry by a goldsmith, a glass artist an architect, as the best play area proposal for this area. This playground design is seen by the serious art community in Denmark to epitomise the playground of the future and was constructed over 1998.

In March of 1999 I visited the site for the first time and made the following observations: On approaching the garden it was clear that the winter had been a hard one on the historic garden and many trees had been cut down. The garden was predominantly a flat plane of grass, not particularly well kept and widely dispersed trees and shrubs. Some sculptures strategically located added a sense of prestige and history. The whole park is basically a large green open circulation space used to get from place A to place B. There is no real invitation to slow down and stay a while. If one didn't know there was a playground behind the hedge one could walk on past - there are no clear signals that there is a place for children and for play.

On finding the playground and entering the gate, the first impression is positive as there sitting in the centre is a fascinating metal egg, shining in the light. Set nearby are two carved wooden dragons which also are visually appealing in their newness. Stretching out from this centre are four arms of rather dull, monotone wood and sand, of low profile so they won't intrude onto the outside garden setting. These four arms are crowned by four metal pavilions that look like they fell down from the sky, and just happened to land in these places. The design is intended to represent a golden egg surrounded by the four kingdoms. A sand filled "moat" runs around the central area with four bridges leading to the arms. In one arm there is a maze of logs and sand, another arm consists of a series of poles standing upright, some carved with motifs, the third arm included a structure of poles and cables and a bridge, while in the fourth are low wood stumps carefully arranged in a sand area. The whole area is quite small approximately 900 sq. meters at most.

This sculptural egg at the centre of the play area fascinates the children – and is just the right size for the children.

A close examination shows the craftsmanship of the goldsmith and the glass worker – there is some finely crafted work here that appeals to both the eye and the tactile sense, at a very detailed level. The colour palette used is very subdued with the metal colours of bronze and aluminium being the strongest, otherwise it is wood of various types, sand and stones. An adult, sophisticated selection that shouts "adult good taste". Nothing moves, nothing changes with the seasons. The egg is appealing to the children and they are attracted to touch it and follow the cracks in the egg. Here is a example of how art created by good artists can challenge the children's imagination and heighten the sense of magic and suspense. It is easy to believe that shortly the egg will break open to hatch out some marvellous thing.

This play area in its care for detailing and ideas of magic and wonder carry positive signs in the development of future playgrounds. However in its disdain for the rich array of movement and explorative aspects in a social setting that comprises children's play, this design does not contribute to the development of a new concept of children's play places. To a great extent the weakness lies with those who set up the conditions for the competition; given freer and more child friendly frames of references I am sure this team could create much better play areas.

In terms of design there is a serious problem with the scale of the place-it is not at a comfortable human scale. The central space is approximately 22 meters by 22 meters with each often arm extending about 15 meters out. In this space there is no object higher than the surrounding hedge which is about 120 cm high. The open horizontal scale is dominant, yet one is hidden behind a hedge so the comfort of openness is lost. The space lacks vertical elements of appropriate proportion to make it a comfortable place – and users move on quite quickly. Even the egg is visually too small for the space, although when one watches a three year old child approach the egg - –it is the right height for the child. The pavilions however are ill proportioned both for the spaces they stand in and are too small be used for anything. If they were a bit larger and made into adult seating or story telling places that brings out the history of the garden then they would start to belong on the site.

A play garden – The Four Seasons

The Four Seasons is a play garden which serves as one of the communal child care institutions in Ringe, Denmark. The focus of the institution is to create a good daily life for both the children and the adults. Both the children and adults are out of doors much of the day in all weathers, engaged in both playful activities and in daily activities such as maintaining the garden, harvesting crops, feeding chickens, playing football, reading a story, building a hide-away, mowing the grass, swinging or playing chase. All can happen. Also outside is where they all eat their meals – except in the very coldest wettest weather.

The Four Season is a large residential-like garden space of approximately 3000 square meters. In the centre is a building with basic facilities occupying around 200 sq. meters. Like the playground in the Kings Garden this play garden takes on the basic motif of a central focal object – in this case the building- surrounded by four "kingdoms", here in the form of four different gardens. It is not an co-incidental selection of motifs; such garden plans with a central place, most often a pool or fountain, surrounded by four gardens has been with us from the beginning of garden history and is often shown as the basic layout for the gardens of Paradise.

The concept for The Four Seasons originated with Tom Lindhardt Wils, a Danish artist and play equipment designer. The overall layout and design for the play garden was created by Barbara Hendricks for Kompan A/S, in conjunction with the staff of the kindergarten. The staff of the gardens have been responsible for much of the creation of the gardens and the

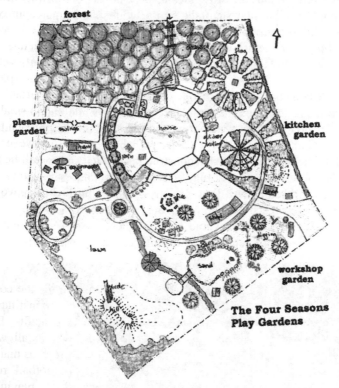

Plan over the Four Seasons play gardens. Drawing by B. Hendricks.

playful, welcoming atmosphere that prevails there (with help from the children of course).

The Four Seasons takes it name from the clear and distinct changes in seasons one experience in Denmark, and the concept is that the children should be aware of, remark upon and celebrate each new season and the changes they bring. So too should the children be able to observe the movement of the sun across the sky, patterns of sunlight and shadow, warm sunny places and cool shady places. Rain and snow and wind as well as fire are part of the children's experiences, as is the growing cycle of plants and animals. The garden is a working balance between the beauty of nature exemplified by the flower gardens, herbs, berries, flowering and fruiting trees, the chickens and the functionality of natural spaces – playing with water, with mud, digging holes, sliding, hiding and construction. Children's playful use of the space is always in the forefront with a rich variety of places and things to do. Children can choose to ride various wheeled toys, play house, paint, dig in the sand, play chase, find their own corner and "do their own thing", talk, be silly, swing, play house, climb, run, watch the trucks on the adjacent road, talk to the adults, and many, many more options. Children are encouraged to find their own rhythms and to take responsibility for themselves and their fellows. There are few rules and few routines – only those necessary for good order, good manners and good health.

The design has focussed on creating some clear, strong spatial framework that can keep a semblance of order while supporting a wide range of messy children's activities and changes in plantings and spatial uses. The Gardens consist of a forest with both native trees and a fruit orchard, a kitchen garden area, a construction garden and a pleasure garden where the more conventional play activities that children enjoy are located in a landscaped setting. All four gardens are distinguished by garden walls or fences between each garden, yet all are connected by a flowing ribbon of a pathway that circles the whole garden. These basic frames and garden types suggest types of activities that can take place in each setting however

At the Four Seasons the children and the adults enjoy being outdoors in all weather.

as the place is about a good outdoor life for both the children and the adults there is much blending of uses, as each new use takes up a space not already claimed for other activities.

This garden has a lesson for designers of play spaces in the relationship between design and daily life. While there maybe a temptation for a designer to work in isolation and to push for their ideas to predominate the physical forms of the garden, if the emphasis is on a good life in that space for those who live there on a daily basis, then the designer must give up some of their sovereignty over spatial decisions. It is essential in such situations that the people who live and work in these places have a sense of ownership over the spaces and feel that it is permitted and that they have the ability to make changes in the spaces. The space must belong to those who live there and they must feel in control. The best play spaces come when a designer can work over a period of time with enthusiastic and caring child care specialists who also know something about gardens. This was the case with the Four Seasons.

With the Four Seasons it became very clear that the pedagogues approach to play spaces and structures was very conventional although they were in the process of realising a unconventional play garden. When the decisions were to be made about what piece of play furniture would be placed in the gardens, the choice always was focussed on function and price, not on the aesthetics or design of the play item. Their training seems to have so influenced their judgement that while they would select furniture for their own home with an eye for design, at work in a communal facility for children, design in the outdoor items which the children touched, and played with and on was not an issue.

Good design in the children's spaces is one way the whole society clearly tells children that we really mean it when we say we love them.

The spatial design of the yard was also low on the scale, rather the staff were more interested whether there was room for all the things and activities they wanted. These kind of decisions were made early on in their time with the centre as the work began shortly after they were employed, and after four years their attitudes may have altered somewhat as has the garden.

There is, however, so little emphasis in the daily working of pedagogues on design and beauty for children that the issue takes a very low priority in their professional judgement. In this centre the staff focus on good, positive experiences, challenges and stimulation for the children with an emphasis on outdoor life and a good time with the staff and other children. All these things are very important in the life of children. A designer could also wish that the children and staff would also take the time and consciously enjoy the beauty in the world around them and that adults would, through their work, demonstrate to the children that the play and daily surrounding can also have an aspect of good design. Good design in the children's spaces is one way the whole society clearly tells children that we really mean it when we say we love them.

A quality play area is an excellent expression of civilisation and a fine signal to our children that we really mean it when we say we love them.

New ways to create quality play settings

Trends in playground design should continue to experiment with new ways to create high quality settings for children's play out of doors. In this chapter we have focussed mainly on the work with young children's spaces. The nature playground movement may not be a good solution to children's play needs but it was good that people have tried to make better play areas. Play spaces for older children are also in need of a rethinking. Children need to be given more place in city life– and not left over spaces but carefully created special spaces and opportunities.

Formal academic research is starting to turn to looking at children's play and play spaces as acceptable academic activities. Research in children's reactions to outdoor environments is still a very young academic discipline and research methodology is not well developed. There are now forums for researchers to meet and exchange experiences – such as the Halmstad International Toy Research Conference, The International Council for Children's Play (ICCP) World Conference, and various national conferences of Early Childhood experts. However, in these forums researchers in children's outdoor environments have to fight for place and time with subjects like playful educational techniques, new educational methodologies, art and drama for young children and research on children's consumption and preference for toys, and so forth. If there is a discussion about outdoor play it is all to often dominated by the adult concern for safety regulations. There is at this time, no forum specifically for researchers and designers who work with children's outdoor environments. Interestingly, the International Association of Landscape Architects has completely neglected this area in their conferences and research groups.

Efforts to improve children's play possibilities can follow parallel with developments in academic research in children's response to the outdoors. This area of research is fast growing and can benefit from a central forum for the exchange of information, research methodologies and for positive critiques of work underway. Adults researching children's response to and use of outdoor environments, just like designers of play spaces, come from a wide range of professions and it is this richness that can contribute so much to the outcome if they can avoid in-fighting over which profession really owns the subject of children's outdoor play.

References

Bettleheim, Bruno. (1980), *Surviving and Other Essays*, Vintage Books: New York.
Grahn, P. et al. (1997), *Ute Paa Dagis*, Movium: Alnarp. Sweden.
Hendricks, Barbara. (1995), "Young Children's Playful Interactions in and With Nature in Urban Areas", paper presented at *Building Identities Conference*, Amsterdam, unpublished.
Piaget, Jean. (1977), *The Child's Conception of the World*, Paladin: St Albans.Herts.

13 Magic in the Play Area

Children and the magic world

Children are born with an enormous potential in their brain. They also have skills and abilities over and above the basic instincts needed for survival. It is in the brain of the children that our culture's future lies. Human beings have a long childhood to permit the brain to achieve its full potential before the person is required to make decisions and take action that determine human-kinds survival. The long childhood is not however just a waiting period; it is a period of fervent activity and development of all aspects of mind, body and spirit. It is not enough that children arrive at adulthood with a good education, they must also arrive with an intact spirit, an enthusiasm for life and a set of principles and values aimed at enhancing life on earth.

Throughout the twentieth century adults have studied children and childhood, yet we know so little about what it means to be a child and almost nothing about what it feels like to be a child. Those are lands which we can only know through vague memories from our own childhood for we can not travel to them again as adults. Mental states and capacities alter throughout our life time and our experiences contribute toward forming the next altered state. Children at birth are not blank cards on which experience makes the first marks, they bring into the world with them a complex set of personality traits and a way of seeing and knowing the world. Children sense the world around them and work out their own explanations and understanding of their experiences. They know the world out from their own body and see themselves as the centre of their world. They feel happiness and sadness, warmth and cold, love and anger and many other feelings. They therefore assign other objects with similar capacity for feelings and are capable of feeling empathy for others. Things, we as adults know to be dead, such as unfeeling objects like stones, children know to be living, feeling beings.

Young children are nurtured by adults and come to know that they were made by their parents and assume that all things in the physical world were made by adults. They assign adults an almost god-like power. At the same time when an adult goes away at first the young child thinks that person has gone forever, but soon they come to understand that just because they cannot see a person doesn't mean that person has stopped existing. A person they don't see still exists and still loves them and is their friend. This they know because the adults have assured them it is so and their experience supports this idea. Believing this, they can easily move from believing in the constant existence of someone they occasionally see to having invisible friends that only they can see. They can believe that their grandmother and other loved ones are well and happy when they are in another city and only hear their voice over the telephone, because their parents tell them it is so. They can also believe that their invisible playmates and heroes are out there somewhere and will come to them at certain times when the child needs them. There is no magic in this to the child, it is all part of how it works that people and things appear, go away, and send voices and images.

> Children assign adults an almost god-like power

There is magic in story telling and fairy tales which can absorb children's attention. Their imagination fills out the basic frames to create a magic world of wonders and great beauty.

There is also a power of magic for children. The magic that comes with stories and fairy tales where children become powerful and can solve the most difficult problems where they deal with powers that threaten to take their life or the life of those they love. The magic of the traditional fairy tale and myth holds children enchanted, not because these are pleasant stories but because these stories give the children insight into a world where they can be powerful forces for setting situations to right, where they can take revenge on those who have hurt them.

> Like all great art, fairy tales both delight and instruct, their special genius is that they do so in terms which speak directly to children. At the age when these stories are most meaningful to the child, his major problem is to bring some order into the inner chaos of his mind so that he can understand himself better – a necessary preliminary for achieving some congruence between his perceptions and the external world (Bettlelheim, (1989), p 53).

The actions and characters as well as ideas in these stories are taken up by the children because these stories suggest that it is possible for children to become powerful and deal with problems that otherwise appear overwhelming. Fairy tales, through their telling of magical transformations, tell children there is hope. It is possible that a fairy godmother will come and make all right again, as well as it is possible to turn a mean adult into an ugly troll or a powerless insect. The fairy tale and the child's imagination playing together create a better world order for the child. Playing out some aspects of the stories and characters is one way in which the child can further develop and work out ideas and feelings that they are experiencing.

Landscapes for play that do not deny magical possibilities, ones that permit the children to act out some aspects of fairy tales and stories, can contribute to childhood's wonder and satisfaction. Such landscapes do not need to include a fully developed house in the forest in the style of the house in Hansel and Grethel; they can be much more subtle in their suggestion. Children's pretend play is not a re-enactment of what they have seen or have been told, rather they use images, characters and ideas as tools to work out their own ideas and set order to their world. They do this through playing. Landscapes for playing should not be replicas of fairy tale lands, rather children can play out many ideas in landscapes that are varied with elements that they can assign to be specific places or things; what is important is that the landscape permits the children to become so immersed in their play that all else in the outside world is shut out and does not interrupt or intrude.

This landscape in Iceland is inhabited by small people whose presence can be felt by sensitive adults and who can be seen by young children who believe in magic.

Magical imagination and the play environment personality

Children are born with some inherent personality traits, develop other traits from experiences within the family and home and take on other aspects of personality as a result of interaction in the environment. People behave differently and take on different characters in different settings. Environmental personality refers to the ways in which a person behaves in a specific setting or situation. The play environment personality is a set of behaviours in a playground and continues as an influence of memories at play on one's behaviour throughout a lifetime.

Children are very sensitive to signals of appropriate behaviour and want to learn what is appropriate behaviour in public spaces. While the drive to play is so urgent in children that they will play anywhere, even in refugee camps in the middle of a war, the play experience and the forms of play are influenced by the character of the environment. Where children are permitted to play freely, with few rules and in the presence of various materials to be used in play, imaginative and dramatic play develops quickly and children become very engrossed in their play. Where children are required to play in accordance with rules of appropriate behaviour, where there is limited time to play and limited materials to play with, play is often limited to physical/explorative activities. The reason that play on traditional playgrounds is limited to swinging and sliding and rocking, is not inherent in the character of the swings, slides and rockers but is attributable to the fact that children have a limited time to play in these places, and are required by adults to use these structures in accordance to the rules and that there are no other materials to integrate into the play. Alternative playgrounds which consist of only fixed structures such as tree trunks and mounds and with play safety rules will result in the same kinds of restricted play behaviours.

Magic and reality

The magic and imagination in play comes about when children can manipulate and change things. There is an idea in certain early childhood specialist circles that objects and spaces that represent elements from life or fairy stories in some ways restrict children's fantasy and imagination in a way that simple, abstract objects do not. There is no proof to this belief – in fact there seems to be proof of just the opposite. Objects and elements that suggest or communicate something relating to a real life object or a fairy tale serve as stimuli to imaginative play. This happens because these objects or suggestions signal to the children that it is okay to be imaginative here. For younger children objects with some suggestive aspect of reality are necessary to keep the play going. When these objects can be moved, sat upon, furnished, used to make a pretend meal or to travel to new lands, then the children's imagination and play has transformed them "just like magic". It seems what is important is the clear signal to the children that childhood and play are welcome here – the rest the children will take care of. It is better to include in the play area design some objects that are realistic, which the children can relate to as part of play than to provide the children with abstract non-representational objects that have no connection with childhood or playfulness. Children's imaginations are not so weak that they can't turn a boat into a rocket ship, but they are allowed to play freely as children in so few places that they need signals that reinforce the permission to play.

> Magic and mystic comes from within as well as from outside. True magic is not technological tricks.

Play items and play spaces that visually suggest real-life objects such as riding horses and play trains do not restrict the child to only one kind of imaginative play. A playship will not always be a ship in the child's imagination but it clearly tells the children that fantasy and imagination are legitimate play tools in this environment. It is not so important whether it is a ship or a castle, what is important is that it is child friendly, comfortable for the child and signals to the child that imaginative play is what the place is about. A dead tree trunk laying on a pile of dirt does not communicate fantasy and imagination to children, whereas images from stories they have been told do so. Soft rounded shapes and designs that are characteristic of other elements in the childhood culture are understood by the children to mean that childhood is welcome in this place and that there is potential for magic things to happen. Playing with ideas, emotions and magic are powerful and deeply felt experiences for children, and they need environments that clearly signal that such play is okay, otherwise they will seek out hidden corners where the adults can't see them or be deprived of an important play opportunity.

Play environments should include small spaces that clearly suggest that "here is a space where magical things happen".

In the past such signals for play that supported imaginative play were not so vital to play happening as there was always some safe haven hidden away from the adults that the children could take over – such places had the additional magic of being "found" or discovered places. Today there are few of these kinds of spaces left in cities where children are permitted to play safely. Play of all kinds is limited to the public play spaces – and play area designers need to bring in new approaches to play. The way previous generations played and the places they played in as children are part of a past childhood culture; play provision for today's children should be based in today's childhood, not yesterdays, and the public play area is expected to provide spaces and places for all kinds of play – a demanding role not filled by traditional play spaces. Among the elements missing is the potential for something magical to happen there.

Magic landscapes

There is a fascination and a power in certain landscapes, and some form of expression in all. Feng Shui, from the orient and the many western myths and folk beliefs confirm that humans have always felt these forces from the earth although our scientific era has not been able to measure and describe them. Some forms of landscapes influence us in certain ways, some good, some not so good. The Icelandic belief in invisible people living in rocks and hills and the widespread belief in monsters living in deep waters are some examples of the relationship between landscapes and human responses. In her novel *Shirley*, Charlotte Brontë in 1849, describes the Fieldhead Hollow, a place where the last of the fairies lived, in this way: "A lonesome spot it was – and a bonny spot – full of oak trees and nut trees." (Brontë, (1985), p. 599).

Not only wild nature has magic; for centuries people have tested the magic of fountains and streams, tossing in coins and wishing. Places of special magic qualities have become destinations for pilgrimages and places to go for cures. Water is often present in magical places with the well, spring, fountain or lake serving as a home for the magical force. Oriental teachings on special forces in the landscape also recognise the special qualities in water. In fact, the oriental term *Feng Shui* means wind and water.

Landscapes specifically created for playful activities for children could be so much richer if we developed ways in which we bring to the children some of the power and suggestion that is present in the kinds of landscapes that have some magical character. The study of magic landscapes has not interested many western landscape architects until recently. They have been more interested in the landscapes of adult power and influence.

The potential for magic in a landscape is influenced by the amount of variation in the landscape and is not limited to natural features; magical places can also be built urban and cultural places. It is important however to distinguish between an adult design creating a stage setting for acting out a play or for amusement of the viewers – such as seen in various amusement parks, Disneylands and Legolands. This is one kind of magic – a reference to magic in known stories. The kind of magic in children's play areas should be suggestive of children being able to script their own stories and make their own transformations, rather than a faithful retelling of a

Suggestions of magical happenings in children's play areas should suggest fantasy yet permit children to make up their own stories and transformations.

specific story. It is true that children find comfort in the exact repetition of a favourite tale. In this case, the comfort is in the telling and the predictability of the events. At play the children need to take control because the play is dealing with their inner feelings and ideas, not repeating a story. For this reason, while play area magic can be suggested though symbols that make connections to fairy tales and magic characters, the landscape must also include appropriate spaces and facilities for the children to create their own stories.

Magic landscapes can be little hidden nooks, gardens with flowering shrubs and plants where the fairies dance, caves and dens where the invisible people live. In northern and western Europe many mythological and supernatural beings live the forest and it is not surprising therefore that some Northern European adults today believe that forests are more supportive of children's imaginative play than are urban streets. For the child however this is not necessarily the case. Local childhood myths and traditions can create magic places within the neighbourhood and on the institutional or school playground.

Elves in the form of Nisse (Danish) or tomte (Swedish), still live in the modern mythology of Scandinavian countries. They are small, teasing little people that live in the attic and come to the fore at Christmas time. Santa Claus is seen as a type of Christmas Nisse. The belief in Nisse in Scandinavian countries originally had them living alongside people on farms, however today Nisse have moved into the city and live quite comfortably in all suburbs. Most adults, when faced with other serious adults, will say they do not believe in Nisse but they enjoy the continuation of the belief through telling stories to their children and acting out situations where the nisse play a part. Such situations are tremendously important signals to the children that the fantasy and magic elements of their life are acceptable. That many of the adult Nisse supporters are women is a indicator that women do not feel the pressure to hold themselves to the scientific and measurable world in a way that many men do. In Iceland it is also believed that the invisible people who inhabit the land can be seen by young children up to the age of around three and by special adults throughout their life.

There is more magic in the landscape than just invisible people and supernatural beings. A magic or story telling corner or bench in a quality outdoor landscape can be the source of many hours of imaginative play with a magical quality. Such a place, when used to stimulate the children's fantasy through story telling by the adults and through provision of play props, can signal that magic and imaginative play is accepted in this environment – a signal that the children will take up and make many new play routines.

Designs that communicate magic are difficult to define, mainly because "magic" has many meanings and because it has been dominated by commercial interests such as Walt Disney or by technological sleight of hand for the entertainment of viewers. Magic designs for play are ones where the design addresses the children's magic world of make-believe, not the entertainment industry's. Magic landscapes are places where invisible forces are felt, where there is a mythology of beings and doings that is part of the local childhood culture, and where the magic is played out by the children not performed for them.

> Magic designs for play are ones where the design addresses the children's magic world of make-believe, not the entertainment industry's.

Magic is not a standard requirement in a neighbourhood park playground, nor do school children ask for magic when consulted on a playground renewal scheme. Magic is absent, not because children don't want it – but because they don't know they can ask for it. Children are so good at co-operating with adults that they limit their demands to those elements the adults conventionally provide. Once magic becomes an issue in

234 Designing for Play

playgrounds – children will demand it. Magic landscapes, when they are present in play places makes those places attractive to the children, drawing them into a type of play where they become so absorbed in the play that they forget about the outside real world – and that is magic!

References

Bettelheim, Bruno. (1989), *The Uses of Enchantment, The Meaning and Importance of Fairy Tales*, Vintage Books: New York.
Bronte, Charlotte. (1985), *Shirley*, Penguin Classics: Harmondsworth.

14 Playing with the Future

This is a book for designers about designing for play. Perhaps in the process designers of reading and considering what has been written, they will have also come to play with designing. Playing for children is all about living; that attitude to life need not stop when we become adults. A lifelong playful interaction with living is a full life.

> "A childhood of play allows the plasticity of the mind and the spirit of the child to unfold freely." (Mary Taylor, (1990)).

Adults all too often have discounted the knowledge we have accumulated over the twentieth century about how the child's mind works. This knowledge has not yet been integrated into educational approaches and certainly not into the ways we provide for play. While the rationale for the provision of public play areas and facilities is to develop the child and assist the educational curriculum in the preparation of the child for adulthood, there is no well thought through programme of communicating to the child from the starting point of the child's knowledge of the world or what goes on in the child's mind. Instead we have pushed down on top of childhood another, adult layer of knowledge and skills, squeezing out the child's world and the child's confidence in their minds and abilities.

If we instead worked out from a starting point of the children's minds, the children's competences and allowed them to add additional skills not only would the acquisition of adult knowledge be enjoyed by the children, the character of knowledge and knowing could change. Through playing with ideas where the children's minds and adult way of thinking are set together, the results could be beneficial to both adults and children. In playing with the world, a world that is set out from the children's knowledge of the world, a new concept of living in this world for all society can evolve.

> "Think of the investment that evolution has made in the child's brain.... When I was born, my body was a mere appendage to the head; it weighed only five or six times as much as my brain. For most of history, civilisations have crudely ignored that enormous potential. In fact the longest childhood has been that of civilisation, learning to understand that" (Bronowski , J. (1973)).

The pathway to tomorrow leads through the playground

For many years now wise people have stated that public playgrounds were "dead", meaning there was no future in making more of the same. Before we throw away playgrounds we must develop alternative spaces that have good quality play possibilities where childhood is celebrated. One of the dangers of making places for all ages to be together is that the celebration of childhood is downplayed and de-emphasised. These shared places can remain as just one more place where children are sent signals that they aren't really human yet – they must wait until they are grownup before they can really do what they want. We are a society that is fixated with adulthood and adult view points to such a degree that it is almost anti-child. While children are very good at adapting to adults and will sacrifice a lot to please adults, they shouldn't need to so all the time. Children as young citizens, not as becoming adults, should have places of refuge where they can be themselves, away from the demands of the adult world. A civilised society would make it happen.

Today's playgrounds, for the most could be much better play places. Because adults have not been good at designing for them is no reason to take them away from the children. We need to re-examine our reasons for providing playgrounds. They should be part of the urban landscape not because children need to play but because they are part of what marks a cultured and civilised society. It is necessary to make good playgrounds – for the good of the adults who need to broaden their worldview to include provision for the needs of others, to strengthen society which develops further through play, to foster social and community bonds through playing together in public open spaces. Children too have rights as citizens, even though they do not have the right to vote. In a democratic land provision for those with less empowerment is a sign of a healthy and developed democracy. And finally childhood and children have such a joy of life there simply must be places where they can celebrate this. It is how we know we are human.

Art on the pathway to tomorrow

This is not a practical book in that there are no guides here wherein an adult will find some recipe for their work with children's playgrounds. The work of the adult designer and the demands of the children make for an interesting and challenging working life, but not an easy life. The easy route is to satisfy the minimal adult demands of the day and do only what political and adult management has determined they are prepared to do for children.

There is a large gap between what the adult western cultures are prepared to do for adult artists – painters, sculptors, opera singers, ballet dancers and others who work in the "fine arts" and what they are prepared to do for children. There is a recognised symbolic value in art that does not exist in society in relation to children's play. We see art work for which very high prices have been paid hanging in art collections that consist of nothing more than the word "H E L L". This is high art of the late Twentieth century. Many who look at this will think – "Hell, I can do that myself, but no one would pay me to do that." And that is the case – the value of the works of contemporary visual art is often based in the reputation of the artist and has the value it has to society because it is that specific person who has thought out the idea of the art, who has selected the material and techniques used in the execution of the work. There is not a lot of fine drawing or representational skills involved, there is not a lot of time consuming brushwork or other painterly skill. In contemporary painting and two dimensional art it is no longer an issue of mastering techniques but more an issue of concepts, ideas and of personalities. (Peter Bonde's work "HELL" is in Statens Museum for Kunst, Copenhagen.)

These two issues - what galleries collect in contemporary painting and the low priority of public playgrounds may at first glance seem to be two very separate aspects of modern life. But are they? I see them as a two different positions on the same scale of the values and choices of those in power in western society.

We are living in a time where there is a cult of adulthood, more specifically of younger adulthood with careers. Today is a time where everyone who falls outside of this category: the young, old, sick, unemployed, immigrants from developing countries and refugees, are dealt with in a manner that clearly signals they are second rank. Efficiency and effectiveness rule when these peoples needs are to be considered. Under no circumstances are all their needs met, a few basic ones are minimally satisfied for a time.

The adults who are in power, demand that all their needs be fulfilled, that they have a good life. The good life consists of all the signs of powerful consumption– fashion wardrobes, house at the right address, plenty of space indoors in terms of a big office, big cars, homes with over 150 sq. m of space, the biggest bedroom in the house, big freeways so they can get to work a few seconds faster. They must never have to wait for anything.

Money is the great equaliser and the great divider. Workers in the service sector should be servile and self sacrificing; they are not equal; they don't earn as much money. After all the demands and wishes of this pampered elite have been somewhat satisfied there is not much money for children along with the other "outsiders". The adults have what they need to make their life easy for themselves and have little left over either in terms of money or empathy for those who are not positioned like themselves.

> Having galleries full of contemporary art is a sign of a well functioning society led by persons of high sophistication and superior tastes.

An examination of art works in art galleries working with an in depth knowledge of the way the thinking and concepts of the individual artist can reveal a very harsh criticism of modern society. Similarly a review of playgrounds that society allocates to children, viewed with a knowledge of what children need, also places this modern society in an negative light. There is money for the fine arts because, although these people do not understand what the artist is doing, fine arts symbolise good taste and ownership of art and having galleries full of contemporary art is a sign of a well functioning society led by persons of high sophistication and superior tastes.

That much of contemporary two dimensional art includes a serious critique of this society seems to be a part of the attraction of the art. Having bought the art and hung it is a fine gallery and paid a huge sum to staff the gallery, hired security and paid insurance on the art work, society now has eased its conscience about what is wrong – see they are also very sophisticatedly tolerant as well. The artist message is lost through indulgence and adulation of art by a sector of society who use the art and artist to promote their own values. Prevailing society is deaf to the artists message and see only the symbolic value of the art for their own purposes. Similarly these same groups are deaf to the needs and values of children's play because they do not realise any symbolic value in these things.

> Play is a prerequisite to later adult creativity and in turn the creative adult culture is reflected in the play of the people.

Creating works of art and playing are two related aspects of humanity, the two aspects wherein lies the origins of our western culture and civilisation. Play is a prerequisite to later adult creativity and in turn the creative adult culture is reflected in the play of the people. Play and high art are interrelated and how we deal with these areas of human culture are measures of the quality of our society.

As space designers we have a choice. We can aim to create art that is approved by the adult society and to be entered in art histories to be appreciated by generations of art enthusiasts as a symbol of our cultural period, or we can create art that is lived in and used up while it creates an impression on the users that influences the further development of culture and civilisation.

Play and high art are two related aspects of human aesthetic expression.

Function versus expression
Alessi. Interview in *Politiken*, April 9 1999.
"If it is only function that we are talking about – we have achieved that already a thousand years ago. With Alessi it is the form of expression. I would have to close the factory if we only considered function."

Open space and culture- the search for Paradise

Open space must not be seen as potential building grounds. Rather the space occupied by buildings should be seen to be potential open space. We are sealing off the surface of the planet earth and covering over the only place we know of that is capable of supporting life.

The professional bias of architects has dominated the form of our living spaces for centuries – a profession whose income depends on making buildings, and therefore with every decade we build more, we cover the surface of the earth with boxes, always choosing the best land and locations for these constructions. We cut down trees, drain wetlands to gain access to these lands. What drives us to this – are we still carrying around inside some little cave man who fears attack from wild animals and well armed

Civilisation develops through interaction with society in social setting and public spaces.

enemies and who seeks comfort from bad weather? A small cave in the hillside didn't alter the whole ecology of the land. Today our caveman instincts are turning the whole surface of Planet Earth into a labyrinthine series of caves where we can hide from each other. This direction will not lead to any further development in culture or civilisation – such development and innovations arise in social settings, in group values, in highlighting those aspects of life on earth that humans feel most strongly.

While we may all need our own personal caves – they should be so small to accommodate only the necessary while the shared open social spaces should be as large as possible. Schools and institutions for children should have a minimum of building space and a maximum of well landscaped outdoor space.

Architects, the modern day cavemen, have their place but not as urban planners. Not only do we carry within us the heritage of the caveman we also carry with us the heritage of the gardens of paradise. Much of human history and culture has been touched by our very human dream and longing to Paradise, and Paradise is always a garden, never a building. Human beings are also gardeners, creators of paradise on earth, and the urge to construct must be balanced with the urge to create gardens and forests and open air living spaces as well as well balanced outdoor ecosystems. In this way our civilisations will grow and thrive. If we cover the earth with buildings, we have no possibility to create Paradise.

Children lost the struggle for space before they could walk

Space, land, is one of the signs of power and wealth. Wars all over the globe are fought over land and who controls it. Democratic countries have tried to develop tools for discussion and debate amongst themselves where there are territorial disputes but this is such an emotional issue that violence often arises. The media and public relations people work to realign the citizen's perception of events so that those in power can find a widely based agreement for their viewpoint. Dictators also use the media and their armies to enforce their visions of enough space to satisfy their egos. A huge amount of wealth and peoples lives are sacrificed every year to satisfy the needs of a few men for power over space. The whole problem is that there is a limited amount of land on Planet Earth – and with all our technology we really can't make much more. Yes, we can build high rise buildings so there is more living space by increasing density, but down on the ground there is a limited supply.

Space is also one of the absolutely essential elements in quality outdoor play provision for children. Children need room and play requires space for the big arm movements, for jumping, for running. A report published in a Danish newspaper in March 1999 stated that the amount of indoor space per person in the homes of Danes had been increasing over the century. First because families are smaller today and secondly because modern families demand larger homes. Today, there is an average of 55 sq. m per person in the Danish private home, and less than 4 sq. m per child in a pre-school institution where the children spend most of their waking time. The home stand empty from 7.30 in the morning until 4 in the afternoon. Outdoors it is a similar story. If only we could get 55 sq. m per child in the outdoor play area!

Some cities now have more than 50% of their total land area paved and devoted to roadways, freeways, access road and parking lots. Even though there are more streets and streets are traditionally preferred play space by children; for the most streets are too dangerous for children to use for play - the adults need to go fast.

Outdoor park land is threatened and much of it is no longer open space but built up space with covered tennis courts, pools, centres and of course – parking lots. There is little informal, semi- wild or wild lands left within easy access for children of middle school years to find their own play space. While land inventories may show that there is still the same amount

Adult disregard for adequate open space for playing results in situations such as here where the little outdoor space is filled with a structure which is used mostly for storage.

of recreation and park land in the community as there was earlier in the century the spaces have been highly organised and often taken over by one interest group and are not available for other activities. The result is that there are few places where children can play and the amount of space available per child for playing is very limited – usually just the designated playground. Here there is far less that 55 sq. m per child in the neighbourhood. Most communities allocate much less than 10 sq. m per child resident as designated outdoors space for play – when in fact they should have 50 sq. m (excluding pre-school institutional spaces) depending on their age and where else they can play.

One thing I am convinced that most adults in society will immediately react with the statement that their community cannot afford to provide this kind of space for children's play. This space provision is only met in rural and very unorganised districts. In the urban centres planners don't even give the children a chance to have quality in play spaces, and children have no power to lobby for their needs. They need, and we all need, political leaders with a vision for further development of civilisation and culture.

One hundred and fifty years ago, when western cultures began providing public park spaces for ordinary citizens, the arguments for this provision were based in the health benefits and the improvement in character of the ordinary person as well as the creation of a sense of community and citizenship. Zuylen writes

Napoleon III knew full well that the oases of greenery he inserted in the   restless city of Paris were much more than pleasure grounds, they were part of a political agenda. Public parks held out the prospect of social harmony, or the illusion of it. The aesthetic

Time spent in high quality garden-like settings serve as a neutraliser to the stresses of modern city life.

rationale of modern city parks harks back to the timeless theme of the garden of Eden, in this brilliant variation, it was hoped that relaxation and diversion in a natural setting would act as a safety valve for the tensions of urban life and perhaps neutralize its harmful effects (p 113).

Today we think people have adjusted to the tensions of city life. Political leaders have overlooked the importance of time spent in a high quality garden-like setting as a neutraliser to the stress of the city life. We have neglected how important it is for our children to be outside and in contact with planet earth.

Instead we rely more and more on chemistry to neutralise the harmful effects. Children are give pills so they can concentrate better and schools and all can take a "happy" pill if they feel depressed. We have forgotten how very, very essential it is to the health and well being of the human spirit, for our brain and our body to move about in pleasant outdoor surroundings – often and everyday. In the twenty-first century we also need outdoor places where we can find, not only refreshment, but also the sense of social harmony and feeling of being part of a community. Rather than investing in maintaining a land base of well designed parks within cities we have refocused public funds into health care and medication of the population, including our children. We can and must do better than this. It is civilising to enjoy park-like settings in the company of our fellows in a way that taking a pill is not; it is even more civilising to struggle, to suffer the twinge of minor inconvenience, in order to make life better for our children. Children will not wage war on us because we fail to give them quality spaces for play, they love us and, when young, think of adults as all powerful and almost godlike. We should not fail them, not only for their sake but to civilise ourselves.

Our childhood stays with us for a lifetime.

The future and technology

Many adults repeat the phrase "the future is technology". This is not much of a vision for our future. The twentieth century was defined and shaped by machines, with many improvements and conveniences in life for wealthy western adults. But the costs have been tremendous. Poor people in developing countries are cut off from any possible benefits from modern culture. In the west, the small amount of funding the politicians will allocate for children are channelled into computers, based in the argument that today's children must be computer literate to be able to work in adulthood. Computer technology is changing so fast that by the time these children are adults computers will be world's apart from what they are today. Children of today, to prepare for tomorrow's work life, do not need to spend a lot of time with today's computers; for the sake of a good adult life they should be practising to use their brain in all its facilities and competences. More than anything else they should be developing skills to deal with the new and the unknown.

Life and culture in the twenty first century must integrate more consideration for a balance in living conditions for all beings in all places. Bronowski has written that "the longest childhood has been that of civilisation" in learning to understand the enormous investment evolution has made in the brain. Technology today aims at replicating the brain or at least the performance of the adult brain. There is a much better future for our culture if we were to focus on developing the huge potential in the child's brain.

> Today's children must learn to understand how real-life situations are different from computer simulated conditions.

Our future on this planet will be affected by the way we interact with each other and our surroundings.

Today's children must learn to understand how real-life situations are different from computer simulated conditions. In the computer all is programmed, all games and projects have a precise solution like that of chess or engineering. This is the heritage of the twentieth century machine age – where all problems were solvable if we just put all the tiny pieces together in the right way. Real life doesn't work that way. Real-life is not a chess game, nor is it engineered. It is not a series of pre -programmed events. Real-life means interacting with the forces of life on this planet – people, and living things. More than anything our future on this planet will be affected by the way we interact with each other and with nature.

Children on the pathway to adulthood in tomorrow must understand that real life situations do not have precise, pre-programmed solutions but that they are a living part of the solution. Johnny von Neumann, in his theory of competitive games states "real life consists of bluffing, of little tactics of deception, of asking yourself what is the other man going to think I mean to do." An understanding of real life and an ability to find workable real-life solutions comes from learning about how people behave, how people think. This is not something we learn from a computer, we develop these skills through playing with people.

"Good for computers; no good for life", sayings of a Ukrainian –Canadian grandmother.

Aesthetics and play - summary

In a book on designing for play the issue of aesthetics cannot be ignored. To further develop design for play it can be helpful to look at the origins of art and aesthetics. Art and aesthetics have their origins in the human urge to create, in human fantasy, in the human sense of magic and mysticism. Art and belief are closely connected and art and religion have the same origins. In a time when mankind has discovered that the replacement of spiritual belief with belief in science is not fulfilling, we have turned to art as a element of expression which can move us, and we find identity in consumption of trendy goods and services. Will the twenty first century person be the perennial tourist searching for newer and more exotic experiences? And will they feel empty after is has all been done? "Been there, done that, bought it all." Today's children are new "tourists" in a world full of ordinary wonders. The whole world is exotic to a baby. Like the child, we can all benefit from looking again at the ordinary and seeing the wonders of life on this planet.

Playing at Designing #3
The advantage of playing is that you can test out actions and emotions that would be too dangerous to act out in real life. For a designer playing means he or she can take risks that might other wise affect their professional reputation. When we play we can take enough risk that we can actually invent something new. When we risk enough we learn and make this new knowledge our own.

Good art, however, is more than an expression or an acquisition to express status. Good art gives insight to the individual on life, beauty and the human condition. Good art gives insight on real life conditions. Good art for children must touch and communicate to the children.

Artists play with design elements and ideas as a method of creation. Play for creative adults is a tool for inventiveness. Similarly children's play includes kernels of creation, ingenuity, and holds the potential for future cultural developments. The human urge to play with things is the source of our culture and future developments of our culture will only come about as a result of playful interactions and discoveries. Playing with ideas has been a technique used by inventors and creators as a problem solving technique, such a methodology can also be applied to many other aspects of our culture.

Good design in the children's play spaces would be designs that communicate some insight into life on this planet and the conceptual and imagination's worlds. The design should add to the quality of playfulness of the space and something more – a unique communication between the site, the designer and the players. Playing is living for the young child and for the future.

References

Alessi. (1999), *Politiken*, April 9.

Bronowski, J. (1973), *The Ascent of Man*, Little, Brown and Co.: Boston.

Taylor, Mary. (1990), "Foundations of Early Childhood Education" in Doxey, I. ed. *Child Care and Education, Canadian Dimensions*, Nelson Canada: Scarborough.

Zuylen, Gabrielle van. (1995), *The Garden, Visions of Paradise*, Thames and Hudson Ltd: London.

Appendix 1 Guidelines for Layout of Playgrounds

Prepared by CEN/TC136/SC1 Working Group on Playground Layout.
This Guideline is still in draft form after nearly five years of discussion within a very small group. It has been sent out for comment from the general public. This guideline covers aspects of what is good practise in practical play area layout (not design) and is included here as access to such material is otherwise very limited..

Foreword:
Playground safety is dependent on many factors, including:
1. Equipment for Play
2. Surfacing
3. Ancillary items
4. Layout

Safety of children: Playgrounds which meet the developmental needs of the children and are fun to play on are safer than those which fail to meet the needs of the children.

This guideline is intended to address the broad areas of playground layout related to statistics of injuries occurring on public playgrounds. It is of a general nature and intended to draw attention to areas of concern rather than giving detailed advice. Specific responses should be developed in accordance with national and local practice and regulations.

1. Scope
This guideline gives guidance on play areas intended for public use, including layout, selection and placement of ancillary items.

Normative reference:
This guideline makes reference to European Standards, in particular
EN 1176- 1, Playground Equipment, Part 1 General safety requirements and test methods.

It is intended that this standard be used in conjunction with this guideline.

Items placed in the playground with the intention that children will use them as play equipment should comply with EN1176 parts 1 – 7, Playground Equipment and EN 1177 Impact Absorbing Playground Surfacing. This guideline addresses some of the other elements included in or related to a play area.

2. Location

Playgrounds should not be located in areas where there are environmental hazards or adequate protection against danger provided.

Play activities resulting from local climatic conditions should be considered.

3. Ancillary Items

Ancillary items are elements such as fences, litter bins, cycle racks and seating that are placed within or around a playground.

Ancillary items should comply with the entrapment, protrusion and chamfer requirements in EN1176-1. Refer to Section 4.2.5 Finish of equipment and Section 4.2.7 Protection against entrapment.

Items should also comply with the requirements for structural stability and integrity as set out in EN1176-1 Section 4.2.2 Structural integrity.

Fences and Gates intended as barriers – i.e. children should not easily be able to go over or through them – should conform to EN 1176-1 Section 4.2.4.4. Second paragraph – "there shall be no intermediate horizontal or near horizontal rails or bars that can be used as steps by children attempting to climb. The design of the top of barriers should not encourage children to stand or sit on them, nor should any infilling encourage climbing.

4. Circulation

Children moving around the playground should have sufficient space to move around the playground and equipment. The space used for circulation should not normally intrude into the *free space* and/or *falling space* that compose the minimum use zones around the play equipment. Children should do not need to go through these safety spaces to get to another piece of equipment.

5. **Pathways and circulation areas where there is a forced direction of movement**.
for example a bicycle or tricycle path on a slope, should have provision for a free space around the player in movement similar to that described as free space in EN1176-1 Section 4.2.8.1.2 Dimensions of the Free Space. This free space should be provided to ensure that the user can complete the movement.

6. Surfacing
Surfaces have different slip characteristics and attention should be paid to the interface between surfaces with two different slip characteristics. Loose fill surfaces spilling out onto paved surfaces used for circulation can be particularly hazardous and the layout of the play area should consider means to eliminate or reduce this hazard.

7. Planting
Selection of plant material in the playground should be made bearing in mind that children will be playing with it.

8. Access - General
Access into the play area or sections of the play area where there is a raised perimeter edging should be established with the consideration that very young children may be accessing these areas. Provision should be made for ease of access into those areas intended for use by young children.

9. Separation of play activities.
Separation by age and user skill.
Equipment designed to provide challenging physical play for older children should be placed in the playground so that it is clearly separate from the play opportunities for the younger children. That is to say it should be clear to all who come to the play area that the items which are physically challenging for older children are not part of the young children's play area.

Separation by play type.
Some forms of play- i.e. the quieter creative and manipulative play activities- should be kept separate from those play items where physical movement predominates.

10. Sun orientation

Consideration should be given to sun orientation and shade when placing metal slides cable rides, some swings and other relevant items in the playground.

11. Special needs

Consideration should be given to the needs of children who are differently abled and special layouts and equipment may be called for to meet their developmental requirements.

Appendix 2 Useful Play Organisations and Contacts

This listing of play organisations and contacts is based on those organisations who took the time to return information for inclusion in this book. The author would like to thank these contacts for taking the time to submit the following information:

Dansk Legeplads Selskab/Danish Playground Association
Klerkegade 10B
Denmark
Phone(+45) 33 33 96 97
This organisation was the original roots for the founding of IPA. The current goals of the organisation are to create better play opportunities for children with emphasis on playgrounds such as building playgrounds, adventure playgrounds and "nature" playgrounds. Publishes newsletter *Legepladsen* four times each year.

Nordic Centre for Research on Toys and Educational Media
Halmstad University
Box 823, 301 18 Halmstad, Sweden
Web: www.hh.se/dep/ncflweb.html   E-mail: sekr@ncfl.hh.se
Attached to a university, serves as a research centre and base for academics whose work touches on toys and play. Has organised the first and second International Toy research conference.

Pro Juventute
Secretary General
Seehofstrasse 15, Postfach , 8022 Zurich, Switzerland.
Phone + 251 72 44, fax + 252 28 24
The work of this organisation is oriented toward Swiss conditions and works in the German language primarily. A childhood lobby group oriented towards children's rights and protecting children from violence.

Organisation supports efforts to create a more child oriented environment, through PR work, counselling and fun activities.

The Royal Society for the Prevention of Accidents (ROSPA)
Edgbaston Park, 353 Bristol Road, Birmingham, B5 7ST, UK
Web: www.rospa.co.uk E-mail: Help@rospa.com
Phone + 121 248 2000   fax + 121 248 2001

IPA
(International Association for the Child's Right to Play)
PO Box 219
Huntingdon, PE18 8WE, UK
Phone (+44) 1480 41 13 84   Fax (+ 44) 1480 38 65 10
For membership info: http://ndo.be/encp
E-mail: 100611.512@compuserve.com

There are many more play organisations – most organised around a regional or national base. Government Services for children's play are often placed in under the umbrella of sports and all too often it is the sports aspects that gets the attention and the money. It is difficult however to maintain an up-to-date record of not for profit play organisations addresses as these often change with a change in staff or volunteers.

Appendix 3 Safety Guidelines and Standards for Playground Equipment and Play Spaces

Most western countries now have in place some form of standard or guideline that regulates the manufacture of playground equipment and its placement in the playground. Some countries – like the USA have both a Guideline and a Standard – work is underway to harmonise these so they work together. In some areas there has been efforts to develop a common standard for manufactured equipment as national standard variations often have been used as a means of protecting local industry, a form of trade barrier. This is the case in Europe where 19 of the countries including Norway and Iceland have agreed to be part of a CEN standard group. In the CEN lands there is one standard for the manufacture of equipment but some lands like France and Germany have deviations that deal with space around the play items and the way in which they describe the requirement for safety surfacing under and around the play items.

Standards and Guidelines are for the most developed through a process of voluntary work centered in a non-profit Standard setting organisation and members of the committees behind the standards are representatives from the manufacturers and other interested groups. However as children's lobby groups are usually very under funded they have been hampered from participation in most of these committees which have been dominated by government regulating agencies, accident prevention workers and manufacturers.

The aim of these Standards and Guidelines is to reduce serious injury to children at play though describe a minimum level of safety to be present in all public playgrounds. They also describe a minimum level of professional practise for designers of play items and of playgrounds. In most cases the standards are not mandatory – but are valid where a play provider demands that playgrounds be up to a safety standard. This means that if a city wants there playgrounds to met a safety standard it is the national standard they must use – they cannot devise some new one of their own. The standards are in need of improvement in terms of consideration for play value and risk versus safety, however they are the best we have today and should be adhered to when designing play spaces.

To obtain a copy of the standards for your country contact the local office of the standard setting body.

To obtain other standards:

Handbook for Public Playground Safety
U.S. Consumer Product Safety Commission
Washington D.C. 20207, U. S.A
http://www.cpsc.gov

Standard Consumer Safety Performance Specifications for Playground Equipment for Public Use ASTM F 1487-98
American Society for Testing and Materials
100 Barr Harbor Drive,
West Conshohocken, PA 19428, U.S.A.

Children's Playspaces and Equipment
CAN/CSA-Z614-98
Canadian Standards Association
178 Rexdale Boulevard
Etobicoke, Ontario M9W 1R3, Canada

CEN standard – European Standard
EN 1176 Playground Equipment : parts 1 through 7
European Committee for Standardization
Central Secretariat: rue de Stassart, 36
B-1050 Brussels, Belgium

(official languages of the standard are English, French and German)

CEN Standard- European Standard
EN1177 Impact Absorbing playground Surfacing- Safety Requirements and Test methods

Contact address is same as above for EN1176

Australia and New Zealand
A series of standards related to playground equipment and siting.
Standards Association of Australia
80 Arthur Street
North Sydney, New South Wales 2060
Australia

It is not only western countries which have standards. There are also standards that I am aware of in India, and South Korea. Japan also demands safety standards and appears to accept US and European standards. There is great likelihood that other nations also have established standards – before beginning work on a playground in any land it is best to research of there are any standards that must be met.

A professional designer will always work within the published standards for safety – they serve as the definition of a minimal professional standard. If, as a designer, you find the standards too restrictive to create good play areas – then join in the debates around the standard – take contact with the standard setting body and suggest changes. These standards should always be under revision in light of latest knowledge – and if you have something that will improve the quality of play for children – become part of the movement to change things.

Bibliography

Barnett, Lynn A. (1990), "Playfulness: Definition, Design and Measurement, *Play & Culture*, Vol. 3 No. 4.

Bengtsson, Arvid. (1970), *Environmental Planning for Children's Play*, Praeger Publishers: New York.

Berger, John. (1977), *Ways of Seeing*, Penguin Books: Harmondsworth.

Berrall, Julia S. (1978), *The Garden, An Illustrated History*, Penguin Books: Harmondsworth.

Bettelheim, Bruno. (1989), *The Uses of Enchantment, The Meaning and Importance of Fairy Tales*, Vintage Books: New York.

Bettelheim, Bruno. (1980), "About Summerhill", *Surviving and other Essays*, Vintage Books: New York.

Bronowski, J. (1973), *The Ascent of Man*, Little, Brown and Co: Boston.

Bronté, Charlotte. (1985), *Shirley*, Penguin: Harmondsworth.

Bronté, Charlotte. (1989), *The Professor*, Penguin: Harmondsworth.

Brown, Jane. (1999), *The Pursuit of Paradise, A Social History of Gardens and Gardening*, Harper Collins: London.

Burton, Anthony. (1996), *Children's Pleasures*, V&A Publications: London.

Burton, Anthony. (1998), *Bethnall Green Museum of Childhood*, V&A Publications: London.

Burton, Thomas L. (1976), *Making Man's Environment: Leisure*, Van Nostrand Reinhold Ltd.: Toronto.

Canadian Broadcasting Corporation. (1987), "Play" an Ideas programme, transmitted on CBC June 18.

The Canadian Commission for the International Year of the Child. (1979), *For Canada's Children, National Agenda for Action*, The Commission: Ottawa.

Cassell's New Compact Latin Dictionary. (1963), Cassell: London.

Chawla, Louise. (1994), *In the First Country of Places: Nature, Poetry and Childhood Memory*, Albany, New York: State University of New York Press.

Clark, W.G. and Aldis Wright, W. eds.(no date), *The Complete Works of William Shakespeare, Volume 1*, Nelson Doubleday, Inc: Garden City.

Crystal, David. (1998), *Language Play*, Penguin Books: London.

Davidsen, Thomas. (1996). "Arkitekturen savner kvindelighed" in *Samvirke*, November.

Dudek, Mark.(1996), *Kindergarten Architecture: Space for the Imagination*, E & FN Spon: London.

Education Commission of the People's Republic of China. (no date), *Statute of Kindergartens in the People's Republic of China*, Beijing: Beijing Normal University.

Engholm, Ida og Michelsen Anders.(1999), *Designmaskinen, Design af den nye verden*, Gyldendal: Copenhagen.

Eriksen, Aase. (1985), *Playground Design, Outdoor Environments for Learning and Development*, Van Nostrand Reinhold Co.: New York.

Esbensen, Steen B.(1987), *The Early Childhood Playground, An Outdoor Classroom*, The Highscope Press: Ypsilanti, Michigan.

Fairbrother, Nan.(1974), *The Nature of Landscape Design: As an Art Form, a Craft, a Social Necessity*, Alfred A. Knopf: New York.

Frost, Joe L. and Sunderlin, Sylvia. eds. (1985), *When Children Play*, Association for Childhood Education International: Wheaton, MD.

Frost, Joe L. and Klien, Barry. (1983), *Children's Play and Playgrounds*, Playscapes International: Austin Texas.

Gage, John. (1993), *Colour and Culture*, Thames and Hudson: Singapore.

Grahn, Patrick et al. (1997), *Ute paa Dagis*, Movium: Alnarp Sweden.

Harris, Judith Rich. (1998), *The Nurture Assumption, Why Children Turn out the way they do*, The Free Press: New York.

Heft, Harry. (1988), "Affordances of Children's Environments: A functional approach to environmental description", *Children's Environments Quarterly*, Vol 5, No. 3, (fall).

Hendricks, Barbara. 1994 "No Room for Children- The Changing Dimensions of Provision for Children's Play in Urban Areas," *Leisure: Modernity, Postmodernity and Lifestyles*, Henry, I. ed., LSA Publication no. 48: University of Brighton.

Hendricks, Barbara. (1995), "Politically Correct Play," *Professional and Development Issues in Leisure, Sport and Education*, Lawrence, L. Murdoch, E and Parker, S. eds., LSA Publication no. 56:University of Brighton.

Hendricks, Barbara. (1995), "Young Children's Playful Interactions in and with Nature in Urban Areas", presented at *Building Identities Conference*, University of Amsterdam, April, unpublished.

Heseltine, Peter and Holborn, John. (1987), *Playgrounds, The Planning, Design and Construction of Play Environments*, Nichols: New York.

Hubbard, P. (1996), "Design Quality: A Professional or Public Issue?" *Environments by Design*, Vol 1, No. 1, Jan.

Huizinga, Johan. (1993), *Homo Ludens, om kulturens oprindelse i leg*, translated Niels Christian Lindtner, Gyldendal: Copenhagen.

Jekyll, Gertrude. (1982), *Children and Gardens*, Woodbridge Suffolk: The Antique Collector's Club Ltd.

Jackson, Caroline. (1995), "Play Strategies: The Vision or the Reality?" *Professional and Development Issues in Leisure, Sport and Education*, Lesley Lawrence, E. Murdoch, S Parker eds., LSA Publication no. 56: University of Brighton.

Kamin, Blair. (1995), "Sheltered by Design", *The Chicago Tribune* special section, June 18-June 23.

Kampmann, Jan and Andersen, Peter Ø. (1996), *Børns Legekultur*, Munksgaard,Rosinante: Copenhagen.

Lamb, Trevor and Bourriau, Janine eds. (1995), *Colour: Art & Science*, Cambridge University Press: Cambridge.

Lasdun, Susan.(1983), *Making Victorians, The Drummond Children's World 1827-1832*, Victor Gollancz Ltd: London.

Lehrer, Ruthann and Sparks, Naoma. (1976), *Play Power! The Triumphs & Trauma of Greening the San Francisco Schoolyards*, Volunteers to Beautify Our Schools, Inc: San Francisco.

Lucio-Meyer, JJ de. (1973), *Visual Aesthetics*, Harper & Row: New York.

Lu Pu, ed. (1990), *China's Folk Toys*, New World Press: Beijing.

Manu, Alexander. (1995), *Tool Toys, Tools with an element of play*, Danish Design Centre: Copenhagen.

Moore, Robin C. (1990), *Childhood's Domain, Play and place in child development*, MIG Publications: Berkley.

Nachmanovitch, Stephen. (1990), *Free Play, The Power of Improvisation in Life and the Arts*, Jeremy P Tharcher, Inc.: Los Angeles.

Piaget, Jean.(1977), *The Child's Conception of the World*, St Albans Herts: Paladin.

Qvortrup, Jens. (1991), *Childhood As A Social Phenomenon, An Introduction to a Series of National Reports*, European Centre for Social Welfare Policy and Research: Vienna.

Rand, Harry. (1998), *Hundertwasser*, Taschen: Cologne.

Rogers, Cosby. (1988), *Play in the Lives of Young Children*, Washington DC: National Association for the Education of Young Children.

Rotterdam Municipal Health Dept. (1987), "Being a kid in a BIG TOWN", report no. 82, The Department: Rotterdam.

Rutledge, Albert J. (1971), *Anatomy of a Park*, McGraw-Hill Book Co; New York.

Rydahl, Klaus. (1999), "Yoyo jorden rundt," *Samvirke*, Februar, p 67.

St Sernin, Mademoiselle.(1974), *Healthful Sports for Young Ladies*, originally published by Rudolph Ackerman in 1822, reproduced in facsimile by the Toronto Public Library: Toronto.

Sebba, R. (1991), "The landscapes of childhood : the reflection of childhood's environment in adult memories and in children's attitudes". *Environment & Behaviour*, Vol. 23 No 4: pp. 395-422.

Sutton-Smith, Brian. (1997), *The Ambiguity of Play*, Harvard University Press: Cambridge MA.

Taylor, Mary. (1990), "Foundations of Early Childhood Education" in *Child Care and Education; Canadian Dimensions*, Isabel M. Doxey ed., Scarborough: Nelson Canada.

The Oxford Nursery Book. (1995), Illustrated by Ian Beck. Oxford: Oxford University Press.

Williams, Stephen. (1995), *Outdoor Recreation and the Urban Environment*, London: Routledge.

Williams, Stephen. (1995), "Urban Playgrounds: Re-thinking the City as an Environment for Children's Play," in *Professional and Development Issues in*

Leisure, Sport and Education, Lawrence, L. Murdoch, E. and Parker, S. eds., LSA Publication no 56:University of Brighton.

Zuylen, Gabrielle van. (1995), *The Garden, Visions of Paradise*, Thames and Hudson, Ltd: London.

Index

263